GOD'S SOVEREIGNTY

AND

OUR RESPONSIBILITY

His Heart for All Men

PAMELA K. GOURLEY

PlainFocus Books

ISBN: 978-0-9973578-0-6

Library of Congress Control Number: 2016934973

Cover Design Stock Photo Credits: NASA and 4Max/Shutterstock.com

Author Photo Credit: Patti Buttram Brooks

Scripture quotations [marked NIV1984] are taken from the Holy Bible, New International Version®, NIV®, Copyright © 1973, 1978, 1984 by Biblica, Inc.®. Used by permission. All rights reserved worldwide.

Scripture quotations [marked NKJV] are taken from the New King James Version®. Copyright © 1982 by Thomas Nelson. Used by permission. All rights reserved.

Scripture quotations [marked NASB] taken from the New American Standard Bible®, Copyright © 1960, 1962, 1963, 1968, 1971, 1972, 1973, 1975, 1977, 1995 by the Lockman Foundation. Used by permission. www.Lockman.org.

Scripture quotations marked YLT are from Young's Literal Translation. Scripture quotations marked IGNT are from the Interlinear Greek-English New Testament. Scripture quotations marked KJV are from the King James Version.

"Appendix A" material is copied from the book entitled *Romans: An Interpretive Outline* by Steele and Thomas, ISBN 978-0-87552-443-6. Used with permission of P&R Publishing Co., P.O. Box 817, Phillipsburg, NJ 08865. www.prpbooks.com.

Note: Although I have been true to the renderings of translations, often, for special emphasis, I may have added boldface or italics to special words being considered within those references. Then, although often not specifically noted, *The NIV Exhaustive Concordance* and the internet site for the lexicon *Theological Word Book of the Old Testament* [by Brown, Driver, Briggs, and Gesenius] additionally have been used, alongside other cited lexicons, as references for the names and transliterated spellings of original Greek and Hebrew words.

Acknowledgements

Foremost, I must acknowledge the faithfulness of my Lord. He called me to this, and *He has done it*! And in my weakness, I am trusting that His strength will be known.

As the Lord would have it, the writing of this book has been a very long process, during which time many have helped me to carry this burden. Over the span of several years, many have prayed, and many have strengthened me through timely words of encouragement. In addition to those praying family members and friends who are mentioned below, I desire specifically to acknowledge the following individuals who, over the years, have held up this work in prayer: Pastors Mike and Donna Corrigan, Bowie Curry, David Bradshaw, Bonnie Horn, Teri Buck, Louise Logan, Sissie Lewis, Joanie Barrineau, and Susan Miller. Regrettably, although it will not be possible for me to account for *all* who have prayed, God knows who you are, and I am grateful.

Specially, I want to thank my wonderful family. I want to thank my husband, Mike Gourley, without whose loving support and faithful provision I may not have had the means to follow through with this calling. Also, I want to thank all my children—Marisa, Christi, Ashley, Tara, Erin, Lauren, and Joe—who, with much support and understanding, grew up with this writing as if it was a member of their family. Thank you all for standing with me—for your forbearance, your prayers, your counsel, and your love.

Lastly, I want to thank all those friends and family members—Kim Sawyer, Tara Custalow, Anne Gourley, and Erin Lindsey—who, during the last weeks of the book's preparation, so readily gave of their time either to a final proofing or to the preparation of its cover. Particularly, I want to thank my mother-in-law, Anne Gourley, who, on her own initiative, rose to the task and meticulously combed through the *entire* book, and also my daughter, Erin Lindsey, who so creatively and willingly assisted with the cover.

Table of Contents

SCRIPTURAL INCONSISTENCIES OF CALVINISM

1 Inconsistencies within the Doctrines of *Unconditional Election* and *Limited Atonement*—Part 1:

WHAT *IS*

The *Will* of God

The Sovereignty of God

5 Significant Scriptures Concerning God's Sovereignty—Part 1: Bringing In the Balance

Our Responsibility

An Election According to Foreknowledge

CONCLUSION

APPENDICES

SOURCES

SCRIPTURE INDEX

Introduction

A few years ago, I was shocked when a brother in the Lord (distressed over sins which he saw in his life) confessed a lack of faith to go before God to search and to cleanse his heart. He explained, "Maybe God's not obligated. Maybe I'm not one of the elect."

In two other separate instances, a brother and sister in the Lord similarly made the comment, "I don't even know if *I'm* one of the elect."

Words from the writer of Hebrews resound:

> Beware, brethren, lest there be in any of you an evil heart of unbelief in departing from the living God; but exhort one another daily, while it is called "Today," lest any of you be hardened through the deceitfulness of sin. **For we have become partakers of Christ if we hold the beginning of our confidence steadfast to the end,** (Hebrews 3:14 NKJV)

> [Let] us draw near with a true heart **in full assurance of faith,** having our hearts sprinkled from an evil conscience and our bodies washed with pure water. **Let us hold fast the confession of our hope without wavering, for He who promised is faithful.** (Hebrews 10:22-23 NKJV)

I was so deeply stirred by the comments of my brothers and sisters. In all of the above instances, my brothers and sisters had heard and had received the teaching of *unconditional election,* one of several closely intertwined TULIP teachings of Reformed Theology and Calvinism.[1] I was seeing some of the fruit of the teaching in my friends. *Consequential to the teaching,* their faith—to know that God *will* reward those who diligently seek Him (Hebrews 11:6)—was under serious attack.

On another day, as I was chatting with a friend who did not yet "know"

---

[1] See "Appendix A," where the "five points"/TULIP acronym of Calvinism and Reformed theology are outlaid.

the saving power of Jesus, I was asked about the subject matter of this writing. I hesitated. I was quite cautious about how I could truthfully respond to her question and yet, by her hearing the issues I was addressing, not confuse her image of God and His great love. This should not be! We should not have to hide anything! The gospel of our Savior is glorious!

THE FRUIT OF ANY TEACHING

In the context of Jesus' warning about false prophets, Jesus spoke of the importance of identifying "fruit" when distinguishing between that which may be false and that which is of Him (Matthew 7:15-20). "Every good tree bears good fruit, but a bad tree bears bad fruit. **A good tree cannot bear bad fruit, and a bad tree cannot bear good fruit**" (Matthew 7:17-18 NIV1984). Isn't part of the fruit, which we should be observing in good teaching, that of individuals being *spurred on* and strengthened in the faith—that of individuals becoming more and more sure of the Lord's goodness, His love for them, and His being there when they call? (See Hebrews 10:22-24; 1 John 4:16; and 2 Timothy 1:12.) Paul even spoke of the goal and the fruit of good teaching when he gave to Timothy this instruction:

> [Remain] in Ephesus so that you may instruct certain men not to teach strange doctrines, nor to pay attention to myths and endless genealogies, which give rise to mere speculation rather than **furthering the administration of God which is by faith**. But **the goal of our instruction is love from a pure heart and a good conscience and a sincere faith**. For some men, straying from these things, have turned aside to fruitless discussion . . . (1 Timothy 1:3-6 NASB)

MY HEART

Foremost, the Lord will be esteemed in the greatness of who He is. There is none like Him. He reigns over all. And nothing shall be greater than His covenant to do for *the ones whose hearts are His.*

12

It remains *God's* work. Nonetheless, burning on my heart is the need for professing believers to know *their* need to "continue in the faith"—committing themselves and looking to Jesus until the end (Psalm 37:5; Colossians 1:23; Hebrews 12:2). I see this need as *man's* responsibility and not an automatic thing that will just be "characteristic" of those "predestined" unto election (as Calvinist Reformed teaching conveys). Some brothers and sisters in the faith need strong warning to turn them from their destructive paths; God's love and mercy toward them gives them such warnings. Yet, how can one seriously heed the many warnings of Scripture and take his responsibility—to continue in Christ—when he is unconvinced that it genuinely is his responsibility? Dangerous complacency can set in as a fruit of *unconditional election* and other Calvinist Reformed teachings—and God's loving warnings, intended for life, are undermined.

My desire (what has moved me so greatly in this writing) is to share, in contrast to the teaching of *unconditional election* and other inter-related teachings of Calvinist Reformed theology, what God has laid on my heart concerning *His heart for relationship with all men* and where responsibilities do lie. My life has touched bases with so many people who have either embraced the Calvinist teachings as truth or who are confused by the teachings, and I love these people. Yet, foremost of my reasons for sharing is my love for my Father in heaven. By the teachings of *unconditional election* and *limited atonement*, His name—who He is—is being slandered.

(**From the onset, please note:** I am not a Calvinist, nor am I an Arminian—I hate the labels. I am a follower of Jesus Christ who is after the truth—who simply wants to grow in the knowledge of who He is.

Although the nature of this writing may appear to some as a concerted attack on Calvinist Reformed theology, thereby, making me Arminian, taking sides has not been my aim. Particular teachings being addressed were burning on my heart *long before* I realized they fell under the label of "Calvinism" or "Reformed theology." Although I may primarily address teachings coming from the Calvinist camp, I realize there are also *serious* imbalances within the camp of many professing Arminians.)

DO WE HAVE TO UNDERSTAND?

In the midst of waiting on the Lord, studying, and writing, the Holy Spirit has challenged my heart in many ways. One of the challenges He has given me to consider is this question: "Do you think you have to *understand* everything? Even if My way is shown to be true to the teaching of *unconditional election,* can you still accept Me as 'good' and trust Me?" May my answer be "yes." The truth is: God's ways are higher (Isaiah 55:8-9). We will not always be able to understand.

Thankfully, not all who believe the teachings of *unconditional election* and *limited atonement* appear to be personally weakened by the teachings. Many would say they believe that both the teaching of *unconditional election* and the teaching of *God's provision for all* can somehow be true at the same time. They have made up their minds that they do not have to understand the "how" of both being true. They know that God's ways are higher than our ways. They have received the teaching of *unconditional election* because they think it is what Scripture teaches. Yet, they still stand solid in the Lord. They *know* God is good.

Indeed, God *can* use our responses to *any* teaching as a test of how well we really know Him. As Paul conveyed his concern to Timothy over false teachings' destructive effects on some disciples, he seemed to allude to and be comforted by what *will* be a steadfast and unshakable posture of those who truly have a heart-to-heart relationship with the Lord (2 Timothy 2:19).

SOUND DOCTRINE

Although we will not understand everything, it is clear, however, that we are not to receive just any teaching. Wrong teaching can be very destructive. Paul spoke of **teachings that "destroy the faith of some"** (2 Timothy 2:18 NIV1984). He had earlier invoked Timothy with these words: **"Watch your life and doctrine closely.** Persevere in them, because if you do, you will save both yourself and your hearers" (1 Timothy 4:16 NIV1984).

Over and over again, the apostles warned the early church to be very discerning about what was being taught. The church was to *hold onto and carefully guard* the truth that they had received. Similarly, we also are reminded:

> **See that what you have heard from the beginning remains in you.** If it does, you also will remain in the Son and in the Father. And this is what he promised us—even eternal life. (1 John 2:24-25 NIV1984)

> And you, that were sometime alienated and enemies in your mind by wicked works, yet now hath he reconciled in the body of his flesh through death, to present you holy and unblameable and unreproveable in his sight: **If ye continue in the faith grounded and settled, and be not moved away** from the hope of the gospel, which ye have heard, and which was preached to every creature which is under heaven; whereof I Paul am made a minister. (Colossians 1:21-23 KJV)

Paul prophesied about the relationship between heeding wrong doctrine and *departing from "the faith"* when he said to Timothy: "Now the Spirit speaketh expressly, that in the latter times **some shall depart from the faith**, giving heed to seducing spirits, and doctrines of demons" (1 Timothy 4:1 KJV). For sure, sound doctrine is important to "continuing in the faith."

Paul spoke soberly of the dangers of our even receiving "another gospel" (and of the judgment upon many who would spread it). (See 2 Corinthians 11:4 and Galatians 1:6-9.) Jude, in his letter to the church, urged to "**contend for the faith** that was once for all entrusted to the saints" (Jude 3 NIV1984). What is "the gospel"/"the faith" that we are told to hold onto and to "contend for"? Evidently, *it is to be distinguishable from that which is not of Him.*

I believe there are distinguishable differences between Calvinist Reformed teaching's portrayal of God's work in sending Jesus and that of the gospel message first given and received. **According to Calvinist Reformed teaching, the "good news" of the gospel is that provision for salvation through the death of Jesus is *not* available to all**—but only to the elect ones who were *unconditionally* predestined unto salva-

15

tion by God. The gospel message I first received, however, was quite different. According to that gospel, God loves all men, and provision for salvation has been made available, through the work of Jesus, to all who would humble themselves to receive Him.

VERY SACRED GROUND

When speaking about teachings over which we disagree, we are treading upon *very sacred ground*. The Lord loves His church, and He is very jealous over her—His house—which is being built for His glory. Indeed, "**if anyone destroys God's temple, God will destroy him**; for God's temple is sacred, and [we] are that temple" (1 Corinthians 3:17 NIV1984). Furthermore, we also are commanded: "Make every effort to keep the unity of the Spirit through the bond of peace" (Ephesians 4:3 NIV1984). As I present these writings, therefore, I am very sober and mindful of my responsibility. By what I present, I ask myself: Am I building up or am I tearing down God's temple? Am I being wrongly divisive by what I say?

Zealously and surely, we *must* guard the unity that we have in the Spirit. Although, in the process of our growing in the knowledge of the Lord, Satan would have us divide, we must not be a part of causing such a division. Never should we let what is "good" become "evil." To the contrary, as Philippians 2:1-3 would urge:

> If there be therefore any consolation in Christ, if any comfort of love, if any fellowship of the Spirit, if any bowels and mercies, fulfill ye my joy, that ye be like-minded, having the same love, being of one accord, of one mind. Let nothing be done through strife or vainglory; but in lowliness of mind let each esteem other better than themselves. (KJV)

Significantly today, I believe the church is in a crucial time of history. The Lord is building us to look *as we should look*. Part of that building, I believe, is our even being brought into a place where we reach clarity and unity concerning important doctrines. The following words especially excite me:

> It was he who gave some to be apostles, some to be prophets, some to be evangelists, and some to be pastors and teachers, to prepare God's people for works of service, so that the body of Christ may be built up **until we all reach unity in the faith and in the knowledge of the Son of God and become mature, attaining to the whole measure of the fullness of Christ. Then we will no longer be infants, tossed back and forth by the waves, and blown here and there by every wind of teaching** and by the cunning and craftiness of men in their deceitful scheming. Instead, speaking the truth in love, we will in all things **grow up into him who is the Head, that is, Christ.** From him the whole body, joined and held together by every supporting ligament, grows and builds itself up in love, as each part does its work. (Ephesians 4:11-16 NIV1984)

There is a glorious promise before the church! Yet even so, as Ephesians asserts, key to the church growing up into Him in all things is our guarding the unity, which we have in Christ, and our having dialogue "in love" with one another. Constantly, the Lord has reminded me of the crucial importance of walking "in love" with the brothers and sisters with whom I have disagreed. We may speak of differences we have on doctrine. We may make judgments on doctrines. But we are *not* to judge one another.[2] Only God knows the motives of each one's heart. (See Matthew 13:24-30; 1 Corinthians 4:3-5; and 2 Timothy 2:19.)

AT REST

We do not need to get anxious and, by our anxiousness, do destructive works of the flesh. We *can* rest knowing that, if a person's heart is after

---

[2] Note: In the church, we are to make judgments toward brothers or sisters caught in sin—for the sake of discipline and for the sake of retaining holiness in the church (1 Corinthians 5:9-12). These judgments, however, are not final and condemning "you are this" types of judgment. Furthermore, righteous judgments are even made with hopes of future restoration (1 Corinthians 5:4-5).

the Lord, the Holy Spirit *will* make everything clear. He *will* lead into all truth. If a person is looking to the Lord and not unto men, trusting the Holy Spirit as his teacher, the Lord *will* guard him and bring clarity (Psalm 25:3; Philippians 3:15; John 16:13; 1 John 2:26-27). Paul spoke the following words to Timothy, which speak of the confidence we can have in *the Lord's ability* to keep those who love Him—who entrust their lives wholly to Him:

> I know whom I have believed, and am convinced that **he
> is able to guard what I have entrusted to him for that
> day**. (2 Timothy 1:12 NIV1984)

The Lord has reminded me of these words so many times to give me rest (because I have been so greatly alarmed by the Calvinist Reformed doctrines being widely taught). Although God may call us to speak on issues that are on His heart, we can still maintain hearts at rest—knowing *He is bigger than it all.*

ONLY THE WORD OF GOD

From the onset, I have felt the Lord speaking to me this important re-minder, as a guide preceding anything that I might share with others:

> **"Do not go beyond what is written."** (1 Corinthians
> 4:6 NIV1984)

Truly, it does not matter what man may think. For God's ways are higher than our ways. And never are we to take our journey into the "wisdom of men." "For it is written: 'I will destroy the wisdom of the wise. The intelligence of the intelligent I will frustrate' " (1 Corinthians 1:19 NIV1984). The intent of this writing, therefore, is to share *based on scriptures,* and not my own thoughts or presumptions, what I believe the Lord has firmly stated are His will and His provision for all men.

Moreover, within this writing, I have endeavored to look at *all* Scrip-ture in my consideration of doctrines. Consider anew the words of Paul to Timothy:

All Scripture is God-breathed and is useful for teaching, rebuking, correcting and training in righteousness, so that the man of God may be thoroughly equipped for every good work. (2 Timothy 3:16-17 NIV1984)

Clearly, as Paul states, "all Scripture" is useful for our instruction. None is to be disregarded. Even the past is recorded in Scripture for our example (helping us to know patterns of God's ways and dealings with men—from which we can learn). *All* Scripture, therefore, will be open to consideration.

Notwithstanding this, although all Scripture should be available when considering "right" teaching, all Scripture also should only be considered within the *context* of its writing. I am greatly troubled by the flippant way some people handle Scripture. Many teachings have been built by pulling one scripture from here and one scripture from there, without being careful to understand the context. Yet, in contrast, Paul spoke of the workman who did not need to be ashamed as one who "correctly handles the word of truth" (2 Timothy 2:15 NIV1984). He grieved concerning the ones who would rise up and "distort the truth" (Acts 20:30 NIV1984).

Significantly as well, as many doctrines in the church have been mainly built by taking words *from letters* written by the apostles to the early church, it is also important, when studying any letter of the Bible, first to slowly read through from the beginning to the end. We must handle letters as the letters they are—the writer is sharing his heart! As there would be danger of misrepresentation from just taking tiny snippets of an interview with someone who had gone into great detail to develop and to share his full heart, so there is danger of distorting the intent of a writer in his letter to the church.

Indeed, the apostles themselves were quite familiar with the distortion of things they had to say. Aware of such, Paul spoke to the Romans concerning such misrepresentations (Romans 3:8). Moreover, Peter even spoke thus, with respect to some of Paul's writings: "His letters contain some things that are **hard to understand, which ignorant and unstable people distort**, as they do the other Scriptures, to their own destruction" (2 Peter 3:16 NIV1984). Particular words of Scripture *have* been distorted—but may we not do the same.

Then additionally, desiring to rightly divide, I have aimed to be true to the original texts by studying scriptures in light of Greek and Hebrew lexicons, the Interlinear Greek-English New Testament, the Septuagint, and other scriptures where the same original Greek or Hebrew words are found. Especially, during this study, I have noticed the diversity in the way different English translations represent the meanings of the actual Greek and Hebrew words found in the original Old Testament and New Testament texts—and, consequently, think that variance from the original words and their specific shades of meaning is what, many times, also has led to critical misunderstandings and formation of wrong doctrine. Hence, although the analytical word studies contained within this work may appear time consuming and unnecessary for some, for others, the studies may be just the key needed to understand certain scriptures. Often, therefore, I have supplied the original Greek or Hebrew words, *in italics*, following words of special significance.

"HARD TO UNDERSTAND" SCRIPTURES

Agreeably, at first, several scriptures do appear to support the Calvinist doctrines of *unconditional election* and *limited atonement*. Terms such as "elect," "election,""chose," and "chosen" do frequently appear in Scripture regarding those who belong to Him. Words like "predestined" also appear. In many of these places, the texts can be complex and, at first, hard to understand.

Just as, in 2 Peter 3:16, Peter warned us of writings that are "hard to understand," and much more open to distortion, I believe many of these scriptures fall into that category. There is important meaning to the references commonly cited in support of *unconditional election*—no scriptures should ever be discounted! So, in following chapters, many of these scriptures will be addressed for consideration of other more likely meanings.

In the meantime, however, it is important, when confronted with difficult passages of Scripture, not to falter in faith because of a lack of understanding, but, instead, to trust the Holy Spirit to make all things clear, precept upon precept, and in their proper time (John 16:13; Philippians 3:15; 1 John 2:27). Until that time, we can hold onto scriptures that *are* clear and explicit (Philippians 3:16). These are the scriptures from which we shall begin.

SCRIPTURAL
INCONSISTENCIES
OF
CALVINISM

Chapter 1

Inconsistencies within the Doctrines of *Unconditional Election* and *Limited Atonement*—Part 1: A Provision for "Whosoever Will"

> But everything exposed by the light becomes visible, for it is light that makes everything visible. (Ephesians 5:13 NIV1984)

If we have nothing else, we have that which the Lord *explicitly* has said about *for whom* He has died. With that understanding, we can discern whether or not it would be consistent to say that God *unconditionally* predestines some, before their births, to know Him and, likewise, some, before their births, not to have opportunity to know Him. With an understanding of what the Lord explicitly has spoken about for whom He has died, we also can discern whether, as Calvinism concludes, it would be consistent to say that Christ's atonement on the cross, consequently, was "limited"—that His atonement was not available to all.

THE CLEAR WITNESS OF SCRIPTURE

The following scriptures are some of the many explicit scriptures—noting *for whom* the Lord has provided salvation. Even so, from discussions with Calvinist friends concerning the meanings of some of these passages, I have become especially aware of arguments used to discount them. Consequently, at times, I may have made comments. To begin, therefore, consider the following:

> Hebrews 2:9
> But we see Jesus . . . now crowned with glory and honor because he suffered death, so that by the grace of God he might taste death **for everyone**." (NIV1984)

> Romans 3:20-24
> Therefore no one will be declared righteous in his sight

by observing the law; rather, through the law we become conscious of sin. But now a righteousness from God, apart from law, has been made known, to which the Law and the Prophets testify. This righteousness from God comes through faith in Jesus Christ **to all who believe**. There is no difference, for **all have sinned and fall short of the glory of God, and are justified freely by his grace** through the redemption that came by Christ Jesus. (NIV 1984)

We are quite familiar with the portion of this scripture that says "all have sinned." (This is a familiar verse used in presenting to the unsaved their need for a savior.) Yet, are we equally as familiar with the rest of Paul's statement, making known God's provision for salvation to all (provided they embrace God's work in their lives)? Notably as well, this writing of Paul is a continuation of the discussion Paul has been having (in the immediately preceding verses of Romans) about the advantage Jews, the ones circumcised and under the law, have over Gentiles, the ones uncircumcised and not under the law. Whatever context one gives to whom Paul is speaking about in Romans 3:10-18, therefore, should be the same for the "all" in verses 22 and 23. Is he differentiating between people groups, that none are righteous before God and any better than the other, or is he speaking about all individuals?

Romans 11:32
For God has bound all men over to disobedience, **so that he might have mercy on them all**. (NIV 1984)

As is discussed in the chapter "Another Look at Romans 3:11," there is much similarity between what Paul is saying in this part of his letter and what he earlier had expounded on in parts of Romans 2 – 4. To help, the Interlinear Greek New Testament translates: "For God shut up [*synkleio*][1] all in disobedience in order that to all He may show mer-

---

[1] E. W. Bullinger, *A Critical Lexicon and Concordance to the English and Greek New Testament* (Grand Rapids, MI: Kregel Publications, 1999; orig. pub. 1908), p. 177.

cy."[2] Just as the Interlinear Greek New Testament clarifies, no one has any claim to giving anything to God that He should repay—in order that He may show mercy. Moreover, even as the "all" who have fallen short of God's glory are justified freely by His grace (Romans 3:23-24), the "all" who are disobedient (Romans 11:32) are the ones to whom God would want to show mercy. The Lord *would* have mercy on all! In His mercy, and not in our works, He receives great glory!

In Response to Israel's Failure to Receive

Consider, again, Paul's discussion regarding Israel—as well as the truth that is given concerning provision for all:

Romans 9:30-32
What shall we say then? That the Gentiles, who did not pursue righteousness, have attained to righteousness, even the righteousness of faith; but Israel, pursuing the law of righteousness, has not attained to the law of righteousness. Why? Because **they did not seek it by faith, but, as it were, by the works of the law.** They stumbled at the stumbling stone. (NKJV)

Romans 10:1-4
Brethren, my heart's desire and prayer to God for Israel is that they may be saved. For I bear them witness that they have a zeal for God, but not according to knowledge. For **they being ignorant of God's righteousness, and seeking to establish their own righteousness, have not submitted to the righteousness of God.** For Christ is the end of the law for **righteousness to *everyone* who believes.** (NKJV, emphasis mine)

Can it be seen, here, that Paul is talking about the *conditions* needed for individual people to be saved? Also, note that verse 5 (which follows) shows the context of Paul's interchange—that he is speaking about the

---

[2] *The Zondervan Parallel New Testament in Greek and English,* 8th ed. (New York: Zondervan Publishing House, 1982), p. 472.

individual man, and not about a people group, by his expressions containing "everyone." Verse 5 reads: "The **man** [*anthropos*] who does those things [lives by the law] shall live by them."[3]

> Romans 10:11-13
> For the Scripture says, "*Whoever* **believes on Him** will not be put to shame." For there is no distinction between Jew and Greek—for the same Lord over all is **rich to** *all* **who call upon Him**. For "*whoever* **calls on the name of the** LORD **shall be saved**." (NKJV, emphasis mine)

Here, Paul continues his discussion, which was begun earlier in Romans 9:1, concerning whether or not God's word to Israel had failed by His, seemingly, lifting His favor to them as a nation and giving it to another. Paul seems to be saying that the ultimate reason only some of his brethren were chosen for God's mercy—and not most of Israel—is that those of *His* choice had submitted to *His* righteousness and not to their own way of their own works. Those who had received and who would receive God's provision for salvation (whether Jew or Gentile) would be those who trusted *only* in Him. They would be those individuals who would call out to Him for *His* help and *His* work in their lives. Never had God spoken of any other way of righteousness. God always had looked toward and always had shown favor toward those whose hope was only in Him (Habakkuk 2:4; Genesis 15:6; Job 1:1; Psalm 25; Psalm 33:12-22).[4]

Pas Anthropos

Although some would argue that the "all" or "all men" references of the previous verses might just possibly be "all nations" (because the Greek only says "all" / *pas*), the immediately following scriptures cannot be argued in such a way. Instead, in the following scriptures, according to the Interlinear Greek New Testament, provision can be seen for *all men*. It can be seen that the references to "all men" (to be itali-

---

[3] See the upcoming discussion of the Greek word *anthropos*.
[4] Later, within the chapter entitled "Our Real Effect upon Our Salvation," more is discussed concerning whether all have had opportunity *to believe* on the Father and, thus, to receive a revelation of Jesus—their salvation.

cized in the following scriptures) definitely are referring to "individuals" and not to "nations." Contextually, nations are not being discussed in any of the upcoming scriptures. Most importantly, however, according to the Greek in the passages, the meaning is *specific*.

Quite significantly, *anthropos*[5] is the word translated as "men" in the immediately upcoming scriptures, and, according to *Bullinger's Lexicon*, means the following: "an 'individual' of the human race, a man or woman, a person, a human being."[6] Then as well, among the 550 times *anthropos* is translated in the New Testament,[7] that same Greek word for "man" or "men" can be noted in scriptures where "individuals" are clearly indicated: Romans 5:12 ("through the one *man* [Adam]"), Romans 5:15 ("the one *man*, Jesus Christ"), and Hebrews 9:27 ("just as *man* is destined to die once").

Not only is there distinction toward "individuals," but, when rendering the meaning of "nation" or "nations," the writers of the New Testament knew about and freely used the Greek word *ethnos*,[8] a word specific for "nations." For instance, within the 1984 New International Version (NIV1984) translation of the New Testament, the Greek word *ethnos* can be seen sixty out of the sixty-two times that "nation" or "nations" is found![9] Moreover, within that translation, never is "nation" or "nations" translated from *anthropos*, and never is "man" or "men" translated from *ethnos*.[10] The writers of the Greek New Testament seemed to know about the distinctions between the words *ethnos* and *anthropos*— and so should we. Even so, sadly, some explanations of these very clear passages still might side-step the importance of the original Greek writings and of what Scripture specifically states about God's provision for all souls.

---

[5] Edward W. Goodrick and John R. Kohlenberger, *The NIV Exhaustive Concordance* (Grand Rapids, MI: Zondervan Publishing House, 1990), p. 1682.
[6] E.W. Bullinger, *A Critical Lexicon and Concordance to the English and Greek New Testament*, p. 476.
[7] Goodrick and Kohlenberger, *The NIV Exhaustive Concordance*, p. 1682.
[8] E. W. Bullinger, *A Critical Lexicon and Concordance to the English and Greek New Testament*, pp. 516-517.
[9] Goodrick and Kohlenberger, *The NIV Exhaustive Concordance*, pp. 783-784.
[10] Ibid., pp. 782-784, 728-730, 746-748.

Romans 5:15
But the gift is not like the trespass. **For if the many died by the trespass** of the one man, **how much more did God's grace and the gift that came by the grace** of the one man, Jesus Christ, overflow to the many! (NIV 1984)

Romans 5:18
Consequently, just as the result of one trespass was **condemnation for *all men*,** so also the result of one act of righteousness was **justification, that brings life for *all men*.** (NIV 1984)

1 Timothy 4:9-10
This is a trustworthy saying that deserves full acceptance (and for this we labor and strive), that we have put our hope in the living God, **who is the Savior of *all men*, and especially of those who believe.** (NIV 1984)

Note: In 1 Timothy 4, Paul differentiates between the ones to whom there is abundant provision and *the ones who receive by believing.* There has been provision, although all do not receive it.

Titus 2:11
For the grace of God that brings salvation has appeared **to *all men*.** (NIV 1984)

1 Timothy 2:4-6
This is good, and pleases God our Savior, **who wants *all men* to be saved and to come to a knowledge of the truth.** For there is one God and one mediator between God and men, the man Christ Jesus, **who gave himself as a ransom for all men**—the testimony given in its proper time. (NIV 1984)

Significantly, within 1 Timothy 2, it can be seen—both God's heart for *all* individuals as well as a statement specifying Jesus' gift as a ransom for *all* individuals![11]

It is God's sovereign "will," His ruling desire, that men fully know Him—and for this He has made abundant provision! The word in the Greek used for "wants," which is *"thelo,"*[12] truly means "to will," "to wish," and "to desire."[13] God desires that all men be saved! And indeed, "this is the confidence that we have in approaching God: that if we ask anything *according to his will*, he hears us. And if we know that he hears us—whatever we ask—we know that we have what we asked of him" (1 John 5:14-15 NIV 1984, emphasis mine).[14]

This now ends the section of scriptures following the *"pas anthropos"* pattern.

As One Died *for All*, All Died

<u>2 Corinthians 5:14-21</u>
For the love of Christ controls us, having concluded this, **that one died for all**, therefore all have died; (15) **and He died for all**, so that they who live might no longer live for themselves, but for Him who died and rose again on their behalf. Therefore from now on we recognize no one according to the flesh; even though we (16) have known Christ according to the flesh, yet now we know Him in this way no longer. (17) Therefore if anyone is in Christ, he is a new creature; the old things passed away; behold new things have come. (18) Now all these things are from God,

---

[11] Note: The last "all men" phrase does not follow the *"pas anthropos"* pattern. The Greek text translated as "all men" has only "all" (*pas*), and not "men," in the "ransom for all men" phrase of 1 Timothy 2:6. Nonetheless, contextually, from verses 4 and 5, where *anthropos is* expressed, it is very evident that Paul is talking about *individuals*.
[12] Goodrick and Kohlenberger, *The NIV Exhaustive Concordance*, p.1730.
[13] Bullinger, *A Critical Lexicon and Concordance to the English and Greek New Testament*, p. 884.
[14] A full discussion of 1 Timothy 2:4-6, emphasizing context, is found in the chapter "Inconsistencies—Part 2."

31

> who reconciled us to Himself through Christ and gave us the ministry of reconciliation, (19) namely, **that God was in Christ reconciling the world to Himself**, not counting their trespasses against them, and He has committed to us the word of reconciliation. (20) Therefore, we are ambassadors for Christ, as though God were making an appeal through us; we beg you on behalf of Christ, be reconciled to God. (21) He made Him who knew no sin to be sin on our behalf, so that we might become the righteousness of God in Him. (NASB)

Paul is referring again to *all individuals* when he speaks of the ones for whom Christ died—the ones for whom he would lay down his life in ministry in order that they might be reconciled to Christ. He is not talking about all nations in these statements, nor is he talking about only the elect. Can there be any doubt as to the important truth of God's provision that Paul conveyed? Some still may have doubts; so I will expound.

Beginning with verse 14, it can be clearly seen that Paul is referring to "individuals," not "nations." As he mentions the "all" for whom Christ has died and the proper result being *for them to die too*, the words of verses 14 and 15 definitely would not make sense with "nations." The message of dying to selves, both in response to His death and in order to have the life of Christ (Romans 6:2-4; 2 Corinthians 4:10-12), is for *individuals*, not nations.

Next, by looking at context (because at this point, in 2 Corinthians 5, Paul has been discussing his and Timothy's *ministry* for a while), clues can also be found which show *about whom* the "all," within verses 14 and 15, is speaking. Just previous to the noted verses, in verse 11, Paul has shared that "we persuade men [*anthropos*[15]/ individuals]." Then later, in verses 20-21, he continues to share the message—the plea God has given him to share with *individuals* about reconciliation and becoming "the righteousness of God." So again, Paul is *not* discussing the gospel going to all *nations* (and nations becoming "the righteousness of God"); he is discussing, here, the good news that is being preached to

---

[15] *The Zondervan Parallel New Testament in Greek and English*, 8th ed., p. 531.

individuals.

In addition, for those who might think Paul's reference to the "all" (for whom Christ died) possibly refers to only "elect," "predestined" individuals, notice the surrounding scriptures. Only a chapter earlier, in 2 Corinthians 4:2-4, *within that same discussion of his and Timothy's ministry*, Paul had spoken very pointedly concerning the ones to whom they gave themselves in ministry—the ones whom they tried to "persuade" (according to 2 Corinthians 5:11):

> [But] by the manifestation of truth commending ourselves to **every man's** conscience in the sight of God. And even if our gospel is veiled, it is veiled to those who are perishing, in whose case the god of this world has blinded the minds of the unbelieving so that they might not see the light of the gospel of the glory of Christ, who is the image of God. (2 Corinthians 4:2-4 NASB)

In this earlier statement, Paul specifically states (according to the Greek)[16] that they commended themselves to *"every conscience of men [anthropos]."* Thus, Paul must also have been speaking later (in 2 Corinthians 5:14-15) about all *individuals* (whether they responded to the message or not), and not only concerning the elect. It is clear because, from 2 Corinthians 4 *until* the section being discussed in 2 Corinthians 5:14-21, the ones to whom Paul and Timothy see themselves in ministry never changes. (Paul does *not* later, towards 2 Corinthians 5:14-21, shift into talking about ministry only to the elect.) Furthermore, as can be seen by this earlier statement (2 Corinthians 4:4), the ones to whom Paul and Timothy commended themselves—the ones whom they tried to persuade—would even include those whom he stated had been "blinded" by Satan[17] towards seeing the light of the gospel.

Also helpfully, Paul's statements of belief, as recorded in 2 Corinthians 5:14-15, lead to the responses and further conclusions by Paul (within the verses immediately following), thus continuing to aid in getting the

---

[16] Ibid.

[17] Concerning those "perishing," see the discussion of 2 Thessalonians 2:10-12, found within the chapter "Inconsistencies—Part 2."

full intent of his statements, which note *for whom* there is provision of Christ's sacrifice. First, in response to Christ's demonstration of love, Paul and Timothy no longer regard themselves the way they once did. As seen in verse 15, they no longer believe in living for themselves (and would encourage others to have the same thinking). Secondly, and quite significantly, *as a result of their belief that Christ died for all*, they no longer see *any* humans "according to the flesh" anymore. They see *all* people as potential new creations in Christ.

(Note: The fact that verses 16 and 17 are related to what was just said in verses 14 and 15 clearly can be seen by the Greek word chosen to connect the latter verses. Notably, the word *hoste* [18]— translated as "so" or "therefore"—was used in both verses 16 and 17. That Greek word, accordingly, means "so as that" and marks "a result."[19])

Most significantly, however, it can be seen that Paul is referring to all *individuals*, for whom Christ died, in that *he also chose to put Christ with those* whom they may have once regarded only "according to the flesh." Because he was referring to all *humans* that might be regarded "according to the flesh," he even included Christ—because Jesus Christ came "in the flesh." Paul knew what he was saying. His conclusions regarding *all human beings* came as a result of what he was convinced of—that Christ had died for all!

A Reconciliation of "All Creation"

The next portions of Scripture to be noted are much alike. All are very inclusive in their statements of for whom and for what Christ died and made provision. While Calvinist Reformed teaching limits God's provision, these scriptures seem to be doing the opposite—expanding His provision even beyond man!

2 Corinthians 5:18-19
Now all these things are from God, who reconciled us to

---

[18] Goodrick and Kohlenberger, *The NIV Exhaustive Concordance*, p. 1809.
[19] Bullinger, *A Critical Lexicon and Concordance to the English and Greek New Testament*, p. 783.

Himself through Christ and gave us the ministry of reconciliation, namely that God was in Christ **reconciling the world to Himself**, not counting their trespasses against them, and He has given to us the word of reconciliation. (NASB)

2 Corinthians 5:19 is so significant in that it states: "God was in Christ reconciling the world to Himself." God was reconciling *the world*! Indeed, according to Bullinger's Lexicon, *kosmos*,[20] the Greek word used for "world," wholly renders the following:

The ordered universe, the ordered entirety of God's creation, but considered as separated from God. Then, the abode of humanity, or that order of things in which humanity moves or of which man is the centre; then, mankind as it manifests itself in and through such an order; then, that order of things which, in consequence of and since the Fall, is alienated from God, as manifested in and through the human race.[21]

Paul wrote a very broad word to speak for whom God was providing reconciliation. He did not limit the provision with a word such as "nations" or "elect" here. He could have, or he even could have written *anthropos*, for "individuals"—but he did not. Perhaps instead, Paul was asserting, by his statement, that God *not only* sent Jesus to pay for the sins of *all individuals*—in order to bring them back into relationship—but God's plan and provision were there to even reconcile *all creation* back into its former glory through Jesus. Notwithstanding Paul's likely intent, it is clear that the "world," which God was reconciling back to Himself through Jesus, would certainly include *every **human being**—* **provided he willingly respond** to God's initiatives.

Colossians 1:17-20
He is before all things, and in him all things hold togeth-

---

[20] Goodrick and Kohlenberger, *The NIV Exhaustive Concordance*, p. 1744.
[21] Bullinger, *A Critical Lexicon and Concordance to the English and Greek New Testament*, pp. 900-901.

er. And he is the head of the body, the church; he is the beginning and the firstborn from among the dead, so that in everything he might have the supremacy. **For God was pleased** to have all his fullness dwell in him, and through him **to reconcile to himself *all* things**, whether things on earth or things in heaven, by making peace through his blood, shed on the cross. (NIV1984, emphasis mine)

"All things" refers to the "all creation" (v. 15), of which *all men* are a part. Contextually, even verses 15, 16, and 18 show clearly that men are a part of the "all creation" that Jesus is over.

John 12:47
"And if anyone hears My words and does not believe, I do not judge him; for I did not come to judge the world but **to save the world**." (NKJV)

Again, Jesus came to save the world—which accordingly, in the Greek, is *kosmos*![22] Even so, although all creation is being restored through the work of the cross,[23] when Jesus shares His mission for coming and His provision for *the world*, He seems to be talking about *individuals*. When His statement is made, Jesus is explaining the reason why the *person* failing to embrace His words is not right away being judged (see verse 48).

An Atonement for the *Whole* World

1 John 2:2
And **He Himself is the propitiation for our sins**, and not for ours only but **also for the whole world**. (NKJV)

This passage of Scripture, alone, is so full. Yet, for the sake of those who would still doubt Christ's *full* provision—His abundant provision

---

[22] Ibid.

[23] Concerning the reconciliation of *all* creation, see also the discussion entitled "The Most Valued of All Creation," found within the chapter "Inconsistencies—Part 2."

for the whole world (if they will receive)—note the actual Greek words used in the Greek text. The Greek word used for "propitiation" is indeed *hilasmos*,[24] which renders the following: "conciliation, expiation."[25] Agreeably, Webster's Dictionary defines "expiation" as the following: "atonement; making amends for wrongdoing or guilt." To "expiate" is to "pay the penalty of."[26] Next, the Greek word translated as "whole" is *holos*,[27] rendering the following: "the whole, all, meaning every part."[28] Finally, and in agreement, the Greek word used for "world" is again *kosmos*[29] (which previously has been defined). Surely, this scripture must mean what it says!

IN CONCLUSION

And let him that is athirst come. **And whosoever will, let him take** the water of life freely. (Revelation 22:17 KJV)

Clearly, Christ's atonement is only limited by one's own failure to embrace His initiatives and to desire Him. **His atonement for life has been *available* to all.** The teaching of *limited atonement* as proclaimed by TULIP's "L"—that Christ's atonement was not for all—that it was limited to only the "elect" individuals whom God had predestined and chosen *unconditionally* before birth—cannot be an accurate doctrine according to Scripture.[30]

---

[24] Goodrick and Kohlenberger, *The NIV Exhaustive Concordance*, p. 1733.

[25] Bullinger, *A Critical Lexicon and Concordance to the English and Greek New Testament*, p. 608.

[26] *Webster's New World Dictionary of the American Language, College Edition* (Cleveland and New York: The World Publishing Company, 1968), p. 512.

[27] Goodrick and Kohlenberger, *The NIV Exhaustive Concordance*, p. 1763.

[28] Bullinger, *A Critical Lexicon and Concordance to the English and Greek New Testament*, p. 879.

[29] Ibid., pp. 900-901.

[30] Concerning scriptural inconsistencies with the doctrines of *unconditional election* and *limited atonement*, see also the chapters "Inconsistencies—Part 2" and "Discrepancies of Various TULIP Teachings—2 Peter 2."

Chapter 2

Inconsistencies within the Doctrines of *Unconditional Election* and *Limited Atonement*—Part 2: Do We *Know* the One in Whom We Have Believed?

Would it be consistent with *who God is* to say He destines ahead of time some individuals unto wrath and judgment and some unto life eternal—regardless of any responses they might make in life? Would that be in line with what we know Scripture does say about who He is—what brings Him delight and how He feels about things? Can we not know God and even grow in the knowledge of the Lord (2 Timothy 1:12; Hebrews 8:11; John 17:3; Ephesians 1:17; 1 John 5:20)? Are we not even experientially supposed to know Him in such a way, through the Holy Spirit, that we can detect that which is counterfeit and not true (1 Corinthians 2:11-12; 1 John 2:20-21, 26-27; Jude 10)? When we get to know someone, getting to know his heart, are we not able to resist slanderous accusations that are false about that person? Do we know the one in whom we have believed?

There are so many places in Scripture that are inconsistent with the "predestination unto wrath" that Calvinist Reformed theology suggests with its doctrine of *unconditional election*. Unlike the chapter "Inconsistencies—Part 1" (where scriptures are cited that specifically state God's provision of salvation *to all men*), the purpose of this chapter is to show the inconsistencies such "predestination unto wrath" would have with other scriptures. Significantly, the notion that God would "unconditionally" predestine some unto wrath is inconsistent with what the Word clearly tells us about who God is (His heart for all men, what brings Him joy, and His ways), as well as with what our own experiences tell us—as we daily receive *His heart* placed upon our hearts.

MAN'S REFUSAL OF AVAILABLE GRACE

To begin with, there is inconsistency with the teaching of *unconditional election* in that Scripture says God *does* reveal Himself so that all men may fully know Him and glorify Him. Also, as can be seen by the immediately following scriptures, Scripture is very clear in identifying *man* as the one who carries the responsibility for whether he receives God's provision of life or not. The responsibility squarely is given to man, because of *his* responses to God's revealed truth, and not to a predetermined decision of God (one that cannot be thwarted).

First and quite significantly, within the following section of Scripture, we are given a detailed description of the relationship that God *has* begun with all men, as well as the progression that relationship has taken with some (in bringing on His revealed wrath).

Romans 1:18-32

The wrath of God is being revealed from heaven against all the godlessness [*asebeia*] and wickedness of **men** [*anthropos*] **who suppress** [*katecho*] **the truth by their wickedness,** (19) **since what may be known** [*gnostos*] **about God is plain to them, because God has made it plain to them.** (20) For [*gar*] since the creation of the world God's invisible qualities—his eternal power and divine nature—have been clearly seen, being understood from what has been made, so that **men are without excuse.** (21) For **although they knew** [*ginosko*] **God, they neither glorified him as God nor gave thanks to him, but their thinking** [*dialogismos* / "reasoning through"][1] *became* **futile** [*mataioo* / "useless, empty"][2] **and their foolish hearts were darkened.** (22) Although they claimed to be wise, they *became* fools (23) and exchanged the glory of the immortal God for images made to look like mortal man and birds and animals and reptiles. (24) **Therefore God gave them over in the sinful desires of their hearts** to sexual impurity for the degrading of their bodies with one another. (25) **They exchanged the truth of God for a lie**, and worshiped and served created things rather than the Creator—who is forever praised. Amen. (26) **Because of this, God gave**

---

[1] E.W. Bullinger, *A Critical Lexicon and Concordance to the English and Greek New Testament* (Grand Rapids, MI: Kregel Publications, 1999; orig. pub. 1908), pp.401, xiii.

[2] Ibid., pp. 844, xiii.

them over to shameful lusts. Even their women exchanged natural relations for unnatural ones. (27) In the same way the men also abandoned natural relations with women and were inflamed with lust for one another. Men committed indecent acts with other men, and received in themselves the due penalty for their perversion. (28) Furthermore, **since** [*kathos*] **they did not think it worthwhile** [*dokimazo*] **to retain** [*echo* / "to have and hold"][3] **the knowledge** [*epignosis*] **of God,** *he gave them over to a depraved [adokimos] mind,* to do what ought not to be done." (29) They have become filled with every kind of wickedness, evil, greed and depravity. They are full of envy, murder, strife, deceit and malice. They are gossips, (30) slanderers, God-haters, insolent, arrogant and boastful; they invent ways of doing evil; they disobey their parents; (31) they are senseless, faithless, heartless, ruthless. (32) **Although they know** [*epiginosko*] **God's righteous decree that those who do such things deserve death, they not only continue to do these very things but also approve of those who practice them.** (NIV 1984, emphasis mine)

Contextually, in this section of Romans 1, Paul is recounting how, as God is revealing His righteousness through the gospel of Jesus (v. 17), He also is revealing His wrath against all the "godlessness and wickedness of men who suppress the truth by their wickedness" (v. 18). Perhaps, even, Paul is thinking about the case of many of his own Jewish brothers, who had dismissed the knowledge they *had* received of God, when he begins his discussion of God's judgment displayed. (See Psalm 106:20 and Romans 2:9-10.) At any rate, it is then that Paul proceeds to show the judgments given by God for wrong responses that are made by men.

Romans 1:18-32 is so pointed in what it speaks! Yet importantly, and in order to get its full meaning, it is helpful to understand more precisely the meanings of some of the Greek words used by Paul. Thus, even beginning with verse 18—and lest one should argue that Paul is refer-

---

[3] Ibid., pp. 644, xiii.

41

ring to "nations," and not to "individuals"—the root word used in the Greek for "men" is *anthropos*. Accordingly, Bullinger's Lexicon describes the meaning of *anthropos* as follows: "an 'individual' of the human race, a man or woman, a person, a human being."[4] Then as well, in verse 18, the Greek word used for "suppress," *katecho*, means "to have and hold down."[5] Hence, to begin with, according to the apostle Paul, *all men* have had truth; yet, *some have held down the truth* by their wickedness. (With similarity, verse 25 likewise makes the issue that the ones receiving God's wrath were ones who "exchanged the truth [which they had] for a lie.")

Equally, notice also, as the section proceeds, the constant use of words that show cause and effect—words such as "since" (v. 19), "for" (v. 20), "for" (v. 21), "therefore" (v. 24), "because of this" (v. 26), and "since" (v. 28). A study of the words used does indeed show verses 19, 21, 24 and 26, as translated, to be consistent with the Greek. (Verses 19 and 21 use the same Greek word, *dioti*, which means "for this reason,"[6] and verses 24 and 26 similarly use the same Greek word,[7] *dio*, which means "on which account."[8]) With the use of all of these words and phrases, Paul *definitely is* connecting judgments rendered with responses first wrongly made (and not with unconditional determinations by God). The cause and effect words used for verses 20 and 28 (the words "for" and "since"), however, rate additional mention because of the special meanings and inferences that are made by their original Greek.

Notably, the Greek word actually used for the "for" in verse 20, the word *gar*, renders *a strong reason* for what was just spoken in previous verses. Its meaning, and perhaps a better translation, is "the fact is, in fact." Just as Bullinger's Lexicon notes concerning the word: "[It has] a more extensive meaning than the [English] 'for,' expressing the reason,

---

[4] Bullinger, *A Critical Lexicon and Concordance to the English and Greek New Testament*, pp. 476, xiii.
[5] Ibid., pp. 378, xiii.
[6] Ibid., pp. 86-87.
[7] *The Zondervan Parallel New Testament in Greek and English*, 8th ed. (New York: Zondervan Publishing House, 1982), pp. 446-447.
[8] Bullinger, *A Critical Lexicon and Concordance to the English and Greek New Testament*, pp. 871, xiii.

cause, motive, principle, etc. of what has been previously said."[9] Thus, in view of this, verse 20 can read: "[The fact is] since the creation of the world God's invisible qualities—His eternal power and divine nature—have been clearly seen, being understood from what has been made, so that men are without excuse" (NIV 1984). In short, the apostle Paul clearly wanted it to be known: The ones to whom God's wrath was being revealed—the ones being given to "depraved" minds—likewise *had* been given opportunity to "know" God, who shows Himself through things He has made.

Also, and very important to note, found within verse 28 is the Greek word from which "since" was translated, the word *kathos.* According to Bullinger's Lexicon, it has a meaning of "like as, according as."[10] (Most often it is even translated in the NIV 1984 as "just as," and "as.")[11] Subsequently, therefore, the specific use of the word *kathos* not only shows *the reason for becoming* depraved *after* a knowledge of God, but the actual meaning may be stronger—denoting a direct correlation of the judgment rendered (of having a "depraved"/"unapproved" mind) to the fact that *they* had not "approved" (*dokimazo*) to have God in "full knowledge." (Read the note about "full knowledge" in the upcoming paragraph on *epignosis.*) Just as some have not approved of "having *and* holding" God in "full knowledge," God, in turn, has rendered a judgment on them of having an "unapproved" (*adokimos*)[12] knowledge holder—the mind.

Next, and of importance, notice the verbs which precisely denote the change that happened to the wicked *as a result of* their wrong responses—words such as "became futile" (v. 21), "were darkened" (v. 21), "became fools" (v. 22), "gave . . . over" (v. 26), and "gave . . . over" (v. 28). Clearly, the ones on whom God's wrath was revealed did not start out in the same depraved state in which they ended up (as *is* the teaching of some). They *became,* as part of God's rightful judgment.

---

[9] Ibid., pp. 296, 298, xiii.
[10] Ibid., pp. 258, xiii.
[11] Edward W. Goodrick and John R. Kohlenberger, *The NIV Exhaustive Concordance* (Grand Rapids, MI: Zondervan Publishing House, 1990), p. 1735.
[12] Bullinger, *A Critical Lexicon and Concordance to the English and Greek New Testament*, pp. 640, xiii.

Very distinctly, the Calvinist Reformed teaching of *total depravity* asserts that all are so "totally depraved" from birth that they are unable to see or even want to seek God. Indeed, verse 21 does fit this picture, but only somewhat. The ones receiving God's wrath *are* people whose ability for "reasoning through" (*dialogismos*)[13] has become "useless, empty" (*mataioo*).[14] Yet, significantly, the Greek verb tense used denotes "*became*"[15]—and not "was" (as a condition that might have been from birth). Their "futile" thinking was *because* of their wrong responses to God.

Then, verses 19, 21, 28, and 32 are similar in that they all contain related Greek words (*gnostos, ginosko, epignosis, and epiginosko*)—words of the root meaning "know." Moreover, all these verses also are alike in that they give important insight as to whether those—who, in the end, do receive God's wrath—equally have had the revelation needed for a proper response to the Father (*in order* to receive further revelation from the Father of just who Jesus is). Significantly, as is with verse 19 (having the Greek word *gnostos*), the Greek words used together for "what may be known" clearly do render a meaning of "that which is known, capable of being known, knowable."[16] Hence, it also becomes clear: **that which is capable of being known about God—His greatness and that He is God—*has* been manifested to everyone alike**. No one has been excluded.

Additionally, the word *ginosko*, rendered as "knew" in verse 21,[17] also is particularly revealing and in alignment with verse 19. Unlike *oida* (also translated as "know" in Scripture), in which "knowing" is only that of "having a knowledge of," possibly even just "from hearsay,"[18] *ginosko* "denotes *a personal and true relation between the person knowing and the object known . . .*" (emphasis mine). To *ginosko* is "to perceive, observe, obtain a knowledge of or insight into."[19] Thus, from

---

[13] Ibid., pp. 401, xiii.

[14] Ibid., pp. 844, xiii.

[15] *The Zondervan Parallel New Testament in Greek and English*, 8th ed., p. 447.

[16] Bullinger, *A Critical Lexicon and Concordance to the English and Greek New Testament*, pp. 437, xiii.

[17] Ibid., pp. 434-435, xiii.

[18] Ibid., pp. 434, xiii.

[19] Ibid., p. 434.

this it can be seen that, **before "their thinking became futile and their foolish hearts were darkened," the wicked (and depraved ones)** *had* **personally had revelation of the greatness of God and His place to be worshipped.** Faithfully, God had taken an interest in these individuals and had revealed Himself to them.

Lastly, the Greek words used for "knowledge" and "know," within verses 28 and 32, are very important to note—as they are even stronger in meaning than the former "knowing" words examined. With significance, the word *epignosis*, which corresponds to verse 28, often is translated "*full* knowledge"—as the prefix renders a "full" sense to the Greek root *gnosis* (the noun form related to *ginosko*). According to Bullinger, *epignosis* carries the specific meaning:

> Clear and exact knowledge . . . [It] is more emphatic than [gnosis], because it expresses a more thorough participation on the part of the knower, with the object of knowledge. [It is] a knowledge that has a powerful influence on the knower.[20]

Indeed, even consistently, within other places of Scripture, we can see a connection between those who have a *full* knowledge of the Lord and those who have a relationship with Him (e.g., Colossians 1:10 and 2 Peter 1:2-3)! **According to verse 28, therefore,** *they* (the wicked ones) had decided it not worthwhile—they had not "approved" (*dokimazo*) of God—"to have and hold" (*echo*) Him in full knowledge. *They* had refused the opportunity to have (*echo* / "implying continued holding and lasting possession")[21] the life of God and to truly know Him. Then, likewise—just as the Greek word *epiginosko*, within verse 32, similarly gives fullness to its root word, meaning ". . . to give heed, to notice attentively, to know fully or well"[22]—even while being depraved and under God's judgment, those who go their own way and do the things listed in verses 29 to 30 still *fully* know that God is God and that to disobey Him is worthy of death!

---

[20] Ibid., pp. 436, xiii.
[21] Ibid., pp. 644, 954, 378, xiii.
[22] Ibid., pp. 435, xiii.

Romans 1:18-32 speaks so clearly! All men have had opportunity for life *and* to fully know and to glorify Him as Father. Individuals who do not know Him will have only themselves to blame. "*Men* are without excuse" (v. 20). God has manifested to all men the knowledge that He Is and that He should be fully known. God's grace *has* been available. Only, some have resisted. Some have not wanted to have Him in full knowledge, and, thus, have become separated from the life of God. If one has become depraved in mind, it is because *he* has chosen not to regard what *could* be known about God—choosing, instead, to go his own way. *Because that one* did not respond to what was given, what he had was taken away (Mark 4:25).[23]

Other scriptures also follow that further show *why* some do not have God's life, as well as inconsistencies there are with saying opportunities to know the Lord have been *unconditionally* predestined.

> Romans 2:5-11
> But **because of your stubbornness and your unre-pentant heart**, you are storing up wrath against yourself for the day of God's wrath, when his righteous judgment will be revealed. **God "will give to each person according to what he has done."** To those who by persistence in doing good seek glory, honor, and immortality, he will give eternal life. But **to those who are self-seeking and who reject the truth and follow evil**, there will be wrath and anger. There will be trouble and distress for every human being who does evil: first for the Jew, then for the Gentile, but glory, honor and peace for everyone who does good: first for the Jew, then for the Gentile. *For [gar] God does not show favoritism.* (NIV 1984, emphasis mine)

This Scripture follows immediately after the previous section of Scripture mentioned. Contextually, as these statements are being made, Paul is rebuking those who would personally pass judgment on the ones

---

[23] Note: more is discussed concerning "depravity" in the chapter entitled "Our Real Effect upon Our Salvation."

whom he had just stated were under God's wrath. Paul states, in Romans 2:2-3, "Now we know that God's judgment against those who do such things is based on truth. So when you, a mere man, pass judgment on them and yet do the same things, do you think you will escape God's judgment?" (NIV 1984). The ones under Paul's rebuke appear to be the type who would teach others the law, but not obey it themselves.

Moreover, it is evident that the ones to whom Paul is speaking here are not yet in the same condition as those mentioned in Romans 1:32. It is evident that they do not "approve of" nor take pleasure in those who so sin (Romans 1:32 NIV 1984 and KJV) because, instead, they are prone to judge. Clearly, these ones have not yet been given over to "depraved mind[s]." Even so, their condition before God is still not settled. They are warned that they, too, have choices to make.

According to Paul's words in Romans 2, the responsibility clearly is *on man* as to whether he receives eternal life through Jesus or stores up wrath for the Day of Judgment. God renders to each person *"according to what he [the person] has done"* (v. 6). God is no respecter of persons. If one does not receive eternal life, it is because of his *own* actions—his *own* rebellion and rejection of the truth that is offered (vv. 6-8).[24]

Finally, verse 11, in itself, is very emphatic that, as God has done to one, He *will* do to another, thus dismissing the assertion that God unconditionally predestines some, before birth, unto eternal life and others unto wrath. Paul refers to this fact as an essential part of the warning he has just made (in verses 5-10). Even pointedly, where the NIV 1984 states, "For God does not show favoritism," the "for" is the word *gar* in the Greek (previously discussed, in relation to Romans 1:20, and rendering a meaning of "the fact is, in fact" and presenting "the reason, cause, motive, principle, etc., of what has been previously said"[25]). So then, *in the context of eternal life*, Paul concludes that, void of any re-

---

[24] **Importantly**, these words and the words that follow are a needful reminder to the one who would become complacent even after receiving a full knowledge of Jesus Christ. See also Matthew 16:27, James 2:14- 26, Revelation 2:23, and Revelation 3:1-6.
[25] Bullinger, *A Critical Lexicon and Concordance to the English and Greek New Testament*, pp. 296, 298, xiii.

pentance, the ones prone to judging others, and yet doing the same things, should expect similar consequences of wrath from God (as given in Romans 1:18-32)—*for the fact that* "**God does not show favoritism**" (v. 11).

> ### 2 Thessalonians 2:10-12
> **They perish because they refused to love the truth and so be saved.** For this reason God sends them a powerful delusion so that they will believe the lie and so that **all will be condemned who have not believed the truth but have delighted in wickedness**. (NIV 1984)

Have all had opportunity to know the truth and be saved? Have all been given truth? This portion of Scripture is powerful in what it states. According to the KJV (a more literal translation to the Greek here[26]), the reason some perish is "because *they received not* the love of the truth" (v. 10).

Indeed, further study into the Greek word actually used for "received" is quite revealing. According to Bullinger's Lexicon, the Greek word used, *dechomai,* means "to take to one's self what is presented or brought by another, to accept, embrace, receive hospitably . . . ." Furthermore, it is to "admit, approve, allow." "[It] implies a subjective reception, showing that a decision of the will has taken place with respect to the object presented . . . ."[27] Now, in order for something to be welcomed and accepted, does it not first have to be made available? In agreement with Romans 1:18 and 25, and Romans 2:8, it appears evident: *All have been given truth to which they can respond.* It is only because certain ones do not willfully "embrace" truth—because they "will" not to love truth—that they miss the opportunity to be saved and so perish.

(Note: Because of the exactness of what the Greek word *dechomai* implies, further study of the word is presented. The word *dechomai* is un-

---

[26] *The Zondervan Parallel New Testament in Greek and English*, 8th ed., pp. 608, 609.
[27] Bullinger, *A Critical Lexicon and Concordance to the English and Greek New Testament*, pp. 626, xiii.

like *lambano* and other Greek words of the *lambano* root. *Lambano*, also often translated as "receive," just has to do with being given something—"to take, take hold of, apprehend . . . to take what is given . . . pointing to an objective reception."[28] *Dechomai*, on the other hand, gets into *the will* of the person—the subject who is to receive what is presented. To differentiate between their specific meanings, examples of the usage of *dechomai* can be seen in Matthew 10:41, Matthew 11:14, Matthew 18:5, and Luke 18:17. Examples of the usage of *lambano* can be seen in John 19:30, Mark 11:24, and Mark 12:40 [KJV]. Additionally, Matthew 10:41 contains *both* words Greek words twice—in the pattern of *dechomai, lambano, dechomai, lambano*.[29])

Then, as the prophet Jonah repents and praises God for His great mercy, he also utters the following words that speak of the *opportunity* of God's grace, which all have had, and *why* some do not obtain it:

Jonah 2:8
"Those who cling [*shamar*][30] to worthless idols [*shav'*][31] **forfeit** [*'azab*][32] **the grace** [*checed*][33] **that could be theirs.**" (NIV 1984)

This passage of Scripture indicates that *there is grace available* which some forfeit by their own actions. The grace "could be theirs"! Yet, as do other translations, the KJV translates this passage differently. The KJV reads: **"They that observe** [*shamar*] **lying** [*shav*] **vanities** [*hebel*] **forsake** [*azab*] **their own mercy** [*chesed*]."**

To be sure, even though other translations may translate a bit differently, a look at the Hebrew proves very helpful in verifying this statement of Jonah concerning God's "abundant provision of grace" (Romans 5:17) for those who would receive. To begin with, according to *Strong's Complete Word Concordance*, the word translated as "cling"

---

[28] Ibid., pp. 626, xiii.
[29] Ibid., pp. 626-627.
[30] Goodrick and Kohlenberger, *The NIV Exhaustive Concordance*, p.1643.
[31] Ibid., p. 1631.
[32] Ibid., p. 1565.
[33] Ibid., p. 1454.

in the NIV1984 and "observe" in the KJV is the Hebrew word *shamar*, which means "to watch, to keep, to preserve, to guard . . . ."[34] Certainly, "to keep" and "to preserve" is "clinging to"—not letting go! Next, according to Strong, the Hebrew word translated for the word "worthless" in the NIV1984 and "lying" in the KJV is *shav*, which means "emptiness, vanity, evil, ruin, uselessness, deception, worthless."[35] Then comparably, the Hebrew word used for "idols" (NIV1984) and "vanities" (KJV) is *hebel*, meaning: "emptiness or vanity."[36] Further, *azab*, the Hebrew word translated as "forsake" (KJV) and "forfeit" (NIV1984) means "to leave, to abandon, to forsake, to loose."[37] Next, the Hebrew word used for "mercy" and "grace" is *chesed*, meaning: "kindness, lovingkindness, mercy, goodness, faithfulness, love, acts of kindness."[38] Finally, the NIV1984 rendering—"that could be theirs"—is just a paraphrase, stressing the fact that "their own mercy" (KJV) is no longer *because of being forsaken*.

Truly, God's mercy is initially available for all—it is theirs! Nonetheless, because some will cling to things other than God—even worthless things that cannot fill—they abandon the grace that can be theirs.

From Jonah's words, can it be seen that God does *not* predestine unto certain ones a void in available grace? *All* have had opportunity to receive His grace and mercy. It *has* been theirs to have.

WHO GOD IS—HIS HEART FOR *ALL* MEN

In the Word, we can get to know our Father—His nature and what His will and desires are. Moreover, in our knowledge of Him, we also can differentiate between what would be "in character" with God and what would not. Significantly, in the immediately following scriptures, we are given *God's desire for the salvation of all men*, to which an "*unconditional* predestination of individuals unto wrath" (by way of their

---

[34] James Strong, LL.D., S.T.D., *Strong's Complete Word Study Concordance* (Chattanooga, TN: AMG Publishers, 2004), pp. 1056, 1990.

[35] Ibid., pp. 918, 1979.

[36] Ibid., pp. 1580, 1842.

[37] Ibid., pp. 518, 1933.

[38] Ibid., pp. 970, 1860.

50

not being one of the "unconditionally elected") would be greatly inconsistent.

His Pleasure in Life

Ezekiel 18:23
"**Do I have any pleasure** [*chaphets*][39]**at all that the wicked should die?**" says the Lord GOD, "**and not that he should turn from his ways and live?**" (NKJV)

Ezekiel 18:31-32
"Cast away from you all the transgressions which you have committed, and get yourselves a new heart and a new spirit. For why should you die, O house of Israel? **For I take no pleasure** [*chaphets*][40] **in the death of one who dies,**" says the Lord GOD. "**Therefore turn and live!**" (NKJV)

According to Ezekiel, our Sovereign Lord gives man an opportunity to repent and to affect his future because He takes *"no pleasure in the death of one who dies,"* but, instead, would prefer to give life.[41]

What about 1 Samuel 2:25?

Within 1 Samuel 2:25, some have seen what appears to be a contradiction to the above statement that God takes "no pleasure in the death of one who dies." 1 Samuel 2:25 reads: "They [Eli's sons] did not heed the voice of their father, **because** [*hoti* / Greek Septuagint rendering][42] **the LORD desired** [*chaphets* / Hebrew][43] **to kill** [*muwth* / Hebrew][44]

---

[39] Goodrick and Kohlenberger, *The NIV Exhaustive Concordance*, p. 1455.
[40] Ibid., p. 1455.
[41] Concerning God's sovereignty, see the chapter "Our Real Effect upon Our Salvation"; the chapter "The *Will* of God—Differentiating Between God's *Desires*, God's *Determinations*, and God's *Pre-Ordained Purposes*; and the chapter "Significant Scriptures Concerning God's Sovereignty—Part 1: Bringing In the Balance."
[42] R. Tan and D. A. deSilva, *The Lexham Greek-English Interlinear Septuagint* (Bellingham, WA: Logos Bible Software, 2009), 1 Kgdms 2:25.
[43] Goodrick and Kohlenberger, *The NIV Exhaustive Concordance*, p. 1455.
[44] Ibid., p. 1512.

them" (NKJV). So, according to this scripture, and in contrast to Ezekiel 18:32, God sometimes *does* want the death of "the wicked" and not their repentance.

Understandably, the thought that God may deliberately harden and keep from repentance some individuals is a challenging truth for some (as it once was for me)—and, seemingly, is also in contradiction to Ezekiel's words. Yet, a look at the original Hebrew words used, and also a look at the Greek Septuagint, does confirm the translation of the last part of 1 Samuel 2:25. Firstly, according to the Greek Septuagint translation of the Old Testament, the word that was translated as the English word "because" corresponds to the Greek word *hoti*, which, according to Bullinger's Lexicon, rightly *is* used "with emphasis on the cause"[45] and "points in general to some existing fact, something which lies before us, and hence answers to 'that' as well as 'because'. . . ." [46] (Additional New Testament passages where the Greek word *hoti* is demonstrated are as follows: Mark 7:19; Mark 8:2; Mark 8:16, and Mark 8:17.)[47] Next, the Hebrew word *chaphets* (used within *both* Ezekiel 18 and 1 Samuel 2) clearly does mean "to delight."[48] Then thirdly, according to *Wilson's Old Testament Word Studies*, the Hebrew verb *mut* renders the meaning: "to die, to be slain; to make to die."[49] Accordingly, therefore, it appears quite clear: the sons of Eli were *made* not to be able to listen to their father *because* the LORD desired to kill them.

Context is so important for avoiding confusion! Upon reading the details from 1 Samuel 2, *the type* of evil in which Eli's sons had been involved is clearly seen. Significantly, Eli's sons not only had been in fornication with women who were stationed by the doorway to the tabernacle (1 Samuel 2:22), but they had treated "the LORD's offering with contempt" (NIV1984). By threats, they had compelled people to offer *first* to them the meat from sacrifices that were first to be offered to the Lord. Even as 1 Samuel states: "This sin of the young men was very

---

[45] Bullinger, *A Critical Lexicon and Concordance to the Greek and English New Testament*, p. 769.

[46] Ibid., pp. 85-86, xiii.

[47] Ibid., p. 86.

[48] William Wilson, *Wilson's Old Testament Word Studies* (Peabody, MA: Hendrickson Publishers, 1993), p. 482.

[49] Ibid., p. 123.

great in the LORD's sight, for they were *treating the LORD's offering with contempt*" (1 Samuel 2:17 NIV1984, emphasis mine). Notably as well, concerning the magnitude of their sins, Eli, himself, had spoken the following to his sons: "If one man sins against another, God will judge him. But *if a man sins against the LORD, who will intercede for him?*" (1 Samuel 2:25 NKJV, emphasis mine).

Indeed, the sins of Eli's sons were very serious. Their sins were very great and contemptuous toward God. Perhaps it was in light of the seriousness of the sins *toward God Himself* that the sons of Eli were given no mercy. (See Numbers 15:30-31 and 1 Chronicles 13:10.) For sure, the Lord has *no tolerance* for the desecration of things sacred to Him. The tabernacle and the sacrifice were very sacred, and they were being defiled.

The Lord is Holy. Foremost, His name will be revered and lifted to the highest place. This purpose will never be thwarted. Although God would rather see repentance than the death of the wicked, He would much more rather have His name exalted than bring reprieve and mercy for some deeds. Some must have judgment. There are times when God is most honored by visible vengeance—so that all will know Him and fear.

In particular, the sins of Eli's sons had been greatly flaunted. They had been known among the people (1 Samuel 2:24). God had spoken earlier that such individuals were to be cut off from among the people (Numbers 15:30-32). Consequently, it is no strange thing that God would *desire* to uphold His name and to kill the sons of Eli.

There is indeed sobering truth that should be considered from God's dealings with Eli's sons. For sure, we should never presume upon God's indefinite patience. Today, if we hear His voice, we should repent because there is a point where God may no longer grant repentance. Instead, *He may harden. He may deafen ears*—leaving that one to judgment.

Back to His Pleasure in *Life*

Although 1 Samuel 2:25 speaks of God's desire, at times, for judgment that results in death, God's greater pleasure is certainly in "life"! Importantly, the context of all of Ezekiel 18 (and expressly verses 27 and 28) is the "soul death," not the physical death of individuals (as is mentioned in 1 Samuel 2:25). With *most* sins of men, God would rather have repentance. Just as Ezekiel 18:23 says, it is, rather, *with a preference towards individuals repenting*—towards individuals turning from their ways to live—that He takes no personal delight or pleasure in the death of any. Therefore, it is inconsistent to think God would take any pleasure in predestining certain ones to wrath and death—regardless of choices they might make. Instead, God would prefer, through their repentance, to have individuals know Him, love Him, and glorify Him as Father. *What greater honor can one know personally—to his name— than to have the love of another?*

Further scriptures noting God's great compassion and desire for the salvation of all men follow. With them also comes the inconsistency there would be in unconditionally predestining, regardless of choice, some unto life and some unto wrath.

> 1 Timothy 2:4-6
> [Speaking of our need to interceed in prayer for all, Paul states why we should and could pray in faith.] This is good, and pleases God our Savior, **who wants** [*thelo*][50] **all** [*pas*][51] **men** [*anthropos*][52] **to be saved and to come to a knowledge** ["full knowledge"/ *epignosis*][53] **of the truth**. For [*gar*][54] there is one God and one mediator between God and men, the man Christ Jesus, **who gave himself as a ransom for all men**—the testimony given in its proper time. (NIV1984)

Here in 1 Timothy 2:4, we see God's perfect will for *all* men to be saved. Certainly, God would not start out, ahead of time, unconditional-

---

[50] Bullinger, *A Critical Lexicon and Concordance to the English and Greek*, p. 884, xiii.
[51] Ibid., pp. 38, 40, xiii.
[52] Ibid., pp. 476-477, xiii.
[53] Ibid., pp. 436-437, xiii.
[54] Ibid., pp. 296, 299, xiii.

ly predestining individuals to eternal wrath, against His perfect will.[55] Also, in case one has doubts about whom Paul was speaking in 1 Timothy 2:4, "*pas anthropos*" is the Greek wording that signifies the recipients of God's affections. Quite significantly, the Greek does not just say "*pas*" (which, perhaps, might leave room for some to argue). Instead, by the Greek word *anthropos*,[56] the recipients are clearly defined as "individuals," and not "nations."

Sadly, however, some still would try to confuse the simplicity of matters. They would argue that the "all men" of God's desire only refers to kings and those in authority. Indeed, immediately before the statement (in verse 4) there is instruction (in verses 1 and 2), specifically identifying "kings" and "all who are in authority" as ones for whom we can pray. Notwithstanding, even if Paul is mostly singling out the need for believers to pray for kings and authorities, this still does not take away the glaring statements of truth that are made—with regard to God's heart for all men.

Contextually, in 1 Timothy, Paul's heart seemed to be *full* with concern that the church (and Timothy, his son in the Lord) remain pure and strong in the Lord and that *faith not be shipwrecked* (1 Timothy 1:19) by unbelief or sin. Paul's concern that the church keep "faith and a good conscience" (1 Timothy 1:18-20) likely was a trigger that brought prayer to Paul's mind. In addition, because Paul understood the temptation of wrath and vengeance—especially towards authorities that can make life difficult—Paul may have just added "kings" and "authorities" as good representatives of peoples for whom we should pray. He would counsel men to lift up "holy" hands, in prayer towards God for *His* works in all—and this, "without wrath or doubting" (1 Timothy 2:8 KJV).

---

[55] **Important for understanding**: please note the differentiation between God's *will/desire* and His pre-ordained *purposes*, as is discussed in the chapter "The *Will* of God—Differentiating between God's *Desires*, God's *Determinations*, and God's *Pre-Ordained Purposes*."

[56] Refer to earlier discussions of this Greek word both in this chapter and in "Inconsistencies—Part 1."

Importantly, Paul wanted the church to be "holy" (*hosios*)—"pure from all crime"[57](v. 8). Even according to the definition of *orge*, the corresponding Greek word for "wrath" (v. 8), Paul was concerned that God's people not have "anger together with the desire for revenge."[58] Instead of directing vengeful wrath toward men, Paul would instruct Timothy of God's better way—that of *praying* for them, even for their salvation.

There is power in our prayers and intercessions! Yet, *in order to pray to an end, in order to "fight the good fight of faith,"* a knowledge of God's perfect desire is needed (1 Timothy 1:18; 1 Timothy 6:12; 1 John 5:14-15). Hence, such a knowledge of God's "perfect will" probably was the catalyst driving Paul to write the words of 1 Timothy 2:4—because he knew that prayers must be made "in faith" (1 Timothy 2:8), believing things requested have been possible.

Truly, our prayers are ineffective where there is doubting (James 1:5-8; Matthew 21:21-22). As Paul instructs Timothy to pray for *all men*, it is as if he is aware of even Timothy's need to be strengthened in the faith concerning God's heart for all men. Then also is when the words proceed from Paul—the words that are stated in the text of 1 Timothy 2:4-6 (being examined).

Significantly, the Greek word *gar* (see discussion of *gar* in earlier Romans 1 and Romans 2 discussions) additionally is used by Paul, in verse 5, to emphasize the truth of what he just stated. Following his words about God, "who wants all men to be saved and to come to a knowledge ["full knowledge"] of the truth" (v. 4), Paul wants to make sure *the truth* of what he has just said is known. So he emphasizes: "[*Gar* / **"The fact is"**] there is one God and one mediator between God and men, the man Christ Jesus, **who gave himself as ransom for all men**—the testimony given in its proper time" (vv. 5-6).

Paul understood the difficulty many have (including, perhaps, Timothy) in regarding others—particularly difficult people—from God's point of view. Understanding men's vulnerabilities and the need for faith-filled

---

[57] Bullinger, *A Critical Lexicon and Concordance to the English and Greek*, pp. 380, xiii.

[58] Ibid., pp. 905, xiii.

prayer, he likely continued, at that point, to emphasize the truth of his previous statements about God's desire and provision for the salvation of *all* individuals. Noticeably even, verse 7 follows with: "And for this purpose I was appointed a herald and an apostle—*I am telling the truth, I am not lying*—and a teacher of the true faith to the Gentiles" (NIV1984, emphasis mine). Then, as is seen in the Greek[59] and in other translations, Paul again recaps in verse 8—even introducing it with the word "therefore" (*oun* / "marking the logical or formal inference")[60]— what was the charge and the motivation for the whole discourse within 1 Timothy 2:1-7, declaring: **"I will *therefore* that men pray everywhere, lifting up holy hands, *without wrath and* doubting"** (1 Timothy 2:8 KJV, emphasis mine).

Today, Paul would say the same thing to the church about doubting God's concern for all men, and he would note the ineffectiveness such doubting brings to our fighting the good fight in our intercessions for others.

2 Peter 3:9

The Lord is not slow in keeping his promise, as some understand slowness. He is patient with you, **not wanting anyone to perish, but everyone to come to repentance.** (NIV1984)

Importantly, note that the Greek word used for "wanting" is "*boulomai.*" According to Bullinger, *boulomai* more accurately renders the meaning: "to have a wish, intention, or purpose, formed after mature deliberation; to deliberately purpose after careful consideration."[61] So, it can be seen more specifically: **The Lord has *not* deliberately purposed or decided best that any should perish.**[62]

---

[59] *The Zondervan Parallel New Testament in Greek and English*, pp. 614-615.

[60] Bullinger, *A Critical Lexicon and Concordance to the English and Greek*, pp. 783-784, xiii.

[61] Bullinger, *A Critical Lexicon and Concordance to the English and Greek New Testament*, pp. 884, xiii.

[62] See further the discussion of the word *boulomai*, found within the chapter "The *Will* of God."

Some say this statement was possibly only directed to the ones to whom Peter was writing the letter. Agreeably, from an examination of the rest of Peter's words surrounding this section and an examination of the way the actual Greek writing flowed (using the Interlinear Greek New Testament), it *is* possible Peter was being specific in his statement. Contextually, in the truth that God is "not wanting [determining best] anyone to perish but everyone to come to repentance," the "anyone" and the "everyone" could be referring to the "you" just addressed. Nevertheless, such a conclusion still does not change important truth that can be received from these words of Peter.

Noticeably, if one reads fully the whole letter of 2 Peter, it becomes very evident that Peter had great concern that the individual believer *continue* in the way. He had great concern that the individual believer **not forget "that he [had] been cleansed from his past sins"** (2 Peter 1:9) and that the **"beloved"** one (2 Peter 3:17), who fully knew Him (having *"epignosis"*/ "a full knowledge"[63] "of Him who called us" / 2 Peter 1:3), **not fall from his secure position** (2 Peter 3:17). It is in this short letter to the ones whom he is addressing—**the ones who had "received a faith as precious as [his]"** (2 Peter 1:1)—that Peter also penned such statements as follows:

> For [*gar* / "the fact is"][64] if you possess these qualities [found in verses 5-7] in increasing measure, they will keep you from being ineffective and unproductive in your knowledge of our Lord Jesus Christ. But [*gar* / "the fact is"][65] if anyone does not have them, he is nearsighted and blind, and has forgotten that **he has been cleansed from his past sins.** (2 Peter 1:8-9 NIV1984)

> Therefore, my brothers, **be all the more eager to make your calling and election sure.** For [*gar* / "the fact is"][66] if you do these things [in verses 5-7], you will never fall, and you will receive a rich welcome into the eternal king-

---

[63] Bullinger, *A Critical Lexicon and Concordance to the English and Greek New Testament*, pp. 436-437, xiii.

[64] Ibid., pp. 296, 299, xiii.

[65] Ibid., pp. 123-124, xiii.

[66] Ibid., pp. 296, 299, xiii.

dom of our Lord and Savior Jesus Christ. (2 Peter 1:10-11 NIV1984)

So I will always remind you of these things [in verses 5-11], even though you know them and are firmly established in the truth you now have. I think it is right to refresh your memory as long as I live in the tent of this body, because I know that I will soon put it aside, as our Lord Jesus Christ has made clear to me. And I will make every effort to see that after my departure you will always be able to remember these things. (2 Peter 1:12-15 NIV1984)

But there were also false prophets among the people, just as there will be false teachers among you. They will secretly introduce destructive heresies, even denying the sovereign Lord who bought them—bringing swift destruction on themselves. Many will follow their shameful ways and will bring the way of truth into disrepute. (2 Peter 2:1-2 NIV1984)

[Concerning false teachers . . .] **If they have escaped the corruption of the world by knowing** [*epignosis* / "a full knowledge"][67] **our Lord and Savior Jesus Christ and are again entangled in it and overcome, they are worse off at the end than they were at the beginning.** [*Gar* / "For," "The fact is" / according to the Greek][68]It would have been better for them not to have known [*epiginosko* / "to know fully"][69] the way of righteousness, than to have

---

[67] Bullinger, *A Critical Lexicon and Concordance to the English and Greek New Testament*, p. 436; Goodrick and Kohlenberger, *The NIV Exhaustive Concordance*, pp. 632, 1721; *The.Zondervan Parallel New Testament in Greek and English*, pp. 700-701.

[68] Bullinger, *A Critical Lexicon and Concordance to the English and Greek New Testament*, pp. 296, 299, xiii; *The Zondervan Parallel New Testament in Greek and English*, pp. 700-701.

[69] Bullinger, *A Critical Lexicon and Concordance to the English and Greek New Testament*, p. 435; Goodrick and Kohlenberger, *The NIV Exhaustive Concordance*, pp. 632, 1721; *The Zondervan Parallel New Testament in Greek and English*, pp. 700-701.

known [*epiginosko* / "to know fully"][70] it and then to turn their backs on the sacred commandment that was passed on to them. Of them the proverbs are true: "A dog returns to its vomit," and, "A sow that is washed goes back to her wallowing in the mud." (2 Peter 2:20-22 NIV1984)

Context is so important! *Just prior* to the 2 Peter 3:9 scripture being discussed, Peter entreated Christians not to scoff, as would others, at the Lord's delay in coming. He spoke:

First of all, you must understand that in the last days scoffers will come, scoffing and following their own evil desires. They will say, "Where is the 'coming' he promised?" (2 Peter 3:4 NIV1984)

Then, *just following* the words of 2 Peter 3:9, and giving clear context to the words, Peter made the upcoming statements:

But the day of the Lord will come like a thief. The heavens will disappear with a roar; the elements will be destroyed by fire, and the earth and everything in it will be laid bare. **Since everything will be destroyed in this way, what kind of people ought you to be? You ought to live holy and godly lives** as you look forward to the day of God and speed its coming. (2 Peter 3:10-12 NIV1984)

So then, dear friends, since you are looking forward to this ["a new heaven and a new earth, the home of righteousness" / v. 13], **make every effort to be found spotless, blameless and at peace with him.** (2 Peter 3:14 NIV1984)

Therefore, dear friends, since you already know this, **be on guard so that you may not be carried away by the error of lawless men and fall from your secure position.** (2 Peter 3:17 NIV1984)

---

[70] Ibid.

Peter seemed to know that, although one is "called," it *is* possible for him to fall from his "secure position." His election is not made "sure," automatically (2 Peter 1:10; 2 Peter 3:17). Peter seemed to desire others to take heed and to understand these truths as well. The tone of the whole second letter of Peter is that of a sober reminder and warning, to those loved by God, of the possibilities of being carried away by the error of wicked men, and of the need to, instead, "grow in the grace and the knowledge" of the Lord (2 Peter 3:18).

Within the context of Peter's concern and within the resulting letter, then, fall the words of 2 Peter 3:9. Perhaps this is the intent of Peter's statement (answering those who would scoff at the slowness of Christ's return):

> **The Lord is patient with us, not quickly coming and rendering judgment to the world, because God determines it best that people** (or, as is the exception of some, the ones to whom Peter was writing—those who had had a "full knowledge" of Him) **be given opportunity to repent rather than perish.** (My Paraphrase)

Could this glimpse of what the Lord determines as best (what He wants) be similar to what He determines as best and so counsels [*symbouleuo* / "to counsel with anyone . . . to advise"][71] the church in Laodicea (Revelation 3:14-18)? Might those bought by Christ's sacrifice benefit to know God's counsel that they repent?

In any event, *even if* the "anyone" statement of 2 Peter 3:9 only refers to those being addressed in the letter, we can still glean important truth that dismisses *unconditional* election of individuals. Although one *can* so fall away that his end is worse than the beginning (2 Peter 2:20), **if anyone does fall away from his secure position, it is *not* because God has decided it best or purposed it.** God has been longsuffering and very merciful to all.

---

[71] Bullinger, *A Critical Lexicon and Concordance to the English and Greek New Testament*, pp. 190, xiii.

God's love and His compassions are so great! Even as God demonstrated His compassion to the people of Ninevah, we also can get a further glimpse of its characteristics, and hear the prophet Jonah's knowledge of it, as is recorded in the following scripture:

> Jonah 3:10 — 4:2
> Then God saw their works, that they turned from their evil way; and God relented from the disaster that He had said He would bring upon them, and He did not do it . . . [Jonah] prayed . . . ". . . I know that **You are a gracious and merciful God, slow to anger and abundant in lovingkindness, One who relents from doing harm**." (NKJV)

Would the idea of God *unconditionally* predestining certain individuals unto the demonstration of His wrath be in line with what Jonah says about who God is? Also, note that it was *after* the Ninevites turned from their sin that God had compassion and changed the course of His planned action. The Ninevites took action before God did. Although God mercifully gave the Ninevites a warning, *He did not make them repent* and then have compassion and change His mind. The compassion came *after* He saw their own decisive response as a nation.[72]

Further scriptures noting who God is, His heart and His ways, continue.

> Exodus 34:5-7
> Then the LORD came down in the cloud and stood there with him and proclaimed his name, the LORD. And he passed in front of Moses, proclaiming, "**The LORD, the LORD, the compassionate and gracious God, slow to anger, abounding in love and faithfulness, maintaining love to thousands, and forgiving wickedness, rebellion and sin**. Yet he does not leave the guilty unpunished, he punishes the children and their children for the sin of the fathers to the third and fourth generation." (NIV 1984)

---

[72] For a discussion on God's "purposes" and dealings with mankind, see the chapter "The *Will* of God."

Hosea 6:6
"For **I desire mercy and not sacrifice**, and the knowledge of God more than burnt offerings." (NKJV)

Psalm 130:3-4, 7
If You, LORD, should mark iniquities, O Lord, who could stand? **But there is forgiveness with You, that You may be feared.** . . . O Israel, hope in the Lord; **for with the LORD there is mercy, and with Him is abundant redemption.** (NKJV)

With God, there is forgiveness and mercy! This attribute of God is very important to esteem. According to the Psalmist, noting God's forgiveness causes us to even fear Him. Properly recognizing this quality of who God is brings us into the right place of reverencing and lifting Him to the Highest Place! The Lord is great! And there is none merciful like our God!

The Greatness of His Heart

Psalm 145:8-9
The LORD is gracious and full of compassion, slow to anger and great in mercy. The LORD is good to all, and **His tender mercies are over *all* His works.** (NKJV, emphasis mine)

Psalm 145:17-18
The LORD is righteous in all His ways, **gracious in all His works**. The LORD is near to all who call upon Him, to all who call upon Him in truth. (NKJV)

The Lord has compassion! He has tender mercies toward *all* He has made—and not just toward animals!

The *Most Valued* of All His Creation

A few years ago, our dog of 16 years, died. My heart was grieving so deeply for the animal I had loved and cared for, like a child, for so many years. I cared about how she was doing. (Her condition for the last year of her life had been so difficult to watch.) The evening following her death, I was thinking of words the Lord had spoken to my heart, just a few months earlier, concerning His care and involvement in the lives of *even* the animals. I was so comforted to know that even my dearly loved pet was in God's hands—for even a sparrow "shall not fall on the ground without [the] Father" (Matthew 10:29 KJV and IGNT).

More significantly, however, immediately after remembering God's care for Fifi, the Lord spoke His heart to me concerning my neighbors who may not know Him. He spoke: *"If I care about the death of Fifi, do I not care even more about the eternal deaths of your neighbors, if they do not know Me?"* At that moment, the Lord affirmed to me who He is and His care for all the lost. I was to know even more His heart for the lost and to make it a priority to share. Confirming what I was thinking, I furthermore was reminded of Jesus' words in reference to the sparrows: **"[You people] are of more value than many sparrows"** (Matthew 10:31 NKJV).

Also, during the "Sermon on the Mount," Jesus similarly had expressed the greatness of the Father's care—even for the birds. He had spoken the following, while encouraging people not to worry about their lives:

> "Look at the birds of the air, for they neither sow nor reap nor gather into barns; yet your heavenly Father feeds them. **Are you not of more value than they?**" (Matthew 6:26 NKJV)

Truly, we are *all* of much value to the Father. Still sadly, some might bring the debate: "Jesus was talking only to His disciples, and not to everyone, when He made an address to "you." So sadly, some may doubt the simplicity of Jesus' statement, noting that all of "man"—having been made in God's image (Genesis 1:26)—are of much more value than birds.

Rightly, when Jesus mentioned sparrows falling to the ground, He was addressing the disciples. According to the Luke account, when Jesus was encouraging people not to worry, but to receive from God even as the birds receive, He may have just been talking to the disciples (later for them to share). To confirm the validity that *all* people are worth more than many sparrows, however, note that Jesus also spoke similarly to the Pharisees one day: **"Of how much more value then is a man than a sheep?"** (Matthew 12:12 NKJV).

Furthermore, Paul's account of the Lord's words, as found in Colossians 1:19-20, also sheds light on God's heart and provision: "For it pleased [*eudokeo* / "well pleased"][73] the Father . . . **by Him to reconcile *all* things to Himself, by Him, whether things on earth or things in heaven** having made peace through the blood of His cross" (NKJV, emphasis mine). Significantly, "all things" include the **"all things . . . created through Him and for Him"** (NKJV) mentioned just four verses earlier (v. 16). Surely all people—the part of His creation whom He had said were of much more value than His created sparrows, birds, and sheep—also were to be included in His provision for reconciliation.

I am newly envisioned and excited about the full work of restoration for all creation that was accomplished through Jesus' blood, shed on the cross. *All God's creation* is precious to Him! Upon completion of all His creation—"it was good" (Genesis 1)! All God's creation is His handiwork and *all His works* praise Him (Psalm 145:10)!

The Lord would restore all of His creation back to its former glory! The Lord has never been defeated—and all the effects of sin, unto which His creation was unwillingly subjected, shall be undone! Even concerning the expectation of God's creation, the apostle Paul declared:

> For I consider that the sufferings of this present time are not worthy to be compared with the glory which shall be revealed in us. **For the earnest expectation of the creation eagerly waits for the revealing of the sons of God.** For the creation was subjected to futility, not willingly, but because of Him who subjected it in hope; **because the creation itself also will be delivered from the bondage of corruption into the glorious liberty of**

---

[73] Bullinger, *A Critical Lexicon and Concordance to the English and Greek New Testament*, pp. 588, xiii; *The Zondervan Parallel New Testament in Greek and English*, p. 587.

the children of God. For we know that the whole creation groans and labors with birth pangs together until now. Not only that, but we also who have the firstfruits of the Spirit, even we ourselves groan within ourselves, eagerly waiting for the adoption, the redemption of our body. (Romans 8:18-24 NKJV)

Again, *all* men are as precious to God as the animals—and even more so. If God has been pleased enough to provide for animals' freedom from the bondage handed down from Adam's sin (Colossians 1:19-20), is it not right to think that He would equally care that all men have the opportunity to know that same freedom? Man, however, has a will and must desire to respond to the God's initiative.

HIS DEMONSTRATION OF LOVE

Scriptures specifically attribute God's provision on the cross—for all who would respond to Him—with His demonstration of love for the world. Consider the following scriptures:

John 3:16
For God so loved the world that he gave his one and only Son, that whoever believes in him shall not perish but have eternal life. (NIV1984)

Ephesians 2:4
But **because of his great love for us, God, who is rich in mercy**, made us alive with Christ even when we were dead in transgressions—it is by grace you have been saved. (NIV1984)

1 John 4:8-10
Whoever does not love does not know God, because **God is love. This is how God showed his love among us: He sent his one and only Son into the world that we might live through him.** This is love: not that we loved God, but that **he loved us and sent his Son as an atoning sacrifice for our sins**. (NIV1984)

Romans 5:8
But God demonstrates his own love for us in this: While we were yet still sinners, Christ died for us. (NIV1984)

1 John 3:16
This is how we know what love is: Jesus Christ laid down his life for us. (NIV1984)

God is Love (1 John 4:16). Significantly, according to the words of Scripture, God's greatest demonstration to us of what His love is like is that He would send His own Son to die for our sins—even "while we were yet sinners." Certainly, therefore, *it would not be in character* with His demonstration of love to predestine some individuals not to have any potential for life. God would not be a God of love to them if that were so. The Lord's provision on the cross *for all men* is part of His demonstration of love for all.

Not only would an unconditional predestination unto wrath be in direct contradiction to God's demonstration of love, but there is also inconsistency between the doctrine of *unconditional election* and other characteristics attributed to *agape* love. Consider the following:

1 Corinthians 13:6
Love does not delight in evil, but rejoices in the truth. (NIV1984*)*

God does not delight in evil. Unlike the implications of *unconditional election*, the fact that *God does not take pleasure in anyone's death* (Ezekiel 18:31-32*), but desires all men to come to repentance and a full knowledge of the truth* (1 Timothy 2:4) is very much "in character" with who He is—Love.

Some have concluded, however, because of their belief that Scripture teaches *unconditional election*, that God can still be love (because Scripture clearly says *He is love*) and simply desire, as a necessary display of His glory, certain numbers to receive His wrath (no matter how they, if given a choice, would ever respond to Him). Some have gone so far even to say that God created sin and is ultimately the one who causes men to sin. (How far will this go?) Again, according to the definition of love, found in 1 Corinthians 13:6, God does *not* delight in evil. Thus, God should never be held responsible for man's sin.

Then significantly, and in agreement, Scripture also states the following:

> James 1:13
> When tempted, no one should say, "God is tempting me." **For God cannot be tempted by evil** nor does he tempt anyone. (NIV1984)

In truth, God *does* use the hardened sinfulness in men's hearts to carry out some of His schemes of judgment. Also, God *does* cause the hardness in some individuals' hearts—so they cannot "see" any longer. If such conditions of hardness are present in individuals, however, it is not because God predestined and took delight in—causing them to be. *It is because of the deceitfulness of men's own sins and their own rebelliousness* that they have become so hardened (Hebrews 3:12-13; Isaiah 44:20).[74]

HIS CONSISTENCY AND IMPARTIALITY

Would it be in line with what the Lord has said about Himself and about *His consistency* to conclude that He differs in His desires towards individuals—with regard to having loving relationships? Again, the issue is whether all men have been given an *opportunity* to know Him, to glorify Him, and to have His life—not whether all can count on the same number of chances as another, with respect to getting it right. (See Romans 9:15, 18 and Hebrews 3:13, 15.) Consider the following:

> Malachi 3:6
> **"I the LORD do not change.** So you, O descendants of Jacob, are not destroyed." (NIV1984)

---

[74] Concerning God's involvement in "evil schemes," see also the chapters "The *Will* of God"; "Significant Scriptures—Part 1"; and "God's Sovereignty Over the Hearts of Men."

James 1:16-17
Don't be deceived, my dear brothers. Every good and perfect gift is from above, coming down from the Father of the heavenly lights, **who does not change like shifting shadows.** (NIV 1984)

2 Timothy 2:13
If we are faithless, he will remain faithful, for **he cannot disown himself.** [He cannot go against who He is.] (NIV 1984)

Romans 2:9-11
There will be trouble and distress for every human being who does evil: first for the Jew, then for the Gentile; but glory, honor and peace for everyone who does good: first for the Jew, then for the Gentile. **For God does not show favoritism.** (NIV 1984)

Ephesians 6:9
And masters, treat your slaves in the same way. Do not threaten them, since you know that he who is both their Master and yours is in heaven, and **there is no favoritism with him.** (NIV 1984)

Colossians 3:25
Anyone who does wrong will be repaid for his wrong, **and there is no favoritism.** (NIV 1984)

1 Peter 1:17
Since you call on a Father **who judges each man's work impartially,** live your lives as strangers here in reverent fear. (NIV 1984)

Psalm 67:4
May the nations be glad and sing for joy, for **you rule the peoples justly.** (NIV 1984)

Psalm 96:10
He shall judge the peoples righteously. (NKJV)

Psalm 98:9
He will judge the world in righteousness and the peoples with equity. (NIV 1984)

Psalm 99:4
The King's strength also **loves justice; You have established** [*kuwn* / "to stand firm"][75] **equity** . . . . (NKJV)

God is consistent. He does not change. He is an impartial and just judge of *all* men—and, thus, an example for us all. It would be inconsistent, therefore, with these qualities of God's nature, to say that He is partial—predestining some individuals unto salvation, and then some others *not*, regardless of any of their responses.

Then as well, consider the lesson that Peter learned:

Acts 10:28
[Peter] said . . . "God has shown me that **I should not call any man common or unclean.**" (NKJV)

Acts 10:34
Then Peter opened his mouth and said: "In truth I perceive that **God shows no partiality**." (NKJV)

Significantly, after the apostle Peter's call to minister to the Gentiles, Peter gained understanding never again to call a person "common" or "unclean." Three times, he had heard from heaven: **"What God has cleansed you must not call common"** (Acts 10:15 NKJV). Likewise, we also should take care with our attitudes concerning those for whom Christ died—for *the sacrifice of his blood was holy* (Hebrews 10:29). Truly, the Lord shows no partiality—except that one must fear Him. Just as Peter learned, so should we: "In every nation, **whoever fears**

---

[75] Goodrick and Kohlenberger, *The NIV Exhaustive Concordance*, p. 1484; William Wilson, *Wilson's Old Testament Word Studies*, p. 149.

Him and works righteousness [responding to the Lord's initiatives] **is accepted by Him**" (Acts 10:35 NKJV).

THE HIGHEST HONOR

According to Calvinist Reformed theology, within the acronym TULIP (given for quick reference to its doctrine of salvation), the "I" refers to the teaching of *irresistible grace*.[76] It is the teaching that holds that the only reason one might come to want the Lord, and thus receive His gift of life, is that God has wooed and "irresistibly" drawn him. Conversely, the reason why others have *not* come to know Him is that He did not choose to irresistibly draw them—or to give them that desire to know Him. (Note: although I affirm that no one can come unto Jesus unless the Father has first drawn him, revealing who Jesus is, Jesus' references to being "drawn" were in the context of *ones who had both "desired" and "heard" the Father's previous teaching.* See John 6:43-45 and John 7:16-17.)

The teaching of *irresistible grace* is packaged to look very desirable. By acknowledging that man has *no* responsibility and God takes *all* responsibility, the teaching of *irresistible grace* would conclude: God gets all the glory. Does He really, though—or can it be that the glory of who God is becomes altered?[77]

May we consider the story of Job? Job was a righteous man who feared God. Also, he was a man who had been given much by God. Satan was well aware of the things God had given Job. Even once, as angels were presenting themselves before God, Satan also appeared to God with the following accusations:

> "Does Job fear God for nothing? Have you not made a
> hedge around him, around his household, and around all
> that he has on every side? You have blessed the work of

---

[76] Refer to "Appendix A" for statements on the teachings of TULIP.

[77] Note, as well, the chapter entitled "Our Real Effect upon Our Salvation," where the issues of "boasting" and of one's faith are considered.

his hands, and his possessions have increased in the land. But now, stretch out Your hand and touch all that he has, and he will surely curse You to Your face!" (Job 1:9-11 NKJV)

For sure, those who love God are under His special protection! Knowing this, however, Satan took issue—stating that Job would *only* continue to follow God *if* God continued to work His favor in Job's life. Satan reasoned that God would receive *less* glory and honor if such was proven true.

Understanding the significance of Satan's accusations, God, thus, allowed the blessings of Job to be stricken by Satan. He removed His hedge of normal protection. In so doing, God seemingly agreed with the premise: He would be *more greatly honored* with the recognition that Job had chosen—on his own initiative—to love and to follow Him.

Truly, a person is most honored when he is freely loved by another because the lover chooses to—and not because of compulsion or anything else which is done. Even as Paul reminded in 2 Corinthians 9:7, it remains so:

> Let each one give *as he purposes in his heart, not grudgingly or of necessity*; for **God loves a cheerful giver**. (NKJV, emphasis mine)

TRUTH

Consider the issue of *truth*.

> Psalm 51:6
> Surely you desire truth in the inner parts . . . . (NIV 1984)

> Ephesians 4:25
> Therefore each of you must **put off falsehood and speak truthfully to his neighbor**, for we are members of one body. (NIV 1984)

There is great discrepancy with how those who believe in the *unconditional* election of individuals typically deliver the gospel message. They share the gospel—and often with many converts. The gospel is proclaimed as "good news" for all to whom the one is speaking (if they will repent). The listeners are entreated with words of *God's love for them*—that Jesus died on the cross in order that *they* might have life. Yet, when is the *other* knowledge about *limited atonement* shared? When is it shared that Christ's atonement was not for all—that it was limited to only "elect" individuals, predestined and chosen *unconditionally?* As one well known Calvinist Reformed theologian puts it:

> The doctrine of election, like every truth about God, involves mystery and sometimes stirs controversy. But in Scripture it is a pastoral doctrine, brought in to help Christians see how great is the grace that saves them, and to move them to humility, confidence, joy, praise, faithfulness, and holiness in response. *It is the family secret of the children of God* [emphasis mine].[78]

Concerning truth, the Word of God has much to say: Jesus is "the way, *the truth*, and the life" (John 14:6 NKJV). The Holy Spirit, "the Spirit of *truth*," leads us into "*all truth*" (John 16:13 NKJV). Therefore, as we know *the truth*, "*the truth* shall make [us] free (John 8:32 NKJV). Yet, in contrast, the Word of God firmly also warns: Satan is "the father of lies" (John 8:44 NIV1984).

The apostle Paul gave us instruction to forsake all falsehood (Ephesians 4:25). Likewise, the apostle John directed us to "walk in the light" (1 John 1:7). Would God then contradict Himself and call us to be *false* witnesses of His love, His grace, and His abundant provision in the death of Jesus (for all who will receive Him / Romans 5:17) if we cannot know, for sure, its real availability for the ones to whom we speak? Would He call us to speak "empty words"—words spoken in vain—that might not be true for the ones to whom we speak (Ephesians 5:6; Psalm 127:1; 1 Corinthians 15:2; 1 Corinthians 15:58)?

---

[78] J.I. Packer, *Concise Theology: A Guide to Historic Christian Beliefs* (Tyndale House Publishers, Inc., 2001), p. 150.

In Isaiah 45:19 the words of the Lord proclaim:

> **"I have not spoken in secret, in a dark place of the earth; I did not say to the seed of Jacob, 'Seek Me in vain'; I, the LORD, speak righteousness, I declare things that are right."** (NKJV)

It is even within the context of our "seeking" the Lord that God would speak concerning the truthfulness of His words. There is no hidden secret. His words mean what they say.

Likewise, even as the apostle Paul was challenged by a false teaching—a teaching that taught "no resurrection"—he declared to us the following concerning *integrity* in our words:

> And if Christ has not been raised, our preaching is useless and so is your faith. More that that, **we are then found to be false witnesses about God,** for we have testified about God that he raised Christ from the dead. (1 Corinthians 15:14-15 NIV 1984)

Certainly, God would not call us to say something is true when we do not know it is so. Such would be lying. Even as Paul spoke:

> We have **renounced secret and shameful ways**; we **do not use deception, nor do we distort** the word of God. On the contrary, **by setting forth the truth plainly** we commend ourselves to every man's conscience in the sight of God. (2 Corinthians 4:2 NIV 1984)

Paul knew the ways of our Father. He knew that one of God's ways is to bring *"hidden things" to light*—and he knew that God would have others walk in that same light. (See Luke 8:16-17, Mark 4:21-22, Matthew 10:26-27, Luke 12:1-3, and 1 John 1:7.) He knew that, because God exposes, He even calls us to expose the truth (while allowing the truth also to be exposed in our own lives). In his letter to the Ephesians, Paul spoke:

Let no one deceive you with empty words, for because of such things God's wrath comes on those who are disobedient. Therefore **do not be partners with them**. For you were once darkness, but now **you are light in the Lord. Live as children of light** (for the fruit of the light consists in all goodness, righteousness and truth) and find out what pleases the Lord. Have nothing to do with the fruitless deeds of darkness, but rather **expose them**. For it is shameful even to mention what the disobedient do in secret. But **everything exposed by the light becomes visible, for it is light that makes everything visible**. (Ephesians 5:6-14 NIV1984)

Paul did not use "secret and shameful ways" (2 Corinthians 4:2 NIV1984). To the contrary, he was emphatic about truth—forsaking all falsehood (Ephesians 4:25). According to Paul, his ministry was "in truthful speech and in the power of God" (2 Corinthians 6:7 NIV1984). Surely, as we follow Paul's example, we can learn much about God's ways.

The gospel message *is* effective—it "is the power of God for the salvation of everyone who believes" (Romans 1:16 NIV1984). Thankfully, people will respond to the message that Jesus died for them—even if the messengers fail to know it for sure.

IN CONCLUSION
His Heart upon Our Hearts

Scripture reveals inconsistencies with the doctrines of *unconditional election* and *limited atonement* and should be the highest authority for truth. Indeed, God's ways are "higher than our ways" (Isaiah 55:8-9), and it really does not matter what we think. Nonetheless, although we must accept the limitations of our understanding, *our hearts* should bear witness to that which is or is not true about our God. The writer of Hebrews even shared the following concerning that which the Lord would place upon our hearts:

> "This is the covenant I will make with the house of Israel after that time, declares the Lord. **I will put my law in their minds and write them on their hearts.** I will be their God, and they will be my people. No longer will a man teach his neighbor, or a man his brother, saying, 'Know the Lord,' because they will all know me, from the least of them to the greatest." (Hebrews 8:10-11 NIV1984)

In accordance with the New Covenant, God has now liberated us from "the written code," instead, to be "led by the Spirit"—as He places *His heart* upon our hearts (Colossians 2:14; Hebrew 8:10-11; Romans 8:1-5; Galatians 5:16-18 NIV1984). Being led by the Spirit, we can be assured of doing His will. We can move in faith by the witness within our hearts. Even from our own hearts—from the things He may place there—we can grow in our knowledge of who He is.

Consider, therefore, what is the Father's heart, not only from what the Word speaks about it, but from the fruits that He would bring forth by His Spirit in us. The apostle Paul commended God's heart to us when he spoke: **"Each of you should look not only to your own interests, but also to the interests of others"** (Philippians 2:4 NIV1984). Likewise, Jesus spoke: **"Love your neighbor as yourself"** (Matthew 22:39). Then, in 1 John 3:16-20, the apostle John described a God kind of love that would sincerely care about the needs of another:

> **This is how we know what love is:** Jesus Christ laid down his life for us. And we ought to lay down our lives for our brothers. **If anyone has material possessions and sees his brother in need but has not pity on him, how can the love of God be in him?** Dear children, let us not love with words or tongue but with actions and in truth. This then is how we know that we belong to the truth . . . . (1 John 3:16-19 NIV1984)

With certainty, God's love in us is not self-centered. How do we react to the thought of others being unconditionally destined for hell? Is it not right to care that others have the same opportunity for what we have come to know in the Lord?

Consider, also, Paul's words of exhortation to the Romans:

> Now may the God of patience and comfort grant you to
> be like-minded toward one another, according to Christ
> Jesus [who did not just think of Himself, but others],
> that you may with one mind and one mouth glorify the
> God and Father of our Lord Jesus Christ. **Therefore, re-
> ceive one another** [let no one be left out], **just as
> Christ also received us**, to the glory of God. (Romans
> 15:5-7 NKJV)

Even as God has called us to do, He also would receive all who are
willing. Is a servant greater than his master (John 15:20)?

Because we know that Jesus was like the Father (John 14:9) *and* that
we are being conformed into the likeness of Jesus (Romans 8:29), can
we not conclude that any character we are called to emulate, in our own
dealings with others, begins, first, with that of the Father? Is God not at
work within us to place His law within our hearts (Hebrews 8:10-11)—
to work in our hearts *to will and to do what pleases Him* (Philippians
2:13)? If we are called to receive one another, to have the same care for
others (Philippians 2:2-4), to love our neighbors as ourselves (Matthew
22:39), and to show mercy to others, instead of judgment (James 2:13),
has God not been equally as concerned about those same people and
been willing to demonstrate His love through His mercy toward them?

After being in His presence and entrusting ourselves to Him, if we find
our hearts growing in love for and in concern for the lost to know Him,
surely that heart is found in us because it first was the heart of the Father. *It is from the heart of the Father that mercy comes*—and His
"mercy triumphs over judgment" (James 2:13 NIV 1984).

77

Chapter 3

Discrepancies of Various TULIP Teachings: Revelation from 2 Peter 2

Consider the following portions of text from 2 Peter 2:

> But there were also false prophets among the people, just as there will be false teachers among you. They will secretly introduce destructive heresies, **even denying** [*arneomai* / "to deny, disown"][1] **the sovereign Lord who bought** [*agorazo*][2] **them—bringing swift destruction upon themselves.** . . . (13) They will be paid back with harm for the harm they have done. Their idea of pleasure is to carouse in broad daylight. They are blots and blemishes, reveling in their pleasures while they feast with you. (14) With eyes full of adultery, they never stop sinning; they seduce the unstable, they are experts in greed—an accursed brood! (15) **They have left** [*kataleipo* / "to leave behind . . . to forsake, abandon"][3] **the straight** [*euthys* / "straight . . . right, true"][4] **way and wandered off** [*planao* / "to wander, roam about . . . to be misled, to err, be mistaken"][5] to follow the way of Balaam son of Beor, who loved the wages of wickedness. . . . (17) These men are springs without water and mists driven by a storm. Blackest darkness is reserved for them. (18) For they mouth empty, boastful words and, by appealing to the lustful desires of sinful human nature, they entice people who are just escaping from those who live in error. (19) They promise them freedom, while they themselves are slaves of depravity [*phthora* / "a

---

[1] E.W. Bullinger, *A Critical Lexicon and Concordance to the English and Greek New Testament* (Grand Rapids, MI: Kregel Publications, 1999; orig. pub. 1908), pp. 215, xiii.
[2] Ibid., pp. 125, xiii.
[3] Ibid., pp. 304, xiii.
[4] Ibid., pp. 647, xiii.
[5] Ibid., pp. 74, xiii.

spoiling, corruption, destruction . . . the bringing or being brought into a worse state"][6]—for [*gar* / "the fact is"][7] a man is a slave to whatever has mastered him. (20) [*Gar* / **"the fact is"** / word actually contained in the Interlinear Greek New Testament and other translations][8] **If they have escaped** [*apopheugo* / "to flee away from"][9] **the corruption** [*miasma* / "stain, defilement"][10] **of the world by knowing** [*epignosis* / "clear and exact knowledge"][11] **our Lord and Savior Jesus Christ** and are again [*palin* / "again, once again"][12] entangled in it and overcome, they are worse off at the end than they were at the beginning. (21) **It would have been better for them not to have known** [*epiginosko* / "to give heed, to notice attentively, to know fully well"][13] **the way of righteousness, than to have known** [*epiginosko*][14] it and then to turn their backs on [*hypostrepho ek* / "to turn back out of"][15] the sacred command that was passed on to them. (22) Of them the proverbs are true: "A dog returns to its vomit," and, **"A sow that is washed** goes back to her wallowing in the mud." (NIV1984)

Consider the teachings of the Calvinist TULIP (see "Appendix A"). The "L" of Calvinist Reformed theology's TULIP acronym (for its teachings on God's work of salvation for men) stands for *limited*

---

[6] Ibid., pp. 189, xiii.

[7] Ibid., pp. 296, 299, xiii.

[8] Bullinger, *A Critical Lexicon and Concordance to the English and Greek New Testament*, pp. 296, 299, xiii; *The Zondervan Parallel New Testament in Greek and English*, 8th ed. (New York: Zondervan Publishing House, 1982), p. 701.

[9] Bullinger, *A Critical Lexicon and Concordance to the English and Greek New Testament*, pp. 255, xiii.

[10] Ibid., pp. 590, xiii.

[11] Ibid, pp. 436-437, xiii.

[12] Ibid., pp. 34, xiii.

[13] James Strong, LL.D., S.T.D., *Strong's Complete Word Study Concordance* (Chattanooga, TN: AMG Publishers, 2004), pp. 828, 2075; Bullinger, *A Critical Lexicon and Concordance to the English and Greek New Testament*, p. 435.

[14] Strong, *Strong's Complete Word Study Concordance*, p. 436; Bullinger, *A Critical Lexicon and Concordance to the English and Greek New Testament*, p. 436.

[15] Bullinger, *A Critical Lexicon and Concordance to the English and Greek New Testament*, pp. 824-825, x, xiii.

atonement. This doctrine of *limited atonement* concludes (from the TULIP doctrine of *unconditional election*) that, because provision for salvation is not available for all, but only for the individuals specifically and unconditionally "predestined" for salvation, Jesus' atonement for sin was, therefore, *limited* and not available to all men. Additionally, according to the TULIP acronym, the "P" stands for *perseverance of the saints*. Instead of saying that followers of Christ are "called" to persevere, the emphasis of this "P" doctrine is that all the ones "unconditionally elected" and "atoned for" will be *made* to persevere (and thus, cannot fall away to the point of losing their salvation). And yet, *if* these two doctrines are true, how can the previous section of Scripture in 2 Peter 2 be explained?

WHO ARE THE *FALSE TEACHERS* OF 2 PETER 2?

"Bought"

Peter is speaking and warning God's people about certain false teachers—as well as the destructiveness of their teachings—when he gives very enlightening truths and descriptions of just who some of the false teachers would be. Firstly and significantly, we are told—they will deny the Sovereign Lord **"who bought them"** (v. 1).

Indeed, with accuracy of translation, these teachers were "bought"! For aid in establishing the intent of the word Peter used for "bought," notice the way the same Greek word, *agorazo*, is used in the following scriptures[16]:

> Do you not know that your body is a temple of the Holy Spirit, who is in you, whom you have received from God? You are not your own; **you were bought [*agorazo*] at a price**. Therefore honor God with your body. (1 Corinthians 6:19-20 NIV 1984)

> You were **bought [*agorazo*] with a price**; do not become slaves of men. (1 Corinthians 7:23 NIV 1984)

---

[16] Ibid., p. 125.

81

> From now on those who have wives should live as if they had none; those who mourn, as if they did not; those who are happy, as if they were not; those who **buy** [*agorazo*] something, as if it were not theirs to keep; (1 Corinthians 7:29-30 NIV1984)

> "You say, 'I am rich; I have acquired wealth and do not need a thing.' But you do not realize that you are wretched, pitiful, poor, blind and naked. I counsel you to **buy** [*agorazo*] from me gold refined in the fire, so you can become rich; and white clothes to wear, so you can cover your shameful nakedness; and salve to put on your eyes, so you can see." (Revelation 3:17-18 NIV1984)

In concurrence with the meaning of *agorazo*, all of these passages have to do with something "being acquired." Also, as can be seen, "being bought" was a common way of looking at the ownership that Christ had over those who had received His payment for their sins (or who would later come to know Him and receive His payment). Thus, the statement that our Sovereign Lord bought certain false teachers (2 Peter 2:1) seems clearly to indicate that Jesus, likewise, had purchased *their* salvation. Jesus had "paid" the price for their sins, and, consequently, they had even once begun with and belonged to Him. 2 Peter 2:1 seems plainly, in itself, to indicate that atonement was not only available to them, but it had been received by them.

Having Left "the Straight Way"

Secondly, Peter tells us, in regard to these false teachers who had been "bought": "They have **left the straight way**" (v. 15). Please note, according to Scripture: there is only one straight way, and that is *in Jesus* (John 14:6)—as we acknowledge Him in all our ways (Proverbs 3:5-6).

Having "Fully Known" Christ and Having Been "Washed"

In verses 20-22, Peter continues, by statements he makes, to expound on and to make even clearer the relationship that certain false teachers will have even experienced with Christ. Noticeably, as he describes the fact that these teachers are "slaves of depravity [corruption]" (v. 19), the scenario is given of these false teachers having escaped the corruption of the world, through fully knowing Christ, *before* again being entangled and overcome (v. 20). Peter's statement, in verse 21, stating, "it would have been better for them not to have **known the way of righteousness**," likewise appears very much to the point. Then, in verse 22, Peter concludes the details of their tragic endings by giving the very descriptive proverb of creature, **having been "washed,"** returning to former ways.

Understandably, some might argue that these verses do not relate to the false teachers about whom Peter has been speaking. Frankly, to whomever they refer, the scenarios considered in the statements speak major truths and warnings. With careful study, however, it seems apparent that the words of verses 20-22 *do* relate to the false teachers, because Peter uses the Greek word *gar* to tie his statements, beginning in verse 20, with what he had just said in verse 19. As has been discussed in other chapters, *gar*, meaning "the fact is, in fact," is pointedly a word "expressing reason, cause, motive, principle, etc. of what has been previously said."[17]

Indeed, from an examination of 2 Peter 2:19, to which verse 20 relates, Peter has just mentioned the state of these false teachers being "slaves of [corruption]" when he begins to state the principles for *why* these particular teachers are "slaves of [corruption]." First, beginning in verse 19, Peter states the principle: *"For [gar / "the fact is"] a man is a slave to whatever has mastered him."*[18] Next, in verse 20, Peter continues the principles that govern slavery to corruption with his words: "[*Gar* / "The fact is"][19] *if they have escaped the corruption of the world by knowing . . . and are again entangled in it and overcome, they are worse off at the end than they were at the beginning."* In particular, it is in this context that the truths of verses 20-22 come.

---

[17] Ibid., pp. 296, 299, xiii.

[18] See also Romans 6:1-2, 11-23, and Romans 8:12-14—specifically, Romans 6:14-16, and 21-23—for a similar discussion of the possibility, and yet needlessness, of one's being "enslaved" to sin all over again.

[19] *The Zondervan Parallel New Testament in Greek and English*, 8th ed., p. 701.

Noticeably as well, Peter uses two Greek words in verses 20 and 21, the words *epignosis* and *epiginosko*, which are especially helpful for giving *sure* definition to the relationship of "knowing" that many false teachers will have had with Jesus. Significantly, according to Bullinger's Lexicon, the word *epignosis* (in verse 20) renders the full meaning as follows:

> Clear and exact knowledge . . . [It] is more emphatic than [*gnosis* / which means "knowing, recognition . . ."], because it expresses a more thorough participation on the part of the knower, with the object of knowledge; a knowledge that has a powerful influence on the knower.[20]

Then similarly, *epiginosko*, the verb related to *epignosis*,[21] is used in verse 21. With use of *epiginosko*, Peter is even ascribing to certain false teachers the condition of once having "known ["known *fully*"] the way of righteousness."

Consequently, as is evident from the meanings of *epignosis* and *epiginosko*, Peter is surely describing the false teachers of 2 Peter 2 as ones who had once believed. In Scripture, references to having a "full knowledge of Christ" are found only with regard to those who have received the life of Jesus. (See the following *epignosis* and *epiginosko* scriptures: Ephesians 1:17; Ephesians 4:13; Colossians 1:9, 10; 1 Timothy 2:4; Hebrews 10:26; 2 Peter 1:2, 3, and 8; 1 Corinthians 13:12; Colossians 1:6; and 1 Timothy 4:3.)[22]

Finally, to further bring clarity concerning the relationship that many false teachers will have had with the Lord, Peter gives the analogy (in verse 22): *"A sow is washed."* With certainty, this seems much like a picture of ones who have been "cleansed from [their] past sins" (as is described just shortly beforehand by Peter in 2 Peter 1:9 NIV1984). Hence, it seems clear: not only had there been provision made—

---

[20] Bullinger, *A Critical Lexicon and Concordance to the English and Greek New Testament*, pp. 436, xiii.
[21] Strong, *Strong's Complete Word Study Concordance*, p. 2075.
[22] Bullinger, *A Critical Lexicon and Concordance to the English and Greek New Testament*, pp. 436-437, 434-436.

atonement for these teachers' sins—but **these teachers once had even embraced the atonement and known a "clean" relationship with Christ**.

IN CONCLUSION
A *Great* Contradiction

With an acknowledgement that the false teachers, about whom Peter spoke, were "atoned for" and had experienced a "clean" relationship with Jesus, there appears to be significant discrepancies with several Calvinist Reformed TULIP teachings. Not only is there contradiction with the TULIP doctrine of *limited atonement*, but other doctrines are affected as well.

According to Scripture, individuals cannot "fully know" Christ and the way of righteousness unless they have been *drawn* to Christ, have been *enabled*, and have been *given revelation* of who Jesus is from the Father (John 6: 44, 65; Matthew 16:13-17). Yet, according to the Calvinist Reformed doctrine of *irresistible grace* (the "I" of the TULIP acronym), such a *drawing* unto a "full knowledge" of Jesus only happens to those who are "unconditionally elected" (who, according to the "P" doctrine that is concluded from *unconditional election*, cannot fall away).

In addition, if it can be agreed that these individuals were "atoned for" and had known a relationship with Jesus, there appears to be a great clash between the end reserved for the false teachers and the "P" teaching of the TULIP acronym. According to the "P" of the TULIP acronym, those predestined before birth and "unconditionally elected" are *made* to persevere—they cannot fall away. Yet, the outcome of the false teachers to whom Peter referred appears to be quite different. The teachers mentioned in 2 Peter 2 are *"bringing swift destruction upon themselves"* (v. 1). *"Blackest darkness is reserved for them"* (v. 17). Noticeably also, the case of such like them, who "have escaped" and are "again entangled," is *"worse off at the end than . . . the beginning"* (v. 20).

Clearly, in the beginning, before one knows Christ, he is an "[object] of wrath" (Ephesians 2:3 NIV1984)—under condemnation, in darkness,

85

going to hell, and in need of a savior. For the latter condition to be worse than the beginning, one must be at least in as bad a condition as before he knew Jesus. Only, perhaps now, "no sacrifice for sins is left" (Hebrews 10:26 NIV1984). He has fully known (*epignosis*)[23] the way of truth, and he has "treated as an unholy thing the blood of the covenant that sanctified him" (Hebrews 10: 29 NIV1984).

Specifically, the words from 2 Peter 2 speak about certain false teachers who will lead many astray—and also the destruction that will follow them. Nevertheless, the consequences given for again becoming "entangled" and "overcome" (v. 20), once set free, can be an example for everyone—whether a teacher or not (although, those presuming to teach *should* know their stricter judgment [James 3:1]). Even more importantly, the truths obtained through reading Peter's words can prove significant to one's knowing *the greatness* of Christ's death on the cross and God's *unlimited* love toward all.

---

[23] Strong, *Strong's Complete Word Study Concordance*, pp. 827, 2075.

WHAT IS

The *Will* of God

Chapter 4

The *Will* of God:
Differentiating between God's *Desires*, God's *Determinations*, and
God's *Pre-Ordained Purposes*

Although, in both the New Testament and the Old Testament, many words are often translated interchangeably and regarded simply as indicating God's "will," it is important to differentiate between those select words which *are* specific either to God's desires, His determinations, or His pre-ordained purposes.[1] It is also important to differentiate between the roles God's desires, God's determinations, and God's set purposes play in His dealings with men. Much confusion occurs because of misunderstanding of the differences between the words used in Scripture to express aspects of His "will." Yet, through an examination of several passages of Scripture and the context where different words are used, the shades of meaning do become more defined. It becomes evident that God's perfect "will" is not always decreed; although, if it is His "will," it has been possible.

WORDS EXPRESSING *DESIRE*

Greek Words

Thelema and *Thelo*

From a study of the New Testament Greek, various words can be seen which pertain to "what is wanted"/"what is willed." From those words, and of primary importance, is the distinction seen between the words (in their noun forms) *thelema, boule,* and *prothesis.* So to begin, con-

---

[1] Please note: Because there are so many different Hebrew words used in the Old Testament to show closely related meanings, only a few of those words will be discussed which substantiate the points of difference being noted.

sider the following scriptures where either *thelema* (noun) or *thelo* (verb related to thelema)[2] are used in addressing the "will" of God:

Revelation 4:11
Thou art worthy, O Lord, to receive glory and honour and power: for thou hast created all things, and for thy **pleasure** [*thelema*][3] they are and were created. (KJV)

Matthew 6:10
" 'Your kingdom come, your **will** [*thelema*][4] be done on earth as it is in heaven.' " (NIV1984)

John 7:17
"If anyone **chooses** [*thelo*] to do God's **will** [*thelema*], he will find out whether my teaching comes from God or whether I speak on my own."[5] (NIV1984)

Romans 12:2
And do not be conformed to this world, but be transformed by the renewing of your mind, that you may prove what is that good and acceptable and perfect **will** [*thelema*][6] of God. (NKJV)

Ephesians 5:17
Therefore do not be foolish, but understand what the Lord's **will** [*thelema*][7] is. (NIV1984)

1 John 5:14-15
This is the assurance we have in approaching God; that if we ask anything according to his **will** [*thelema*],[8] he

---

[2] James Strong, LL.D., S.T.D., *Strong's Complete Word Study Concordance* (Chattanooga, TN: AMG Publishers, 2004), p. 2086.
[3] E. W. Bullinger, *A Critical Lexicon and Concordance to the English and Greek New Testament* (Grand Rapids, MI: Kregel Publications, 1999; orig. pub. 1908), pp. 589, xiii.
[4] Edward W. Goodrick and John R. Kohlenberger, *The NIV Exhaustive Concordance* (Grand Rapids, MI: Zondervan Publishing House, 1990), pp. 1255, 1730.
[5] Ibid., pp. 197, 1255, 1730.
[6] Ibid., pp. 1255, 1730.
[7] Ibid.

hears us. And if we know that he hears us—whatever we ask—we know that we have what we asked of him. (NIV 1984)

1 Timothy 2:3-4
This is good, and pleases God our Savior, who **wants** [*thelo*][9] all men to be saved and to come to a knowledge of the truth. (NIV 1984)

John 6:38-40
"For I came down from heaven, not to do mine own **will** [*thelema*], but the **will** [*thelema*] of him that sent me. And this is the Father's **will** [*thelema*] which hath sent me, that of all which he hath given me I should lose nothing, but should raise it up again at the last day. And this is the **will** [*thelema*] of him that sent me, that every one which seeth the Son, and believeth on him, may have everlasting life: and I will raise him up at the last day."[10] (KJV)

Matthew 7:21
"Not everyone who says to me, 'Lord, Lord,' will enter the kingdom of heaven, but only he who does the **will** [*thelema*][11] of my Father who is in heaven." (NIV 1984)

There is a "good, pleasing and perfect will" of God (Romans 12:2 NIV 1984). That is the will we are called to know and to prove concerning the details of our lives. That is the will we are encouraged to understand and to follow (Ephesians 5:17). That is the will for which we may pray and receive. The Greek root word *thelema* is the word used to identify "will" in these scriptures. According to Bullinger's Lexicon, *thelema* means "will, active volition, wish, desire." According to Bull-

---

[8] Ibid.
[9] Ibid, pp. 1260, 1730.
[10] Bullinger, *A Critical Lexicon and Concordance to the English and Greek New Testament*, pp. 883, xiii.
[11] Goodrick and Kohlenberger, *The NIV Exhaustive Concordance*, pp. 1255, 1730.

inger, the verb *thelo* similarly means "to will, to wish, to desire, implying the simple act of volition."[12]

Numerous times *thelema* and *thelo* are also used to refer to the desires/wishes/wills of men. This sampling of scriptures also aids in understanding the distinct meaning that the words *thelema* and *thelo* have:

> Ephesians 2:3
> Among whom also we all had our conversation in times past in the lusts of our flesh, fulfilling the **desires** [*thelema*][13] of the flesh and of the mind; and were by nature the children of wrath, even as others. (KJV)

> 1 Corinthians 7:36-37
> [Paul, speaking concerning marriage during hard days of persecutions.] If anyone thinks he is acting improperly toward the virgin he is engaged to, and if she is getting along in years and he feels he ought to marry, he should do as he **wants** [*thelo*]. He is not sinning. They should get married. . . . But the man who has settled the matter in his own mind, who is under no compulsion but has control over his own **will** [*thelema*], and who has made up his mind not to marry the virgin—this man does the right thing.[14] (NIV 1984)

> (The context related in verse 37 seems to be that of having control over desires and passions [*thelema*].)

> Luke 5:39
> "And no one after drinking old wine **wants** [*thelo*][15]the new, for he says, 'The old is better.' " (NIV 1984)

---

[12] Bullinger, *A Critical Lexicon and Concordance to the English and Greek New Testament*, pp. 883-884, xiii.

[13] Ibid., pp. 218, xiii.

[14] Goodrick and Kohlenberger, *The NIV Exhaustive Concordance*, pp. 1216, 1255, 1730.

[15] Ibid., pp. 1216, 1730.

(Clearly, the context shows that of "desire" and not "plans" for the word *thelo*.)

Luke 8:20
And it was told him by certain which said, Thy mother and thy brethren stand without, **desiring** [*thelo*][16] to see thee. (KJV)

(Jesus' family was not outside "planning" to see Him.)

Luke 10:24
For I tell you, that many prophets and kings have **desired** [*thelo*][17] to see those things which ye see, and have not seen them; and to hear those things which ye hear, and have not heard them. (KJV)

(Because prophets and kings had had no control over whether they would see the Messiah or not, they surely had not made "plans" to see and to hear Him. They had "desired" to see and to hear Him.)

Romans 7:15-16 and 21-23
[Paul, speaking of the bondage He had experienced *before* being set free by Christ—as one enslaved to the sinful nature and unable to fulfill the law (compare v. 14 to Romans 6:6, 14, and 17-18).] I do not understand what I do. For what I **want** [*thelo*] to do I do not do, but what I hate I do. And if I do what I do not **want** [*thelo*] to do, I agree that the law is good. . . . So I find this law at work: When I **want** [*thelo*] to do good, evil is right there with me. For in my inner being I delight in God's law; but I see another law at work in the members of my body, waging war against the law of my mind and making me a prisoner of the law of sin at work within my members.[18] (NIV 1984)

---

[16] Bullinger, *A Critical Lexicon and Concordance to the English and Greek New Testament*, pp. 218, xiii.
[17] Ibid.
[18] Goodrick and Kohlenberger, *The NIV Exhaustive Concordance*, pp. 1216, 1730.

Galatians 4:9
But now that you know God—or rather are known by
God—how is it that you are turning back to those weak
and miserable principles? Do you **wish** [*thelo*][19] to be
enslaved by them all over again? (NIV1984)

(Of course, they were not "planning" to be enslaved by
the law again! Paul was trying to get the Galatians' attention by a question similar to ones we often ask, while
trying to get people to wake up: "Do you *want* to hurt
yourself?" "Do you *want* to hurt somebody?" "Do you
want to mess things up?" We are not asking about
"plans," and neither, most likely, was Paul. *Thelo* most
certainly renders the meaning of "desire" here.)

Hebrew Words

In similarity to the Greek words *thelema* and *thelo,* there are Hebrew
"feeling words" which denote desire/delight/pleasure and are sometimes simply translated as "will." Like the Greek words, they, too,
stand in contrast to the specific words that do bring revelation concerning "determinations" and "plans" God makes. Examples of "delight"
words to be considered are *ratsown* (or *rason* / alternate spelling),
chephets (noun), *chaphets* (related verb form of *chephets*),[20] *leb*, and
lebab.

Ratsown

The Hebrew word *ratsown* has special meaning. It is distinct in its
communication of "desire" within many scriptures. According to *Wilson's Old Testament Word Studies*, *ratsown* means "delight, satisfaction," "will, pleasure, choice."[21] Some Old Testament scriptures that
show the use of this word are as follows:

---

[19] Ibid., pp. 1259, 1730.
[20] Strong, *Strong's Complete Word Study Concordance*, pp. 1860, 1861.
[21] Goodrick and Kohlenberger, *The NIV Exhaustive Concordance*, p. 1621; William
Wilson, *Wilson's Old Testament Word Studies* (Peabody, MA: Hendrickson Publishers, 1993), pp. 314, 482.

Malachi 2:13
Another thing you do: You flood the LORD's altar with tears. You weep and wail because he no longer pays attention to your offerings or accepts them with **pleasure** [*ratsown*][22] from your hands. (NIV1984)

(A "plan" meaning of "will" definitely would not make sense here. One would not accept a gift with "plan"; instead, a gift would be accepted with "pleasure.")

Psalm 40:8
"I desire to do your **will** [*ratsown*],[23] O my God; your law is within my heart." (NIV1984)

Psalm 103:21
Praise the LORD, all his heavenly hosts, you his servants who do his **will** [*ratsown* / "that do his pleasure" in KJV].[24] (NIV1984)

Psalm 143:10
Teach me to do your **will** [*ratsown*],[25] for you are my God; may your good Spirit lead me on level ground. (NIV1984)

Ezra 10:11
"Now make confession to the LORD, the God of your fathers, and do his **will** [*ratsown* / "do his pleasure" in KJV].[26] Separate yourselves from the peoples around you and from your foreign wives." (NIV1984)

---

[22] Goodrick and Kohlenberger, *The NIV Exhaustive Concordance*, pp. 890, 1621.
[23] Ibid., pp. 1255, 1621.
[24] Ibid.
[25] Ibid.
[26] Ibid.

Chephets and Chaphets

The noun *chephets* renders the meaning: "delight; that which is precious as an object of delight . . . ." [27] Similarly, the verb form *chaphets* renders the meaning: "to will that in which one has great delight when accomplished; joined, therefore, with a negative, it implies very great aversion and dislike . . . ." [28] The following scriptures give illustration to the specific meaning of these "delight" words:

Ecclesiastes 5:4
When you make a vow to God, do not delay in fulfilling it. He has no **pleasure** [*chephets*][29] in fools; fulfill your vow. (NIV1984)

Job 22:3
"What **pleasure** [*chephets*][30] would it give the Almighty if you were righteous? What would he gain if your ways were blameless?" (NIV1984)

Malachi 1:10
I have no **pleasure** [*chephets*][31] in you, saith the LORD of hosts, neither will I accept an offering at your hand. (KJV)

Psalm 1:2
[Concerning the *man* who does not walk in the counsel of the wicked . . .] But his **delight** [*chephets*][32] is in the law of the LORD, and on his law he meditates day and night. (NIV1984)

---

[27] Goodrick and Kohlenberger, *The NIV Exhaustive Concordance*, p. 1455; Wilson, *Wilson's Old Testament Word Studies*, p. 314.
[28] Ibid.
[29] Goodrick and Kohlenberger, *The NIV Exhaustive Concordance*, p. 890, 1455.
[30] Ibid.
[31] Wilson, *Wilson's Old Testament Word Studies*, pp. 314-315.
[32] Goodrick and Kohlenberger, *The NIV Exhaustive Concordance*, pp. 272, 1455.

Psalm 16:3
As for the saints who are in the land, they are the glorious ones in whom is all my **delight** [*chephets*].[33] (NIV1984)

Isaiah 53:10
Yet it was the LORD's will [*chaphets* / verb form of *chephets*] to crush him and cause him to suffer, and though the LORD makes his life a guilt offering, he will see his offspring and prolong his days, and the **will** [*chephets*] of the LORD will prosper in his hand.[34] (NIV1984)

Hosea 6:6
"For I **desire** [*chaphets*][35] mercy, not sacrifice, and acknowledgment of God rather than burnt offerings." (NIV1984)

(This scripture is referred to by Jesus more than once— as is indicated by two separate references found in Matthew 9:13 and Matthew 12:7. Interestingly, in place of the Hebrew word *chaphets*, the corresponding Greek word, *thelo*, is given in both Matthew passages. Also, very notably, reference is being made to what God "desires" and not to what He has "planned"/"purposed.")

Isaiah 56:4
[In context of the mercy available to even those who feel excluded from His people, Isaiah declares . . .] For this is what the LORD says: "To the eunuchs who keep my Sabbaths, who choose [*bachar*][36] what **pleases** [*chaphets*][37] me and hold fast to my covenant . . ." (NIV1984)

---

[33] Ibid.
[34] Ibid. pp. 1255, 1455.
[35] Goodrick and Kohlenberger, *The NIV Exhaustive Concordance*, pp. 279, 1455.
[36] Ibid., pp. 197, 1395.
[37] Ibid., pp. 889, 1455.

(Note the similarity of these words to the earlier referenced John 7:17 scripture. Also, more is discussed concerning this scripture in the chapter entitled "Our Real Effect upon Our Salvation.")

Psalm 40:8
"I **desire** [*chaphets*][38] to do your will [*ratsown*],[39] O my God; your law is within my heart." (NIV1984)

Psalm 37:23
If the LORD **delights** [*chaphets*][40] in a man's way, he makes his steps firm; though he stumble, he will not fall, for the LORD upholds him with his hand. (NIV1984)

Ezekiel 18:23
Have I any **pleasure** [*chaphets*][41] at all that the wicked should die? Saith the LORD God; and not that he should return from his ways, and live? (KJV)

(*When compared to a soul that returns from his ways and lives*, God takes no pleasure in the soul death of the wicked! The comparison being made is important because in other scriptures we are told that God *does* desire the death of the wicked [e.g., 1 Samuel 2:25].)[42]

Ezekiel 18:31-32
Cast away from you all your transgressions, whereby ye have transgressed; and make you a new heart and a new spirit: for why will ye die, O house of Israel? For I have no **pleasure** [*chaphets*][43] in the death of him that dieth,

---

[38] Ibid., pp. 279, 1455.
[39] Ibid., pp. 1255, 1621.
[40] Ibid., pp. 273, 1455.
[41] Goodrick and Kohlenberger, *The NIV Exhaustive Concordance*, pp. 1455; Wilson, *Wilson's Old Testament Word Studies*, p. 314.
[42] See the discussion in the chapter "Inconsistencies—Part 2."
[43] Goodrick and Kohlenberger, *The NIV Exhaustive Concordance*, pp. 1455; Wilson, *Wilson's Old Testament Word Studies*, p. 314.

saith the LORD God; wherefore turn yourselves, and live ye. (KJV)

Ezekiel 33:11
Say unto them, As I live, saith the Lord GOD, I have no **pleasure** [*chaphets*][44] in the death of the wicked; but that the wicked turn from his way and live: turn ye, turn ye from your evil ways: for why will ye die, O house of Israel? (KJV)

Isaiah 65:12
I will destine you for the sword, and you will all bend down for the slaughter; for I called but you did not answer, I spoke but you did not listen. You did evil in my sight and chose what dis**pleases** [*chaphets* / "I **delighted** not" in KJV][45] me. (NIV1984)

Isaiah 66:4
"So I also will choose harsh treatment for them and will bring upon them what they dread. For when I called, no one answered, when I spoke, no one listened. They did evil in my sight and chose what dis**pleases** [*chaphets* / "delighted not" in KJV][46] me." (NIV1984)

Leb and *Lebab*

The Hebrew nouns *leb* and *lebab* are closely related to the "desire" words mentioned so far in that they mean "heart."[47] When one's heart is known, one's will—one's desire—can likewise be seen. Although most often translated as "heart," at times the word "will" has even been used. The following examples are given to demonstrate their meanings:

---

[44] Ibid.
[45] Goodrick and Kohlenberger, *The NIV Exhaustive Concordance*, pp. 296, 1456.
[46] Ibid.
[47] Goodrick and Kohlenberger, *The NIV Exhaustive Concordance*, pp. 1499, 1500; Wilson, *Wilson's Old Testament Word Studies*, p. 212.

Exodus 8:15
But when Pharaoh saw that there was relief, he hardened his **heart** [*leb*][48] and would not listen to Moses and Aaron, just as the LORD had said. (NIV 1984)

1 Samuel 16:7
"Man looks at the outward appearance, but the LORD looks at the **heart** [*lebab*]."[49] (NIV 1984)

Deuteronomy 6:5
Love the LORD your God with all your **heart** [*lebab*][50] and with all your soul and with all your strength. (NIV 1984)

Proverbs 4:23
Keep thy **heart** [*leb*][51] with all diligence; for out of it are the issues of life. (KJV)

Proverbs 17:16
Of what use is money in the hand of a fool, since he has no **desire** [*leb*][52] to get wisdom? (NIV 1984)

1 Samuel 13:14
But now thy kingdom shall not continue: the LORD hath sought him a man after his own **heart** [*lebab*],[53] and the LORD hath commanded him to be captain over his people, because thou hast not kept that which the LORD commanded thee. (KJV)

---

[48] Goodrick and Kohlenberger, *The NIV Exhaustive Concordance*, pp. 513, 1499.
[49] Ibid., pp. 513, 1500.
[50] Ibid.
[51] Ibid., pp. 514, 1499.
[52] Ibid., pp. 279, 1499.
[53] Ibid., pp. 513, 1500.

1 Chronicles 17:19
"For the sake of your servant and according to your **will** [*leb*],[54] you have done this great thing and made known all these great promises." (NIV1984)

Lamentations 3:33
For he doth not afflict **will**ingly [*min* + *leb* / "from the heart"][55] nor grieve the children of men. (KJV)

(What an important truth of God's character!)

From the wide array of scriptures given, so far, which represent both New Testament and Old Testament words often "loosely" translated as just "will," hopefully the distinct meaning of "pleasure" or "desire," as it pertains to God's "perfect will," is now more clear. Hopefully, also, some of God's dealings with men can be better understood as well.

It can be seen in Scripture that God's perfect "will"—God's perfect desire—is *not* always accomplished. In Matthew 7:21, Jesus tells the people that only the one "who **does** the will [*thelema* / "desire"][56] of my Father who is in heaven" (NIV1984) will enter the kingdom of heaven. We know, from Scripture, that all will not enter the kingdom of heaven (Matthew 7:14). Similarly, in Mark 3:35, Jesus inferred that God's will/desire is not always done. He separated the many from those whom He would call His "brothers," "sisters," and "mothers" by saying, "Whoever **does** God's will [*thelema* / "desire"][57] is my brother and sister and mother" (NIV1984). We see that God's perfect will (*thelema*) is not always accomplished; for not all does Jesus consider His "brother and sister and mother."

Many times, in references made to the responses which the people of Israel and Judah had made toward God's loving initiatives, it is given that God's will—His desire—was not always done. For instance, God

---

[54] Ibid., pp. 1255, 1499.
[55] Ibid., pp. 1256, 1499, 1519.
[56] Ibid., pp. 1255, 1730.
[57] Ibid.

was angered by Moses, as recorded in Exodus 4:10. He would not have been angered if Moses had been willing to do what He had desired. And, in the previously mentioned scriptures of Isaiah 65:12 and Isaiah 66:4, it can be seen that Israel often did the things in which God "delighted [*chaphets*] not" (KJV).

What is more, according to Jeremiah 32:30-35, the reason God became angry with His people (and the reason He proclaimed judgment) is that they *did not do* His will. Through the prophet Jeremiah, the Lord emphatically spoke these words concerning the people of Israel and Judah:

> "The people of Israel and Judah have done nothing but evil in my sight from their youth; indeed, the people of Israel have done nothing but provoke me with what their hands have made, declares the LORD. From the day it was built until now, this city has so aroused my anger and wrath that I must remove it from my sight . . . They turned their backs to me and not their faces; though I taught them again and again, they would not listen or respond to discipline. They set up their abominable idols in the house that bears my Name and defiled it. They built high places for Baal in the Valley of Ben Hinnom to sacrifice their sons and daughters to Molech, though I never commanded [*tsavah* / see word later],[58] **nor did it enter my mind** [*leb* / "heart"],[59] that they should do such a detestable thing and so make Judah sin." (Jeremiah 32:30-35 NIV 1984)

It never even entered God's heart that the above abominable acts be done! How, then, could those actions have been God's will, and, subsequently, how could they have been *caused* by Him (as some who misunderstand His sovereign ways would say)?

God's willingness and man's willingness are two different things. In Matthew 23:37, Jesus speaks of the distinctions as He cries, "O Jerusalem, Jerusalem, you who kill the prophets and stone those sent to you,

---

[58] Ibid., pp. 219, 1595.
[59] Ibid., pp. 754, 1499.

how often **I have longed** [*thelo*] to gather your children together, as a hen gathers her chicks under her wings, but **you were not willing** [*thelo*]"[60] (NIV1984). Although it is His great desire that His "will" be accomplished, and although it has been possible, it is evident from Scripture that *God restrains Himself* and leaves much of what He would desire up to our responses.

WORDS EXPRESSING *DETERMINATION* AND *COUNSEL*

Although God restrains Himself and leaves much of what happens up to our choices, He does have His thoughts—His knowledge of what is best—on matters. Whereas God's heart—God's desire—is expressed by the words examined thus far (pertaining to God's "will"), the words to follow express *determinations* He makes.

Greek Words

The two Greek words *boule* and *prothesis* (noun forms) are important words to recognize because of the understanding they bring to the meaning of New Testament Scripture. Although both are sometimes represented by the English words "will" or "purpose," and although both *boule* and *prothesis* do involve determinations being made (and not "desire"), both also have their distinct meanings.

Boule and *Boulomai*

According to Bullinger's Lexicon, the Greek noun *boule* most accurately means "determination, decision, decree, counsel." [61] With likeness, the corresponding verb form, *boulomai,* means "to wish, to desire, to have that desire from which [*thelo*] sometimes springs, *to have a wish, intention, or purpose, formed after mature deliberation; to deliberately purpose after careful consideration* [emphasis mine]."[62] One's *boule* is

---

[60] Ibid., pp. 1256, 1730.
[61] Bullinger, *A Critical Lexicon and Concordance to the English and Greek New Testament*, pp. 883, xiii.
[62] Ibid., pp. 884, xiii.

what one determines or judges is best to happen. Yet, as can be seen in some of the following scriptures, one's *boule* is not necessarily a decree that is for sure be made to happen, although the word may be used that way. Often, as in the case of God's "counsel," it is a warning of what He has determined "will happen" *if* there is no change. Some examples that help in interpreting the New Testament word can be found in the following scriptures:

1 Timothy 5:14
So I **counsel** [*boulomai*]⁶³ younger widows to marry, to have children, to manage their homes and to give the enemy no opportunity for slander. (NIV 1984)

(In this case, Paul is giving his counsel—what he has decided is best. He is not commanding and making them to marry. He has no control over that part of their lives.)

Acts 12:4
So when he had arrested him, he put him in prison, and delivered him to four squads of soldiers to keep him, **intending** [*boulomai*]⁶⁴ to bring him before the people after Passover. (NKJV)

(Herod had decided—had determined best—to bring Peter before the people after Passover.)

Luke 23:51
He had not consented to their **decision** [*boule*]⁶⁵ and deed. He was from Arimathea, a city of the Jews, who himself was also waiting for the kingdom of God. (NKJV)

Acts 4:28
"They [Herod and Pontius Pilate] did what your power and **will** [*boule*]⁶⁶ had decided beforehand [*proorizo* /

---

⁶³ Goodrick and Kohlenberger, *The NIV Exhaustive Concordance*, pp. 233, 1695.
⁶⁴ Ibid., pp. 564, 1695.
⁶⁵ Ibid., pp. 267, 1695.
⁶⁶ Ibid., pp. 1255, 1695.

"determine, decree, or ordain beforehand"][67] should happen." (NIV 1984)

(In this example, we can see the usage of two "determination" words. *Boule* is more accurately in the line of counsel, according to the Greek. "What God thought best" was "planned ahead of time to happen.")

Acts 20:27
"For I have not hesitated to proclaim to you the whole **will** [*boule*][68] of God." (NIV 1984)

(During Paul's ministry, he had proclaimed the counsel of God—*what God had determined as "right" in matters.*)

Luke 7:30
But the Pharisees and lawyers rejected the **will** [*boule*][69] of God for themselves, not having been baptized by him. (NKJV)

(**Notably**, God's counsel for the Pharisees and lawyers was rejected. They did not choose God.)

2 Peter 3:9
He is patient with you, not **wanting** [*boulomai*][70] anyone to perish, but everyone to come to repentance. (NIV 1984)

(Perhaps this is the intent of Peter's statement: The Lord is patient with us, not quickly coming and rendering judgment to the world, because God *thinks it best* that people be given opportunity to repent rather than perish.)[71]

---

[67] Ibid., pp. 267, 1782.
[68] Ibid., pp. 1255, 1695.
[69] Ibid., pp. 919, 1695.
[70] Ibid., pp. 1216, 1695.
[71] See the discussion of 2 Peter 3:9 in "Inconsistencies—Part 2."

<u>1 Corinthians 12:11</u>
All these are the work of one and the same Spirit, and he gives them to each one, just as he **determines** [*boulomai*].[72] (NIV1984)

<u>Matthew 11:27</u>
"And no one knows [*epiginosko* / "fully knows" in Greek][73] the Father except the Son and those to whom the Son **chooses** [*boulomai*][74] to reveal him." (NIV1984)

(The determination of who *fully* knows the Father belongs to Jesus. Notably, as the verses that immediately follow verse 27 point out, a condition for such a revelation seems to be one's coming to Jesus and learning from Him. Please note: This decision/determination of what is best is not the same as a perfect desire. Also, the word does not denote, as do other specific words, a predestined intention.)

<u>Ephesians 1:11</u>
Who works out everything in conformity with the **purpose** [*boule*] of his will [*thelema*],[75] (NIV1984)

(*Boule* relays the "counsel"/"determination" tone of will. *Thelema* relays the "desire" meaning of will. This statement is in close similarity with God's statements found in Isaiah 46:10.)[76]

Hebrew Words

As with the specific Greek used in the New Testament, there are also specific Hebrew words used in the Old Testament that, in Scripture,

---

[72] Goodrick and Kohlenberger, *The NIV Exhaustive Concordance*, pp. 282, 1695.
[73] Bullinger, *A Critical Lexicon and Concordance to the English and Greek New Testament*, pp. 435, xiii.
[74] Goodrick and Kohlenberger, *The NIV Exhaustive Concordance*, pp. 197, 1695.
[75] Goodrick and Kohlenberger, *The NIV Exhaustive Concordance*, pp. 919, 1695.
[76] See the references to Ephesians 1:11 and, additionally, to Isaiah 46:10 in the chapter "Significant Scriptures—Part 1."

most accurately denote the "counsel" of God. Yet, they too, like the Greek words *boule* and *boulomai*, often have been simply rendered as "purpose" or "purposed." As with the Greek words, these words also, simply said, have to do with *what is determined as best*. The corresponding Hebrew words to be considered are the related words[77] *etsah* (noun) and *ya'ats* (verb).

Etsah

According to *Wilson's Old Testament Word Studies*, the noun *etsah* means the following: "counsel, including both deliberation and the purpose of doing anything; implying also wisdom, reflection, and skill."[78] With consideration to its distinctive meaning, note the following scriptures where the noun *etsah* is used:

Psalm 1:1
Blessed is the man who does not walk in the **counsel** [*etsah*][79] of the wicked or stand in the way of sinners or sit in the seat of mockers. (NIV1984)

Proverbs 27:9
Perfume and incense bring joy to the heart, and the pleasantness of one's friend springs from his earnest **counsel** [*etsah*].[80] (NIV1984)

Isaiah 16:3
"Give us **counsel** [*etsah*],[81] render a decision . . ." (NIV1984)

Proverbs 12:15
The way of a fool seems right to him, but a wise man listens to **advice** [*etsah*].[82] (NIV1984)

---

[77] Strong, *Strong's Complete Word Study and Concordance*, pp. 1875, 1940.
[78] Goodrick and Kohlenberger, *The NIV Exhaustive Concordance*, p. 1576; Wilson, *Wilson's Old Testament Word Studies*, p. 98.
[79] Goodrick and Kohlenberger, *The NIV Exhaustive Concordance*, pp. 233, 1576.
[80] Ibid.
[81] Ibid.
[82] Ibid., pp. 17, 1576.

Proverbs 19:20
Listen to **advice** [*etsah*][83] and accept instruction, and in
the end you will be wise. (NIV1984)

Jeremiah 18:18
They said, "Come, let's make plans against Jeremiah;
for the teaching of the law by the priest will not be lost,
nor will **counsel** [*etsah*][84] from the wise, nor the word
from the prophets." (NIV1984)

Proverbs 21:30
There is no wisdom nor understanding nor **counsel**
[*etsah*][85] against the LORD. (KJV)

Ya'ats

Very much like *etsah* in meaning and often found alongside is the related verb *ya'ats*. According to *Wilson's Old Testament Word Studies*,
ya'ats means "to deliberate: . . . to lay a scheme, to form a design; to
give counsel, to ask counsel; to take counsel; with or without [*etsah*]."
[86] The following passages (some containing both *etsah* and the verb
ya'ats) also continue to demonstrate the more precise "counsel" and
"deliberation" tone of the words:

2 Samuel 17:11, 15
Therefore I **counsel** [*ya'ats*][87] that all Israel be generally gathered unto thee, from Dan even to Beersheba, as
the sand that is by the sea for multitude; and that thou
go to battle in thine own person. . . . Then said Hushai
unto Zadok and Abiathar the priests. Thus and thus did

---

[83] Ibid.
[84] Ibid. pp. 233, 1576.
[85] Ibid., pp. 887, 1576.
[86] Goodrick and Kohlenberger, *The NIV Exhaustive Concordance*, p. 1473; Wilson,
Wilson's Old Testament Word Studies, p. 98.
[87] Goodrick and Kohlenberger, *The NIV Exhaustive Concordance*, p. 1473; Wilson,
Wilson's Old Testament Word Studies, p. 98.

Ahithophel **counsel** [*ya'ats*][88] Absalom and the elders of Israel; and thus and thus have I counseled. (KJV)

2 Samuel 17:7
And Hushai said unto Absalom, The **counsel** [*etsah*][89] that Ahithophel hath **given** [ya'ats][90] is not good at this time. (KJV)

1 Kings 12:8
But he forsook the **counsel** [*etsah* / "advice" in NIV1984] of the elders which they had **given** [*ya'ats*] him, and **consulted** [*ya'ats*] with the young men who grew up with him, and served him.[91] (NASB)

2 Chronicles 25:16
So the prophet stopped but said, "I know that God has **determined** [ya'ats] to destroy you, because you have done this and have not listened to my [the prophet's] **counsel** [*etsah*]."[92] (NIV1984)

(God had deliberated and had thought best to execute judgment.)

Psalm 16:7
I will praise the LORD, who **counsels** [*ya'ats*][93] me; even at night my heart instructs me. (NIV1984)

---

[88] Goodrick and Kohlenberger, *The NIV Exhaustive Concordance,* p. 1473; Wilson, *Wilson's Old Testament Word Studies*, p. 98.
[89] Goodrick and Kohlenberger, *The NIV Exhaustive Concordance*, p. 1576; Wilson, *Wilson's Old Testament Word Studies*, p. 98.
[90] Goodrick and Kohlenberger, *The NIV Exhaustive Concordance*, p. 1473; Wilson, *Wilson's Old Testament Word Studies*, p. 98.
[91] Goodrick and Kohlenberger, *The NIV Exhaustive Concordance*, pp. 17, 228, 434, 1473, 1576.
[92] Ibid., pp. 233, 282, 1473, 1576.
[93] Ibid., pp. 233, 1473.

Psalm 73:24
You guide me with your **counsel** [*etsah*],[94]and afterward you will take me into glory. (NIV1984)

Psalm 106:13
But they soon forgot what he had done and did not wait for his **counsel** [*etsah*].[95] (NIV1984)

Psalm 107:11
For they had rebelled against the words of God and despised the **counsel** [*etsah*][96] of the Most High. (NIV1984)

From the sampling of scriptures seen so far, it seems that the most literal intent of the Hebrew words *etsah* and *ya'ats* would be that of "counsel" and "counseling." Notably also, as Psalm 106:13 and Psalm 107:11 indicate, **individuals can "wait for" or "despise" God's *etsah* (God's counsel)**. In particular, these words are helpful to understand because of their presence in many significant scriptures that speak of God's sovereignty and how He deals with men.

Also, in like manner, through an examination of both Greek and Hebrew words rendered as "counsel" in Scripture, and through an examination of the context of scriptures containing those words, the meaning of God's "counsel" seems clear. Simply speaking, God's "counsel" is that which He has determined *best* and desires to have done.

WORDS EXPRESSING *PLANS* AND *INTENTION*

God makes determinations on things which He makes plans to do. He determines, first of all, that *it is best* to intervene. He determines, secondly, *how* He wants to intervene. *How He determines to intervene* are His plans.

---

[94] Ibid., pp. 233, 1576.
[95] Ibid.
[96] Ibid.

Greek Words

Prothesis and *Protithemi*

Distinctively, the Greek words *prothesis* (noun form) and *protithemi* (verb form) are words that, in similarity to *boule* or *boulomai*, often are translated as "purpose" or "purposed." Yet, according to Bullinger's Lexicon, *prothesis* renders the meaning: "a setting before or forth, a setting out; then, of what one sets before his mind, proposes to himself, purpose, deliberate resolution."[97] Likewise, the related verb *protithemi*, formed by the preposition *pro* (meaning "before, forward")[98] and *tithemi* (later to be defined), means "to set or put before any one, to set before one's self, propose to one's self, i.e. to purpose."[99]

Unlike the words *thelema* and *boule*, the noun *prothesis* renders the idea of "plan" and "intention." As with man's plans, God's *prothesis* is set ahead of time. (Also, **provided man waits on God and all of God's conditions are met, God's *prothesis* will happen**.) Such places in the New Testament where a form of this word occurs are as follows: Romans 9:11, 2 Timothy 1:9, Romans 1:13, Ephesians 1:9, Romans 8:28, and Ephesians 3:11. Even as an aid in understanding their distinct meanings, consider the following and substitute the words "plan" or "planned" each time *prothesis* or *protithemi* occurs:

> Romans 9:11
> Yet, before the twins were born or had done anything good or bad—in order that God's **purpose** [*prothesis*][100] in election might stand: not by works but by him who calls—she was told, "The older will serve the younger." (NIV 1984)

> ("Purpose"/"plan" is the proper rendering of the Greek. God's *set* intentions will stand. Here we are reminded of God's constant intent concerning who His righteous

---

[97] Bullinger, *A Critical Lexicon and Concordance to the English and Greek New Testament*, pp. 614, xiii.

[98] Ibid., pp. xiii, xx.

[99] Ibid. pp. 614, xiii.

[100] Goodrick and Kohlenberger, *The NIV Exhaustive Concordance*, pp. 919, 1782.

people will be—those who will look to Him and His work, and not unto their own.)

2 Timothy 1:8-9
But join with me in suffering for the gospel, by the power of God, who has saved and called us to a holy life— not because of anything we have done but because of His own **purpose** [*prothesis*][101] and grace. (NIV1984)

(God had His own plan. He had His own purpose—so that He would receive all the praise for the favor totally unearned by us.)

Romans 1:13
I do not want you to be unaware, brothers, that I **planned** [*protithemi*][102] many times to come to you (but have been prevented from doing so until now) in order that I might have a harvest among you, just as I have had among the other Gentiles. (NIV1984)

(Noticeably, the NIV1984 renders the "plan" shade of meaning that this verb form of *prothesis* has.)

Ephesians 1:9-10
And he made known to us the mystery of his **will** [*thelema*][103] according to his good pleasure, which he **purposed** [*protithemi*][104] in Christ, to be put into effect when the times will have reached their fulfillment—to bring all things to heaven and on earth together under one head, even Christ. (NIV1984)

(Here, Paul differentiates between the words *thelema* and *protithemi* [the verb related to *prosthesis*]. Although God's perfect desire is not always carried out, God's

---

[101] Ibid.
[102] Ibid., pp. 887, 1784.
[103] Ibid., pp. 1255, 1730.
[104] Ibid., pp. 919, 1784.

perfect desire *was* fulfilled here. God had planned beforehand how He would redeem the world from the curse of sin and Satan's hold. At just the right time, Jesus was sent into the world to fulfill God's eternal plan.)

Romans 8:28
And we know that all things work together for good to those who love God, to those who are the called according to His **purpose** [*prothesis*].[105] (NKJV)

Ephesians 3:11
According to the eternal **purpose** [*prothesis*][106] which he accomplished in Christ Jesus our Lord. (NIV 1984)

(Sending Jesus had been "planned" for all eternity!)

Then, noticeably, in the following scripture, the Greek words *thelema*, *boule*, and *prothesis* all appear with their distinct meanings:

Ephesians 1:11
In Him also we have obtained an inheritance, being predestined according to the **purpose** [*prosthesis* / plan][107] of Him who works all things according to the counsel [*boule* / determination][108] of His will [*thelema* / desire],[109] (NKJV)

(God purposed ahead of time that, in Him [Jesus], His people would be given a great inheritance. It was His plan. Also, we see, by the words used, that He will work out everything in conformity with *what He decides is*

---

[105] Ibid., pp. 919, 1782. See also the discussion of Romans 8:28-30 within the chapter "Another Look at Various Scriptures."
[106] Goodrick and Kohlenberger, *The NIV Exhaustive Concordance*, pp. 919, 1782.
[107] Bullinger, *A Critical Lexicon and Concordance to the English and Greek New Testament*, pp.614, xiii.
[108] Ibid., pp. 189, xiii.
[109] Ibid., pp. 883, xiii.

best [His *boule*] and what He is pleased to do [His *the-lema*].)[110]

Hebrew Words

Machashabah and *Chashab*

Like the Greek words *prothesis* and *protithemi*, there are also specific words in the Old Testament that render the meaning of "plan" and "planning." Two such words are *machashabah* (noun), and *chashab* (verb). According to *Wilson's Old Testament Word Studies*, the noun *machashabah* renders the meaning: "counsel, purpose, plan, what one meditates or has devised; specially of wicked counsels, devices, machinations."[111] The verb *chashab* similarly has the meaning: "to consider; to design; to contrive with studied thinking."[112] Scriptures that follow demonstrate the particular nature of their meaning:

Esther 8:3
She begged him to put an end to the evil **plan** [*machashabah*][113] of Haman the Agagite, which he had devised against the Jews. (NIV 1984)

Proverbs 21:5
The **plans** [*machashabah*][114] of the diligent lead to profit as surely as haste leads to poverty. (NIV 1984)

Proverbs 20:18
Every **purpose** [*machashabah*][115] is established [*kuwn* / see later discussion][116] by counsel [*etsah*]:[117] and with good advice make war. (KJV)

---

[110] See also the chapter "Another Look at Ephesians 1."
[111] Goodrick and Kohlenberger, *The NIV Exhaustive Concordance*, p. 1514; Wilson, *Wilson's Old Testament Word Studies*, p. 122.
[112] Goodrick and Kohlenberger, *The NIV Exhaustive Concordance*, p. 1459; Wilson, *Wilson's Old Testament Word Studies*, p. 122.
[113] Goodrick and Kohlenberger, *The NIV Exhaustive Concordance*, pp. 887, 1514.
[114] Ibid., pp. 887, 1514.
[115] Goodrick and Kohlenberger, *The NIV Exhaustive Concordance*, p. 1514; Wilson, *Wilson's Old Testament Word Studies*, p. 334.

Jeremiah 49:30

Flee, get you far off, dwell deep, O ye inhabitants of
Hazor, saith the LORD; for Nebuchadnezzar king of Babylon hath taken [*ya'ats* / "deliberated"][118] counsel
[*etsah*][119] against you, and hath **conceived** [*chashab*][120] a
purpose [*machashabah*][121] against you. (KJV)

(Noticeably, within Jeremiah 49:30, a differentiation between *ya'ats/etsah* [closely connected "deliberation"/"counsel" words] and *chashab/machashabah*
[closely related "plan"/"intent" words] can be seen with
the inclusion of each specific word.)

Jeremiah 29:11

[The Lord spoke these words through Jeremiah concerning the future He had "planned" for Israel.] For I know
the **thoughts** [*machashabah* / "plans" in NIV1984][122]
that I **think** [*chashab*][123] toward you, saith the LORD,
thoughts [*machashaba*h / "plans" in NIV1984][124] of
peace, and not of evil, to give you an expected end.
(KJV)

---

[116] Wilson, *Wilson's Old Testament Word Studies*, p. 149.

[117] Goodrick and Kohlenberger, *The NIV Exhaustive Concordance*, pp. 17, 1576.

[118] Goodrick and Kohlenberger, *The NIV Exhaustive Concordance*, p. 1473; Wilson,
Wilson's Old Testament Word Studies, pp. 435, 438.

[119] Goodrick and Kohlenberger, *The NIV Exhaustive Concordance*, p. 1576; Wilson,
Wilson's Old Testament Word Studies, p. 98.

[120] Goodrick and Kohlenberger, *The NIV Exhaustive Concordance*, p. 1459; Wilson,
Wilson's Old Testament Word Studies, p. 90.

[121] Goodrick and Kohlenberger, *The NIV Exhaustive Concordance*, p. 1514; Wilson,
Wilson's Old Testament Word Studies, p. 334.

[122] Goodrick and Kohlenberger, *The NIV Exhaustive Concordance*, p. 1514; Wilson,
Wilson's Old Testament Word Studies, p. 444.

[123] Goodrick and Kohlenberger, *The NIV Exhaustive Concordance*, p. 1459; Wilson,
Wilson's Old Testament Word Studies, p. 444.

[124] Goodrick and Kohlenberger, *The NIV Exhaustive Concordance*, p. 1514; Wilson,
Wilson's Old Testament Word Studies, p. 444.

Jeremiah 26:3

[In the beginning of Jehoikim's rule, following God's call to Jeremiah to speak to the people words of warning, the Lord shares His heart.] "Perhaps they will listen and each will turn from his evil way. Then I will relent and not bring on them the disaster I was **planning** [*chashab*][125] because of the evil they have done." (NIV1984)

(Note: This scripture gives example that *all of the plans* **God has made for individuals** *do not* **happen**. God can change His mind; nevertheless, *if it is God's purpose/plan*, only He can decide to alter it.)

Jeremiah 36:2-3

[The fourth year of Jehoiakim's rule, God spoke these words to Jeremiah.] Take thee a roll of a book, and write therein all the words that I have spoken unto thee against Israel, and against Judah, and against all the nations, from the day I spake unto thee, from the days of Josiah, even unto this day. It may be that the house of Judah will hear all the evil which I **purpose** [*chashab*][126] to do unto them; that they may return every man from his evil way; that I may forgive their iniquity and their sin. (KJV)

(**Significantly**, *if people would have repented*, God may have changed His mind concerning the disaster He was planning for judgment. God so desires to show mercy— but man has a part.)

Lamentations 2:8

The LORD has **purposed** [*chashab*][127] to destroy the wall of the daughter of Zion. He has stretched out a line; He

---

[125] Goodrick and Kohlenberger, *The NIV Exhaustive Concordance*, pp. 887, 1459.

[126] Goodrick and Kohlenberger, *The NIV Exhaustive Concordance*, p. 1459; Wilson, *Wilson's Old Testament Word Studies*, p. 334.

[127] Goodrick and Kohlenberger, *The NIV Exhaustive Concordance*, p. 1459; Wilson, *Wilson's Old Testament Word Studies*, p. 334.

has not withdrawn His hand from destroying; therefore He has caused the rampart and wall to lament; they languished together. (NKJV)

Zamam

The verb *zamam* is another word found in scriptures relaying aspects of God's interactions with men. It, too, demonstrates the power and greatness of God's rule and the determinations—even of judgment—that He does make over men. According to *Strong's Complete Word Study Concordance*, the verb *zamam* renders the meaning: "to plan, usually in a bad sense: consider, devise, imagine, plot, purpose, think (evil)."[128] The following scriptures demonstrate the intent of this word:

Genesis 11:6
[In response to the building of the tower of Babel, *zamam* is used to describe what God said concerning the people of the world.] And the LORD said, Behold, the people is one, and they have all one language; and this they begin to do: and now nothing will be restrained from them, which they have **imagined** [*zamam*][129] to do. (KJV)

Psalm 31:13
For I hear the slander of many; there is terror on every side; they conspire against me and **plot** [*zamam*][130] to take my life. (NIV1984)

Jeremiah 51:12
Set up the standard upon the walls of Babylon, make the watch strong, set up the watchmen, prepare the ambushes: for the LORD hath both **devised** [*zamam*][131] and done

---

[128] Strong, *Strong's Complete Word Study Concordance*, p. 1848.
[129] Ibid., pp. 731, 1848.
[130] Ibid., pp. 367, 1848.
[131] Ibid.

that which he spake against the inhabitants of Babylon. (KJV)

Zechariah 8:14-15
This is what the LORD Almighty says: "Just as I had **determined** [*zamam*] to bring disaster upon you and showed no pity when your fathers angered me," says the LORD Almighty, "so now I have **determined** [*zamam*][132] to do good again to Jerusalem and Judah. Do not be afraid." (NIV 1984)

Alongside scriptural context, the previous Greek and Hebrew words (*prothesis, protithemi, machashabah, chashab, and zamam*) clearly *have* rendered the meaning of either "to plan" or "a plan." Given right conditions, they also clearly *have* been used, contextually, with the notion of God's *making* particular things to happen. Thus, hopefully, from this overview, a greater understanding of the specific intent of many "purpose" scriptures has been achieved—intent that is quite different from those of "desire" or "counsel" scriptures.

WORDS EXPRESSING *DECREE, APPOINTMENT,* OR *FIRM DECISION*

God is on the throne! As with a king, whatever God determines *to do* happens. When God speaks that something shall happen, it happens. Creation, itself, began that way—with a "let there be" and "there was" (Genesis 1:3). Just as Psalm 33:6-9 reminds us:

> By the word of the LORD were the heavens made, their starry host by the breath of his mouth. . . . Let all the earth fear the LORD; let all the people of the world revere him. **For he spoke, and it came to be; he commanded** [*tsavah*],[133] **and it stood firm**. (NIV 1984)

---

[132] Ibid., pp. 1516, 1848.
[133] Ibid., pp. 295, 1953.

Although many words already have been mentioned which have to do with decisions, determinations, and judgments of what is best (often more in line with the word "counsel"), the following words to be noted, when in reference to God, even more specifically *do* speak of God's "decrees" and "appointments" involving particular things that happen.

Greek Words

Boulema

Although this word only occurs two times within the New Testament,[134] the meaning of this noun is especially important to note because the word is contained within a *very significant* section of Scripture. Moreover, when misunderstood in its literal meaning, much confusion can surely occur. Specifically, this noun, which comes from the verb *boulomai*, denotes the idea of "resolve."[135] Additionally, according to Bullinger's Lexicon, the word renders the meaning: "deliberate intention, that which is purposed, designed, planned, or intended." [136] The following scriptures illustrate the precise meaning of the word:

> Acts 27:43
> But the centurion, wanting to save Paul, kept them from their purpose [*boulema*],[137] and commanded that those who could swim should jump overboard first and get to land. (NKJV)

> Romans 9:19
> You will say to me then, "Why does He still find fault? For who has resisted His **will** [*boulema*]?"[138] (NKJV)

> (Understanding the Greek words used here is *so* important. No one has resisted God's *determinations—*

---

[134] Ibid., p. 1000.
[135] Ibid.
[136] Bullinger, *A Critical Lexicon and Concordance to the English and Greek New Testament*, pp. 883, xiii.
[137] Ibid., p. 614.
[138] Ibid., p. 883.

what God has decided to have happen. Yet again, as has been noted, God's perfect and probable desires [His *the-lema*] *can* be resisted.)

Tithemi

The Greek verb *tithemi* is a word often used in the New Testament to give the idea of "appoint." According to Bullinger's Lexicon, *tithemi* renders the meaning: "to put, set, place; then generally to bring a thing into a place; and so, to bring into a situation, to bring about, cause, *metaph.*.to put in a certain place or condition; hence, to appoint." According to Bullinger, one can also *tithemi* one's self: "to cause to put or put for one's self; to assign, determine."[139] The following scriptures, according to context, illustrate the usage of the word:

Revelation 10:2
And he had in his hand a little book open: and he **set** [*tithemi*][140] his right foot upon the sea, and his left foot on the earth, (KJV)

Acts 13:47
[Concerning their placement into service toward the Gentiles, Paul and Barnabus spoke . . .] "For so the Lord has commanded us: 'I have **set** [*tithemi*][141]you as a light to the Gentiles, that you should be for salvation to the ends of the earth.' " (NKJV)

Matthew 22:44
The LORD said unto my Lord, 'Sit thou on my right hand, till I **make** [*tithemi*][142] thine enemies thy footstool . . . (KJV)

---

[139] Ibid., pp. 60, xiii.
[140] Strong, *Strong's Complete Word Study Concordance*, pp. 1312, 2164.
[141] Ibid.
[142] Ibid., pp. 930, 2164.

Matthew 24:50-51
The lord of that servant shall come in a day when he looketh not for him, and in an hour that he is not aware of, and shall cut him asunder, and **appoint** [*tithemi*][143] him his portion with the hypocrites: there shall be weeping and gnashing of teeth. (KJV)

1 Thessalonians 5:9
For God hath not **appointed** [*tithemi*][144] us to wrath, but to obtain salvation by our Lord Jesus Christ. (KJV)

(Clearly, God *has placed us—has brought us into a situation* through Jesus—whereby we no longer need to be recipients of His wrath, but of His salvation!)

John 15:16
Ye have not chosen me, but I have chosen you, and **ordained** [*tithemi*][145] you, that ye should go and bring forth fruit, and that your fruit should remain: that whatsoever ye shall ask of the Father in my name, he may give it you. (KJV)

(The eleven disciples, with whom Jesus was speaking, had been given a very special honor. Jesus had chosen them and *had placed them into their positions* of walking with Him and being his witnesses first hand. He desired them to bear much fruit that would remain.)[146]

2 Timothy 1:11
And of this gospel I was **appointed** [*tithemi*][147]a herald and an apostle and a teacher. (NIV1984)

---

[143] Ibid., pp. 100, 2164.
[144] Ibid., pp. 101, 2164.
[145] Ibid., pp. 1093, 2164.
[146] See further discussion of this verse in the chapter "Our Real Effect upon Our Salvation."
[147] Goodrick and Kohlenberger, *The NIV Exhaustive Concordance*, pp. 76, 1797.

<u>Hebrews 1:2</u>
But in these last days he has spoken to us by his Son, whom he **appointed** [*tithemi*][148] heir of all things, and through whom he made the universe. (NIV1984)

<u>1 Peter 2:7-8</u>
Therefore, to you who believe, He is precious; but to those who are disobedient, 'The stone which the builders rejected has become the chief cornerstone,' and 'A stone of stumbling and a rock of offense.' They stumble, being disobedient to the word, to which they also were **appointed** [*tithemi*].[149] (NKJV)

(God had judged much of Israel, giving "eyes that would not see" and "ears that would not hear" the truth of who Jesus was.)[150]

Tithemi renders the idea most often associated with "appoint." When there is *tithemi*, something is *placed* and *brought into a situation*. Nevertheless, **by itself, *tithemi* does not mean "*predestine*."**

Diatithemai

According to Bullinger, this word has the meaning: "to place separately, arrange, put things in their places. *Middle [diatithemai], as here and in N.T. only*, [is] to arrange as one likes, dispose of."[151] The following scriptures demonstrate the intent of *diatithemai*:

<u>Luke 22:29</u>
And I **appoint** [*diatithemai*][152] unto you a kingdom, as my Father hath **appointed** [*diatithemai*][153] unto me; (KJV)

---

[148] Ibid.
[149] Strong, *Strong's Complete Word Study Concordance*, pp. 101, 2164.
[150] See the discussion of this verse in the chapter "Another Look at Various Scriptures."
[151] Bullinger, *A Critical Lexicon and Concordance to the English and Greek New Testament*, pp. 60, xiii.
[152] Strong, *Strong's Complete Word Study Concordance*, pp. 100, 2054.

Acts 3:25
"You are sons of the prophets, and of the covenant which God **made** [*diatithemai*]¹⁵⁴ with our fathers, saying to Abraham, 'And in your seed all the families of the earth shall be blessed.' " (NKJV)

Noticeably, according to Strong's, *diatithemai* also denotes the idea of *making covenant.*¹⁵⁵ Consider the following scriptures (with *diatithemai* words noted in boldface):

Hebrews 8:10
Because this [is] the covenant which **I will covenant** ["make" in KJV]¹⁵⁶ with the household of Israel after those days, says [the] Lord, giving laws of me into the mind of them, and on hearts of them I will inscribe them, and I will be to them *for* God and they shall be to me *for* a people. (IGNT)

Hebrews 9:16-17
For where there is a testament [*diatheke* / noun form of *diatithemai*],¹⁵⁷ there must also of necessity be the death of the **testator** [*diatithemai*].¹⁵⁸ For a testament [*diatheke* / noun form of *diatithemai*] is in force after men are dead, since it has no power at all while the **testator** [*diatithemai*] lives. (NKJV)

Hebrews 10:16
This [is] the covenant which **I will covenant**¹⁵⁹ to them after days those, says [the] LORD: Giving laws of me on hearts of them, also on the mind of them I will inscribe them . . . (IGNT)

---

¹⁵³ Ibid., pp. 101, 2054.
¹⁵⁴ Ibid., pp. 924, 2054.
¹⁵⁵ Ibid., p. 2054.
¹⁵⁶ Ibid., pp. 931, 2054.
¹⁵⁷ Ibid., pp. 1448, 2052.
¹⁵⁸ Ibid., pp. 1448, 2054.
¹⁵⁹ Ibid., pp. 931, 2054.

Horizo

The Greek word *horizo* is also a very clear and decisive word. According to Bullinger, it renders the meaning: "to make or set a boundary, to bound; then, to mark out definitely, determine."[160] The following passages, likewise, give understanding of this word:

> Acts 11:29
> Then the disciples, each according to his ability, **determined** [*horizo*][161] to send relief to the brethren dwelling in Judea. (NKJV)

> Luke 22:22
> "The Son of Man will go as it has been **decreed** [*horizo*],[162] but woe to that man who betrays him." (NIV 1984)

> (It was God's decree that Jesus should be *given over* and should be put to death for the sins of the people; nevertheless, as is discussed in the chapter "Our Real Effect upon Our Salvation," this does not mean God *unconditionally* predestined the individual, Judas, to betray Him and to receive His wrath.)

> Acts 2:23
> "This man was handed over to you by God's **set** [*horizo*][163] purpose [*boule*][164] and foreknowledge . . ." (NIV 1984)

> Acts 10:42
> "And He commanded us to preach to the people, and to testify that it is He who was **ordained** [*horizo*][165] by God to be Judge of the living and the dead." (NKJV)

---

[160] Bullinger, *A Critical Lexicon and Concordance to the English and Greek New Testament*, pp. 559, xiii.

[161] Strong, *Strong's Complete Word Study Concordance*, pp. 366, 2124.

[162] Goodrick and Kohlenberger, *The NIV Exhaustive Concordance*, pp. 269, 1764.

[163] Ibid., pp. 1023, 1764.

[164] Ibid., pp. 919, 1695.

[165] Strong, *Strong's Complete Word Study Concordance*, pp. 1093, 2124.

Acts 17:26
"From one man he made every nation of men, that they should inhabit the whole earth; and he **determined** [*horizo*][166] the times set for them and the exact places where they should live." (NIV1984)

Acts 17:31
"Because He has appointed a day on which He will judge the world in righteousness by the Man whom He has **ordained** [*horizo*],[167] He has given assurance of this to all by raising Him from the dead." (NKJV)

Proorizo

There is a very important word in Scripture often translated as "predestine." By name, that word is *proorizo*. Very noticeably, it is formed by the aforementioned Greek verb *horizo* prefixed with the preposition *pro* (meaning: "before").[168] By definition and by the context of scriptures where this word occurs, the meaning of this word is very clear. According to Bullinger's Lexicon, *proorizo* has the distinct meaning: "to set bounds before, determine, decree or ordain beforehand."[169] The following scriptures give demonstration to things our Sovereign Lord has predestined:

Acts 4:28
For to do whatsoever thy hand and thy counsel **determined before** [*proorizo*][170] to be done. (KJV)

1 Corinthians 2:7
No, we speak of God's secret wisdom, a wisdom that has been hidden and that God **destined** [*proorizo*][171] for our glory before time began. (NIV1984)

---

[166] Goodrick and Kohlenberger, *The NIV Exhaustive Concordance*, pp. 282, 1764.

[167] Strong, *Strong's Complete Word Study Concordance*, pp. 1093, 2124.

[168] Ibid., p. 2143.

[169] Bullinger, *A Critical Lexicon and Concordance to the English and Greek New Testament*, pp. 597, xiii.

[170] Strong, *Strong's Complete Word Study Concordance*, pp. 366, 2143.

[171] Goodrick and Kohlenberger, *The NIV Exhaustive Concordance*, pp. 280, 1782.

Ephesians 1:5
He **predestined** [*proorizo*][172] us to adoption as sons through Jesus Christ to Himself, according to the kind intention of His will. (NASB)

(God predestined that He would have a people adopted as sons—*through Jesus*, and not their own works.)[173]

Ephesians 1:11
Also we have obtained an inheritance, having been **predestined** [*proorizo*][174] according to His purpose who works all things after the counsel of His will, (NASB)

Romans 8:29-30
For whom He foreknew, He also **predestined** [*proorizo*][175] to be conformed to the image of His Son, that He might be the firstborn among many brethren. Moreover, whom He **predestined** [*proorizo*],[176] these He also called; whom He called, these He also justified; and whom He justified, these He also glorified. (NASB)

There are things "destined" by God and there are things "predestined" by God. Our understanding of this fact is very important to our knowledge of God. Only when we know the power of God's decrees—that they *will* happen—can we see Him fully as He is. Truly, there is none like Him.

The distinction between the meanings of both words, however, must be made. Understanding of who God is, and our relationship with Him, will be greatly affected by any false balance. Likewise, in those scriptures where the original word for "predestine" *does* occur, **distinctions**

---

[172] Strong, *Strong's Complete Word Study Concordance*, pp. 1160, 2143.
[173] See the chapter "Another Look at Ephesians 1."
[174] Ibid.
[175] Ibid.
[176] Ibid.

between *what is* predestined and *what is not* predestined must rightly be made.[177]

Prostasso and *Protasso*

Although "*tasso*" words, by themselves, do *not* render the most commonly associated "decree" meaning commonly associated with "appoint" or "ordain" (see the upcoming discussion of "tasso" words), the words *prostasso* and *protasso* may carry that meaning *when given the right context*. Both words, nonetheless, do carry distinct meanings.

The Greek word *prostasso* renders the strong idea of "commanding." Because of its place in some Greek texts of Acts 17:26 (a scripture demonstrating something being determined beforehand) this word has been included. According to Bullinger's Lexicon, *prostasso* means "to arrange or set in order towards or to any person or thing; hence, to order towards or to any one, to give as a command, to prescribe to."[178] The following scriptures demonstrate the "command" meaning of the word:

Acts 10:48
So he **ordered** [*prostasso*][179] that they be baptized in the name of Jesus Christ . . . (NIV1984)

Matthew 8:4
Then Jesus said to him, "See that you don't tell anyone. But go, show yourself to the priest and offer the gift Moses **commanded** [*prostasso*],[180] as a testimony to them." (NIV1984)

---

[177] Please note: For further discussion of scriptures that speak of "predestination," see the chapters entitled "Another Look at Ephesians 1" and "Another Look at Various Scriptures."

[178] Bullinger, *A Critical Lexicon and Concordance to the English and Greek New Testament*, pp. 169, xiii.

[179] Goodrick and Kohlenberger, *The NIV Exhaustive Concordance*, pp. 4705, 1784.

[180] Ibid., pp. 219, 1784.

Matthew 1:24
When Joseph woke up, he did what the angel of the Lord **had commanded** [*prostasso*][181] him and took Mary home as his wife. (NIV1984)

Acts 10:33
". . . Now we are all here in the presence of God to listen to everything the Lord **has commanded** [*prostasso*][182] you to tell us." (NIV1984)

Acts 17:26
"From one man he made every nation of men, that they should inhabit the whole earth; and he determined the times **set** [*prostasso*][183] for them and the exact places where they should live." (NIV1984)

(This reading is so powerful! God has determined [and has made to happen] the times and the exact boundaries of every nation!)

In some Greek texts of Acts 17:26, a variant word, **protasso,** is found, instead of *prostasso*.[184] In accordance with one of the texts, then, the KJV translates Acts 17:26 as: "hath determined the times **before appointed.**" Notably, according to Bullinger, that word, *protasso*, means "to place or post in front, to arrange one person before another (so as to defend him), pass., to take the lead, go first; generally to appoint or determine beforehand."[185] *Strong's Complete Word Study Concordance* adds: "[The word is] . . . spoken of times or seasons being marked out beforehand." *Protasso* is clearly a decree word; nonetheless, as Strong further shows, it is only used once in Acts 17:26.[186]

---

[181] Ibid.
[182] Ibid.
[183] Ibid., pp. 1023, 1784.
[184] Bullinger, *A Critical Lexicon and Concordance to the English and Greek New Testament*, pp. 60, xiii.
[185] Ibid.
[186] Strong, *Strong's Complete Word Study Concordance*, p. 2145.

Hebrew Words

Charats and *Charuwts*

The related Hebrew words *charats* and *charuwts*[187]are *very strong* words used in the Old Testament to denote decrees which God makes. According to *Wilson's Old Testament Word Studies*, *charuwts* brings the rendering of "decision, judgment."[188] Similarly, according to Wilson, the verb *charats* has the following implications: "to decide . . . "; "to be sharp and pointed; applied to the exact discrimination between justice and injustice, to that which is decreed, fully and irrevocably determined, which admits of no intercession; *that which is stinted, limited, and brought to a settled point.*"[189] Neither *charats* nor *charuwts* are found very often in the Old Testament. (*Charats* is found only ten times, and *charuwts* is found only twice.)[190] Yet, all the times the words are used, and especially regarding God's determinations, the determinations seem very conclusive. Consider, as follows, such times in which *charats* or *charuwts* are used in the Old Testament:

Isaiah 10:22
For though thy people Israel be as the sand of the sea, yet a remnant of them shall return: the consumption ["destruction" in NIV1984] **decreed** [*charats*][191] shall overflow with righteousness. (KJV)

Isaiah 10:23
For the Lord GOD of hosts shall make a consumption ["destruction" in NIV1984], even **determined** [*charats*],[192] in the midst of all the land. (KJV)

Isaiah 28:22
Now stop your mocking, or your chains will become heavier; the Lord, the LORD Almighty, has told me of

---

[187] Ibid., pp. 1863, 1864.
[188] Wilson, *Old Testament Word Studies*, p. 111.
[189] Ibid., pp. 112, 122.
[190] Goodrick and Kohlenberger, *The NIV Exhaustive Concordance*, pp. 1458, 1459.
[191] Strong, *Strong's Complete Word Study Concordance*, pp. 354, 1864.
[192] Ibid., pp. 366, 1864.

the destruction **decreed** [*charats*][193] against the whole land. (NIV1984)

Daniel 9:26
"War will continue until the end, and desolations have been **decreed** [*charats*]."[194] (NIV1984)

Daniel 11:36
"He will be successful until the time of wrath is completed, for what has been **determined** [*charats*][195] must take place." (NIV1984)

Joel 3:14
Multitudes, multitudes in the valley of **decision** [*charuwts*]! For the day of the LORD is near in the valley of **decision** [*charuwts*].[196] (NIV1984)

Tsavah

In similarity to *charats*, the word *tsavah*, when used in certain scriptures speaking of God's actions, also denotes God's sovereign position to appoint and to cause happen those things that He so desires to cause happen. According to *Strong's Complete Word Study Concordance*, the Hebrew verb *tsavah* renders the meaning: "to order, to direct, to appoint, to command, to charge . . ."[197] The following scriptures illustrate very well what is its specific meaning:

Genesis 50:12
So Jacob's sons did as he [Jacob] had **commanded** [*tsavah*][198] them. (NIV1984)

---

[193] Ibid.
[194] Ibid.
[195] Ibid.
[196] Ibid., pp. 352, 1863.
[197] Ibid., p. 1953.
[198] Ibid., pp. 293, 1953.

Lamentations 1:17
Zion spreads out her hands, but no one comforts her: the Lord has **commanded** [tsavah][199] concerning Jacob that those around him become his adversary; Jerusalem has become an unclean thing among them. (NKJV)

Lamentations 2:17
The LORD has done what he planned; he has fulfilled his word, which he **decreed** [*tsavah*][200] long ago. He has overthrown you without pity, he has let the enemy gloat over you, he has exalted the horn of your foes. (NIV1984)

(Here, the Lord's plan was specifically decreed. *Even as His word was decreed*, it was fulfilled.)

1 Samuel 13:14
"But now your kingdom shall not continue. The LORD has sought for Himself a man after His own heart, and the LORD has **commanded** [*tsavah*][201] him to be commander over His people, because you have not kept what the LORD **commanded** [*tsavah*]."[202] (NKJV)

(Here is an example of the more precise "command" meaning of the word. Notably, as was with King Saul, the Lord's **"commands" *unto men* can be disobeyed**. Yet, the command *of His word* surely happens. See also the upcoming discussion of this verse under the word *kuwn*.)

2 Samuel 17:14
So Absalom and all the men of Israel said, "The advice of Hushai the Archite is better than the advice of Ahithophel." For the LORD had **purposed** [*tsavah*][203] to

---

[199] Ibid., pp. 295, 1953.
[200] Ibid.
[201] Ibid., pp. 294, 1953.
[202] Ibid.
[203] Ibid., pp. 100, 1953.

defeat the good advice of Ahithophel, to the intent that the LORD might bring disaster on Absalom. (NKJV)

Jeremiah 32:35
"They built high places for Baal in the Valley of Ben Hinnom to sacrifice their sons and daughters to Molech, though I never **commanded** [*tsavah*],[204] nor did it enter my mind [*leb* / "heart"],[205] that they should do such a detestable thing and so make Judah sin." (NIV1984)

(**Note**: This scripture provides *evidence* **that man has a** *free will*. God does not cause everything that happens. In His rule, He has only chosen to allow that thing which happens.)

The above examples of scriptures containing *tsavah* clearly demonstrate the "command" and "directive" nature of the word. It also can be seen that, **although the "command"** *of God's word* **activates** (note 2 Samuel 17:14, Psalm 33: 6-8, Lamentations 1:17, and Lamentations 2:17), **"commands" toward men are not always fulfilled**. Even so, given the right context, the *sure* power of that which God decrees (the command of His word) can be seen.

Suwm

The Hebrew word *suwm* (alternate s*iym*) renders the idea of one's *making a placement* of someone or something. According to *Strong's Complete Word Study Concordance*, the verb means "to appoint, to bring, to call, to put, to change, to charge, to commit, to consider, to convey, to determine . . . primary meaning . . . to put, to set, or to place."[206] The following verses convey the specific nature of *suwm*:

---

[204] Ibid., pp. 295, 1953.
[205] Ibid., pp. 979, 1888.
[206] Strong, *Strong's Complete Word Study Concordance*, p. 1980.

2 Samuel 7:10
Moreover, I will **appoint** [*suwm*][207] a place for my people Israel, and will plant them, that they may dwell in a
place of the own, and move no more; neither shall the
children of wickedness afflict them any more, as before-
time. (KJV)

Deuteronomy 22:13-14
"If any man takes a wife, and goes in to her, and detests
her, and **charges** [*suwm*][208] her with shameful conduct,
and brings a bad name on her, and says, 'I took this
woman, and when I came to her I found she was not a
virgin,' " (NKJV)

1 Samuel 8:12
"He will **appoint** [*suwm*][209] captains over his thousands
and captains over his fifties, will set some to plow his
ground and reap his harvest, and some to make his
weapons of war and equipment for his chariots."
(NKJV)

1 Samuel 28:22
"Now therefore, please, heed also the voice of your
maidservant, and let me **set** [*suwm*][210] a piece of bread
before you . . . " (NKJV)

Genesis 2:8
The LORD had planted a garden eastward in Eden, and
there He **put** [*suwm*][211] the man whom He had formed.
(NKJV)

2 Samuel 7:10
Moreover, I will **appoint** [*suwm*][212] a place for My people Israel, and will plant them, that they may dwell in a

---

[207] Ibid., pp. 100, 1980.
[208] Ibid., p. 1980.
[209] Ibid.
[210] Ibid., pp. 1310, 1980.
[211] Ibid., pp. 1181, 1980.

place of their own, and move no more; neither shall the children of wickedness afflict them any more, as before-time. (KJV)

Isaiah 61:3
"And **provide** [*siym* / alternate spelling][213] for those who grieve in Zion—to bestow on them a crown of beauty instead of ashes, the oil of gladness instead of mourning . . . " (NIV 1984)

Nathan

Similar to the verb *suwm*, the verb *nathan* also may render the meaning of "appoint"—that of something being placed upon something. According to Strong's word study, the verb, in simplest terms, means "to give, to place."[214] A sampling of scriptures that demonstrates the nature of the word's usage are as follows:

Genesis 3:6
So when the woman saw that the tree was good for food, that it was pleasant to the eyes, and a tree desirable to make one wise, she took of its fruit and ate. She also **gave** [*nathan*][215] to her husband with her, and he ate. (NKJV)

Exodus 30:14
"Everyone included among those who are numbered, from twenty years old and above, shall **give** [*nathan*][216] an offering to the LORD." (NKJV)

Numbers 35:6
"Now among the cities which you will **give** [*nathan*][217] to the Levites you shall appoint six cities of refuge, to

---

[212] Strong, *Strong's Complete Word Study Concordance*, pp. 100, 1980.
[213] Goodrick and Kohlenberger, *The NIV Exhaustive Concordance*, pp. 916, 1624.
[214] Strong, *Strong's Complete Word Study Concordance*, p. 1924.
[215] Ibid.
[216] Ibid., pp. 551, 1924.

which a manslayer may flee. And to these you shall add forty-two cities." (NKJV)

Proverbs 9:9
"**Give** [*nathan*][218] instruction to a wise man, and he will be still wiser; teach a just man, and he will increase in learning." (NKJV)

2 Kings 8:6
And when the king asked the woman, she told him. So the king **appointed** [*nathan*][219] a certain officer for her, saying, "Restore all that was hers, and all the proceeds of the field from the day that she left the land until now." (NKJV)

(An officer was *appointed*—was *placed into a position* to take care of the woman.)

Deuteronomy 11:13-14
" 'And it shall be that if you earnestly obey My commandments which I command you today, to love the LORD your God and serve Him with all your heart and with all your soul, then I will **give** [*nathan*][220] you the rain for your land in its season, the early rain and the latter rain, that you may gather in your grain, your new wine, and your oil.' " (NKJV)

Genesis 17:5
"No longer shall your name be called Abram, but your name shall be Abraham; for I have **made** [*nathan*][221] you a father of many nations." (NKJV)

---

[217] Ibid.
[218] Ibid., pp. 552, 1924.
[219] Ibid., pp. 100, 1924.
[220] Ibid., pp. 551, 1924.
[221] Ibid., pp. 919, 1924.

Jeremiah 1:5

"Before I formed you in the womb I knew you; before you were born I sanctified you; I **ordained** [*nathan*][222] you a prophet to the nations." (NKJV)

(With a foreknowledge of the heart of Jeremiah, even before Jeremiah was born, God *placed* him in a position as a prophet.)

Ezekiel 4:5

"For I have **laid** [*nathan*][223] on you the years of their iniquity, according to the number of the days, three hundred and ninety days; so you shall bear the iniquity of the house of Israel." (NKJV)

As can be seen, in particular by the scriptures using either the words *suwm* or *nathan*, there are *specific* things "appointed" by God—given *and* even caused by Him; nonetheless, as can be seen by the earlier *tsavah* section of scriptures (e.g., Jeremiah 32:35), not all is caused by God.

OFTEN MISUNDERSTOOD WORDS

Greek Words of Special Note—*Tasso* Root Words

All of the immediately following "*tasso*" root words are sometimes translated as "appoint" or "ordain." The specific meanings of the *tasso* words, however, are important to note. **Unless context warrants it, most often** the scriptures containing the *tasso* words do *not* render a meaning commonly associated with "being appointed" or "being ordained"—that of someone or something being placed into something, apart from his own will.

---

[222] Ibid., pp. 1093, 1924.
[223] Ibid., pp. 831, 1924.

Tasso

The Greek word *tasso*, according to Bullinger's Lexicon, brings the meaning: "to arrange, put in order, especially in military sense, to draw up soldiers, array; . . . to appoint or order anything to be done." [224] Some scriptures where the word is used are the following: Matthew 28:16; Acts 22:10; 1 Corinthians 16:15; Romans 13:1; and Acts 13:48.[225]

> Matthew 28: 16
> Then the eleven disciples went away into Galilee, to the mountain which Jesus had **appointed** [*tasso* / "designated" in NASB] for them. (NKJV)

> Acts 22:10
> "And the Lord said to me, 'Arise and go into Damascus, and there you will be told all things which are **appointed** [*tasso*] for you to do.' " (NKJV)

> (Things had been *arranged, put in order* for Paul to do; however, *he could have resisted* and not walked in those things.)

> 1 Corinthians 16:15
> You know the household of Stephanas, that it is the firstfruits of Achaia, and that they have **devoted** [*tasso*] themselves to the ministry of the saints. (NKJV)

> (These people *arranged their own lives* around ministering to the saints.)

> Romans 13:1
> There is no authority except from God, and the authorities that exist are **appointed** [*tasso*] by God. (NKJV)

---

[224] Bullinger, *A Critical Lexicon and Concordance to the Greek and English New Testament*, pp. 60, xiii.
[225] Ibid., pp. 27, 60, 559, xiii.

(God *arranges* and *puts in order* authorities that exist.)

Acts 13:48
Now when the Gentiles heard this, they were glad and glorified the word of the Lord. And as many as had been **appointed** [*tasso*] to eternal life believed. (NKJV)

(Because of its significance, Acts 13:48 is discussed in the chapter entitled "Another Look at Various Scriptures.")

Although often simply rendered with the word "appointed," *tasso* more specifically seems to render the idea of *putting in order* and *arranging* things. Noticeably, also, as can be seen from 1 Corinthians 16:15, *tasso* may be used in the middle sense.[226] **One can either *tasso* himself, or be *tasso*-ed by another.**

Diatasso

Diatasso comes from the *tasso* and the preposition *dia* (which means "through, thorough, between").[227] According to Bullinger, it means "to arrange throughout, to dispose in order; then, to set fully in order, arrange, . . . appoint, ordain."[228] From a look at various scriptures containing the word, *diatasso* most appears to render the idea of "instructing." Some passages of Scripture that contain the word are as follows: Matthew 11:1; Luke 8:55; Luke 17:9 Acts 7:44; Acts 20:13; 1 Corinthians 7:17; and Titus 1:5.

Acts 20:13
[Concerning instructions Paul had given about being picked up.] Then we went ahead to the ship and sailed to Assos, there intending to take Paul on board; for so he

---

[226] Ralph Earle, *Word Meanings in the New Testament* (Peabody, MA: Hendrickson Publishers, Inc., 1997), p. 109.
[227] Bullinger, *A Critical Lexicon and Concordance to the Greek and English New Testament*, p. xx.
[228] Ibid., pp. 60, xiii.

had **given orders** [*diatasso*],[229] intending himself to go on foot. (NKJV)

Titus 1:5
For this reason I left you in Crete, that you would set in order what remains and appoint elders in every city as I **directed** [*diatasso*][230] you, (NASB)

Luke 17:9
"Does he thank that servant because he did the things that were **commanded** [*diatasso*][231] him? I think not." (NKJV)

1 Corinthians 7:17
Only, as the Lord has assigned to each one, as God has called each, in this manner let him walk. And so I **direct** [*diatasso*][232] in all the churches. (NASB)

(Even as an illustration of the indistinct way "*tasso*" words are sometimes rendered, noticeably, the King James Version and New King James Version translated *diatasso* as "ordain" here.)

1 Corinthians 16:1
Now concerning the collection for the saints, as I have **given orders** [*diatasso*][233] to the churches of Galatia, so you must do also. (NKJV)

Acts 7:44
"Our fathers had the tabernacle of testimony in the wilderness, just as He who spoke to Moses **directed** [*diatasso*][234] him to make it according to the pattern which he had seen." (NASB)

---

[229] Ibid.
[230] Ibid.
[231] Ibid., pp. 169, xiii.
[232] Ibid., pp. 559, xiii.
[233] Ibid.
[234] Ibid., pp. 60, xiii.

(God had instructed Moses concerning the pattern of the tabernacle.)

Matthew 11:1
When Jesus had finished **giving instructions** [*diatasso*][235] to His twelve disciples, He departed from there to teach and preach in their cities. (NASB)

Luke 8:55
And her spirit returned, and she got up immediately; and He **gave orders** [*diatasso*][236] for something to be given her to eat. (NASB)

Hebrew Words of Special Note

Yatsar

Yatsar is a significant word. Many times the Hebrew verb *yatsar* connects the reader to the truth of God's involvement and God's plans concerning men. Yet, although interpreted many ways in Scripture (e.g., "purposed," "planned," and "ordained"), the verb *yatsar* most closely renders the meaning: "to form, fashion, or shape, as a potter the clay."[237] Examine the following scriptures:

Isaiah 45:9
Woe unto him that striveth with his Maker! Let the potsherd strive with the potsherds of the earth. Shall the clay say to him that **fashioneth** [*yatsar*][238] it, What makest thou? Or thy work, he hath no hands? (KJV)

---

[235] Ibid., pp. 169, xiii.
[236] Ibid.
[237] Goodrick and Kohlenberger, *The NIV Exhaustive Concordance*, p. 1476; Wilson, *Wilson's Old Testament Word Studies*, p. 158.
[238] Goodrick and Kohlenberger, *The NIV Exhaustive Concordance*, p. 1476; Wilson, *Wilson's Old Testament Word Studies*, p. 158.

Genesis 2:7-8
The LORD **formed** [*yatsar*][239] the man from the dust of the ground and breathed into his nostrils the breath of life, and the man became a living being. Now the LORD God had planted a garden in the east, in Eden; and there he put the man he had **formed** [*yatsar*].[240] (NIV1984)

Genesis 2:19
Now the LORD had **formed** [*yatsar*][241] out of the ground all the beasts of the field and all the birds of the air. (NIV1984)

Psalm 94:9
Does he who implanted the ear not hear? Does he who **formed** [*yatsar*][242] the eye not see? (NIV1984)

Psalm 95:5
The sea is his, for he made it, and his hands **formed** [*yatsar*][243] the dry land. (NIV1984)

Isaiah 45:18
For this is what the LORD says—he who created the heavens, he is God; he who **fashioned** [*yatsar*] and made the earth, he founded it; he did not create it to be empty, but **formed** [*yatsar*] it to be inhabited . . . [244] (NIV1984)

Isaiah 44:2
"This is what the LORD says—he who made you, who **formed** [*yatsar*][245] you in the womb, and who will help you . . ." (NIV1984)

---

[239] Goodrick and Kohlenberger, *The NIV Exhaustive Concordance*, pp. 417, 1476.
[240] Ibid.
[241] Ibid.
[242] Ibid.
[243] Ibid.
[244] Ibid., pp. 381, 417, 1476.
[245] Ibid., pp. 417, 1476.

Jeremiah 33:2
"This is what the LORD says, he who made the earth, the
LORD who **formed** [*yatsar*][246] it and established it—the
LORD is his name:" (NIV 1984)

Because *yatsar* is found in a scripture which, when wrongly interpreted, may wrongly affect a balanced understanding of God's sovereign
rule, it is *very important* to consider its meaning in the most literal
form.[247]

Kuwn

Kuwn is another strong word which, when used regarding God's workings with men, shows the strength of His rule. It is also a word that has
been often misunderstood in its renderings.[248] According to Wilson,
kuwn means "to stand, to be erect; to stand firm, to be established; to be
prepared; to be founded." Similarly, Strong defines its meaning: "a
verb meaning to set up, to make firm, to establish, to prepare . . . primary action . . . to cause to stand in an upright position . . . also means
fixed or steadfast."[249] Indeed, if He so desires, God establishes things;
He causes them to *stand firm*. The following scriptures use the word
kuwn, demonstrate its meaning, and aid in our understanding of who
God is and that which He establishes:

Numbers 23:1
Balaam said, "Build me seven altars here, and **prepare**
[*kuwn*][250] seven bulls and seven rams for me."
(NIV 1984)

Deuteronomy 19:3
Build [*kuwn*][251] roads to them and divide into three parts
the land the LORD your God is giving you as an inher-

---

[246] Ibid., pp. 417, 1476.
[247] See the discussion of Psalm 139:16 within "Significant Scriptures—Part 1."
[248] See "Significant Scriptures—Part 1."
[249] Wilson, *Wilson's Old Testament Word Studies*, p.149; Strong, *Strong's Complete
Word Study Concordance*, p. 1882.
[250] Strong, *Strong's Complete Word Study Concordance*, pp. 1161, 1882.
[251] Ibid.

itance, so that anyone who kills a man may flee to there. (NIV 1984)

1 Chronicles 16:30
Fear before him, all the earth: the world also shall be **stable** [*kuwn*],[252] that it be not moved. (KJV)

Psalm 24:1-2
The earth is the LORD's, and everything in it, the world, and all who live in it; for he founded it upon the seas and **established** [*kuwn*][253] it upon the waters. (NIV 1984)

Jeremiah 51:15
He made the earth by his power; he **founded** [*kuwn*][254] the world by his wisdom and stretched out the heavens by his understanding. (NIV 1984)

Psalm 93:2
Thy throne is **established** [*kuwn*][255] of old: thou art from everlasting. (KJV)

2 Samuel 5:12
And David knew that the LORD had **established** [*kuwn*][256] him as king over Israel and had exalted his kingdom for the sake of his people Israel. (NIV 1984)

Psalm 89:3-4
"I have made a covenant with My chosen, I have sworn to My servant David: 'Your seed I will **establish** [*kuwn*][257] forever, and build up your throne to all generations.' " Selah. (NKJV)

---

[252] Ibid., pp. 1401, 1882.
[253] Ibid., pp. 441, 1882.
[254] Ibid., pp. 442, 1882.
[255] Ibid.
[256] Ibid., pp. 441, 1882.
[257] Ibid., pp. 441.

(God made a covenant with David promising that, by His power, He would make David's seed stand firm forever.)

2 Samuel 7:12-13
[Concerning Jesus, the Lord said to David . . .] "When your days are fulfilled and you rest with your fathers, I will set up your seed after you, who will come from your body, and I will **establish** [*kuwn*][258] his kingdom. He shall build a house for My name, and I will **establish** [*kuwn*][259] the throne of his kingdom forever." (NKJV)

Isaiah 62:6-7
[Concerning Jerusalem being established, Isaiah says to the people . . .] I have set watchmen upon thy walls, O Jerusalem, which shall never hold their peace day or night: ye that make mention of the LORD, keep not silence, and give him no rest, till he **establish** [*kuwn*],[260] and till he make Jerusalem a praise in the earth. (KJV)

2 Samuel 7:24
"You have **made** [*kuwn*][261] your people Israel Your very own people forever; and You, LORD, have become their God." (NKJV)

Psalm 87:5
Indeed, of Zion it will be said, "This one and that one were born in her, and the Most High himself will **establish** [*kuwn*][262] her." (NIV 1984)

Jeremiah 33:2
"Thus says the LORD who made it, the LORD who formed [*yatsar*][263] it to **establish** [*kuwn*][264] it (the LORD is His name):" (NKJV)

---

[258] Ibid.
[259] Ibid., pp. 1401, 1882.
[260] Ibid., pp. 441, 1882.
[261] Ibid., pp. 302, 1882.
[262] Ibid., pp. 441, 1882.

Psalm 9:7
But the LORD shall endure for ever: he hath **prepared**
[*kuwn*][265] his throne for judgment. (KJV)

Psalm 99:4
The King's strength also loves justice; You have **established** [*kuwn*][266] equity; You have executed justice and
righteousness in Jacob. (NKJV)

(Notably, God establishes—He makes stand firm His
equity.)

Psalm 89:2
I will declare that your love stands firm forever, that you
established [*kuwn*][267] your faithfulness in heaven itself.
(NIV1984)

The Hebrew verb *kuwn* is found very often in Old Testament scriptures.
As is noted in "Significant Scriptures—Part 1," understanding *kuwn*'s
distinct shade of meaning can shed new light on the likely intent of so
very many significant scriptures concerning God's sovereignty and
dealings with men (e.g., Psalm 37: 23; Proverbs 16: 9; and Jeremiah
10:23).

"Destiny" Words

Today, we hear many speak of the "destiny" of individuals. Yet, dependent upon one's understanding of God's sovereignty, that term can
mean different things. In Calvinist circles, often the term has inferred
upon it a *predestined* end. In other circles, however, the term is used to
reference the "good and acceptable and perfect" (Romans 12: 2 NKJV)
plans that God has in mind for each individual, dependent upon his responses. Simply put, the "destiny" of an individual is his *end*.

---

[263] Ibid., pp. 518, 1886.
[264] Ibid., pp. 441, 1882.
[265] Ibid., pp. 1161, 1882.
[266] Ibid., pp. 441, 1882.
[267] Ibid.

Although some renderings of "destiny" within scriptures are vague in meaning, there are special words within scripture that do distinctly speak of *the ending state laid up in reserve*. For a better understanding of "destiny" scriptures, therefore, these words shall be considered—as well as other words in Scripture that are less specific to that meaning of "destiny."

Apokeimai

The Greek verb *apokeimai* renders the meaning of "destine" that people often attribute to the word. According to Bullinger's Lexicon, it means "to be laid away; to be laid up in store, be in reserve."[268] The following scriptures show each of the times this word occurs in the New Testament:

> Hebrews 9:27
> Just as man is **destined** [*apokeimai*][269] to die once, and after that to face judgment, (NIV1984)

> 2 Timothy 4:8
> Henceforth there is **laid up** [*apokeimai*][270] for me a crown of righteousness, which the Lord, the righteous judge, shall give me at that day; and not to me only, but unto all them also that love his appearing. (KJV)

> Colossians 1:5
> Because of the hope which is **laid up** [*apokeimai*][271] for you in heaven, of which you heard before in the word of the truth of the gospel. (NKJV)

> Luke 19:20
> "Then another servant came and said, 'Sir, here is your mina; I have kept it **laid away** [*apokeimai*][272] in a piece of cloth.' " (NIV1984)

---

[268] Bullinger, *A Critical Lexicon and Concordance to the Greek New Testament*, pp. 60, xiii.
[269] Ibid.
[270] Ibid., pp. 445, xiii.
[271] Ibid.

Telos

Although, in the 1984 New International Version translation of Philippians 3:19, the Greek noun *telos* has been rendered as "destiny," *telos*, in simplest form, does not render the meaning often attributed to the word "destiny." The noun's most simple meaning is "end." According to Bullinger, *telos* carries the meaning: "the fulfillment or completion of any thing . . . i.e. its end or issue . . ."[273] Additionally, according to Strong, it means "an end, a term, a termination, completion. Particularly only in respect to time." According to Strong, "figuratively, it [also] means end, outcome, result."[274] For illustration of its more specific meaning, consider the following scriptures:

Matthew 10:22
"And you will be hated by all for My name's sake. But he who endures to the **end** [*telos*][275] will be saved." (NKJV)

(The one who continues in Him, finishing the race, shall be saved.)

Matthew 24:6
"And you will hear of wars and rumors of wars. See that you are not troubled; for all these things must come to pass, but the **end** [*telos*][276] is not yet." (NKJV)

(The *completion/fulfillment* is not yet.)

Matthew 26:58
But Peter followed Him at a distance to the high priest's courtyard. And he went in and sat with the servants to see the **end** [*telos*].[277] (NKJV)

---

[272] Ibid.
[273] Ibid., pp. 248, xiii.
[274] Strong, Strong's Complete Word Study and Concordance, p. 2163.
[275] Ibid., pp. 431, 2163.
[276] Ibid.
[277] Ibid.

(Peter desired to see things to the *completion* of the process.)

Mark 3:26
"And if Satan has risen up against himself, and is divided, he cannot stand, but has an **end** [*telos*]."[278] (NKJV)

(Satan would *finish being*. Here, distinctly, the word *telos* is *not* referring to a particular end laid up in store, as would be the case with a use of the word *apokeimai*.)

Luke 1:33
"And He will reign over the house of Jacob forever, and of His kingdom there will be no **end** [*telos*]."[279] (NKJV)

(Jesus' kingdom does not reach a *finish*; it goes on forever.)

Luke 22:37
"For I say to you that this which is written must still be accomplished in Me: 'And He was numbered with the transgressors.' For the things concerning Me have to **end** [*telos*]."[280] (NKJV)

(Before going to the Father, Jesus would *finish* all the things He was called to do [John 19:30].)

John 13:1
Now before the feast of the Passover, when Jesus knew that His hour had come that He should depart from this world to the Father, having loved His own who were in the world, He loved them to the **end** [*telos*].[281] (NKJV)

---

[278] Ibid.
[279] Ibid.
[280] Ibid.
[281] Ibid.

<u>James 5:11</u>
Indeed we count them blessed who endure. You have heard of the perseverance of Job and seen the **end** [*telos*][282] intended by the Lord—that the Lord is very compassionate and merciful. (NKJV)

(James admonished the church, referring to Job. Contextually, we can see that the Lord's intended *end* for all is one of blessing—for He is "very compassionate and merciful." Even so, we must endure—just as did Job— walking out a faith in Him *until the finish*.)

<u>Hebrews 6:8</u>
But if it bears thorns and briers, it is rejected and near to being cursed, whose **end** [*telos*][283] is to be burned. (NKJV)

<u>1 Corinthians 15:24</u>
Then comes the **end** [*telos*],[284] when He delivers the kingdom to God the Father, when he puts an end to all rule and all authority and power. (NKJV)

<u>1 Peter 4:7</u>
But the **end** [*telos*][285] of all things is at hand; therefore, be serious and watchful in your prayers. (NKJV)

<u>1 Peter 4:17</u>
For the time has come for judgment to begin at the house of God; and if it begins with us first, what will be the **end** [*telos*][286] of those who do not obey the gospel of God? (NKJV)

---

[282] Ibid. pp. 432, 2163.
[283] Ibid.
[284] Ibid.
[285] Ibid.
[286] Ibid.

Philippians 3:19
Their **destiny** [*telos*] is destruction, their god is their stomach, and their glory is in their shame. Their mind is on earthly things. (NIV1984)

Whose **end** [*telos*][287] is destruction, whose god is their belly, and whose glory is in their shame—who set their mind on earthly things. (NKJV)

(Contextually, it makes sense that the *end result* of those who set their minds on earthly things is destruction. There is an *outcome* to setting the mind on earthly things. Yet, although the word "destiny" is used in the NIV1984 translation, the "end" destruction is not predestined—apart from one's own doings.)

John 18:37
"For this **cause** [*telos*][288] I was born, and for this cause I have come into the world, that I should bear witness to the truth." (NKJV)

(For the *fulfillment* of His mission, Jesus was sent. Jesus came to fulfill what He was sent to do. To the completion of things—to the very end—Jesus' call was to bear witness to the truth.)

1 Timothy 1:5
Now the **purpose** [*telos*][289] of the commandment is love from a pure heart, from a good conscience, and from sincere faith, from which some, having strayed, have turned aside to idle talk, (NKJV)

(The intended *outcome* of any command or proclamation should be that of good fruit.)

---

[287] Ibid.
[288] Ibid., pp. 431, 2163.
[289] Ibid., pp. 432, 2163.

1 Peter 1:9
[Receiving] the **end** [*telos*]²⁹⁰ of your faith—the salvation of your souls. (NKJV)

(The *outcome* of our faith is the salvation of our souls.)

Sowph and *Miqreh*

The Hebrew words *sowph* and *miqreh* are found in Old Testament scriptures referring to "destiny." According to Strong, and in similarity to the Greek word *telos*, *sowph* simply means "a termination—conclusion, end . . . ."²⁹¹ Then, according to Wilson, the word *miqreh* means "that which befalleth."²⁹² Put together in context, these words speak of that which is *laid up in reserve* for all men. It is even with the words *sowph* and *miqreh* that "death"—the final destiny for all men—is spoken:

Ecclesiastes 7:1-2
A good name is better than precious ointment; and the day of death than the day of one's birth. It is better to go to the house of mourning, than to go to the house of feasting: for that [*death*] is the **end** [*sowph*]²⁹³ of all men; and the living will lay it to his heart. (KJV)

Ecclesiastes 2:14-15
The wise man has eyes in his head, while the fool walks in the darkness; but I came to realize that the same **fate** [*miqreh*] overtakes them both. Then I thought in my heart, "The **fate** [*miqreh*] of the fool will overtake me also. What then do I gain by being wise?" I said in my heart, "This too is meaningless."²⁹⁴(NIV1984)

---

²⁹⁰ Ibid.
²⁹¹ Strong, *Strong's Complete Word Study and Concordance*, 1926.
²⁹² Wilson, *Wilson's Old Testament Word Studies*, p. 150; Strong, *Strong's Complete Word Study and Concordance*, p. 1908.
²⁹³ Strong, *Strong's Complete Word Study and Concordance*, pp. 431, 1926
²⁹⁴ Goodrick and Kohlenberger, *The NIV Exhaustive Concordance*, pp. 381, 1529.

Ecclesiastes 9:2
All things come alike to all: One **event** [*miqreh*]²⁹⁵ happens to the righteous and the wicked . . . (NKJV)

Ecclesiastes 9:3
This is the evil in everything that happens under the sun: The same **destiny** [*miqreh* / "event" in KJV]²⁹⁶ overtakes all. The hearts of men, moreover, are full of evil and there is madness in their hearts while they live, and afterward they join the dead. (NIV1984)

Jeremiah 15:2 and Jeremiah 43:10 -11

The following Scripture passages are important to note:

And if they ask you, "Where shall we go?" tell them, "This is what the LORD says: Those destined for death, to death; those for the sword, to the sword; those for starvation, to starvation; those for captivity, to captivity." (Jeremiah 15:2 NIV1984)

Then say to them, "This is what the LORD says: I will send for my servant Nebuchadnezzar . . . He will come and attack Egypt, bringing death to those destined for death, captivity to those destined for captivity, and the sword to those destined for the sword." (Jeremiah 43:10-11 NIV1984)

Notably, the New International Version's translation of "destined for," in these passages, did not come from an exactly definable word. Only the context warranted the interpretation. Nonetheless, if one reads the surrounding context of these "destiny" type passages, one can see that the destined judgments were not "predestined." God destined the judgments *because* Judah forsook following God's ways and failed to repent. (See Jeremiah 15:5-7 and Jeremiah 44:1-14.)

---

²⁹⁵ Strong, *Strong's Complete Word Study and Concordance*, pp. 449, 1908.
²⁹⁶ Ibid., pp. 280, 1529.

So importantly, we can learn that, **just because something is "destined," it does not mean it was "predestined"** (as *is* the case of death for all men). "Destined for" is merely another way of saying "determined for," and "destiny" is just another way of saying "end." Importantly, the meaning of "destiny" scriptures and statements must be established with respect to context.

IN CONCLUSION

Throughout this chapter, many words have been examined that have particular consequence to understanding God's sovereignty. Just as I have been especially enlightened by this word study, my hope is that the reader also has gained enlightenment into the true intent of words that have been so often misunderstood. *Specific* words render specific meanings. Because very specific words reference God's desires, His determinations, as well as the pre-ordained plans He makes, it is important that unspecific words not apply. We must handle those scriptures that refer to God's sovereignty and our responsibility with particular care and reverence.[297]

---

[297] The chapter "Significant Scriptures—Part 1" outlays many of those scriptures with the specific words as found in the original Hebrew and Greek texts.

The Sovereignty of God

Chapter 5

Significant Scriptures Concerning God's Sovereignty—
Part 1:
Bringing In the Balance

Many of the scriptures that follow are quite familiar as being references that speak of *the sovereignty of God*. Often, however, because of the renderings given in different translations, the meaningful words of Scripture have been misapplied. Many of the passages have been considered as support for the idea that God causes *all* things that happen, instead of for the truth they were meant to convey. "A false balance is an abomination to the LORD" (Proverbs 11:1 NASB)—producing only bad fruit; therefore, we must be vigilant to *bring in* the balance.

Perhaps a better understanding of the original words used within these scriptures,[1] as well as the surrounding context, can lead to different conclusions. Then, as a result, a more balanced view of God's sovereignty—and the loving and equitable ways in which He deals with *all* men—will be effected. So to begin, please reconsider the significant scriptures that follow.

SIGNIFICANT SCRIPTURES

Proverbs 16:9
A man's heart deviseth [*chashab* / plans][2] his way: but the LORD directeth [*kuwn* / makes stand firm / establishes][3] his steps. (KJV)

---

[1] **In preparation for this chapter**, see the word studies of significant Greek and Hebrew words in the chapter "The *Will* of God."
[2] James Strong, LL.D., S.T.D., *Strong's Complete Word Study Concordance* (Chattanooga, TN: AMG Publishers, 2004), pp. 367, 1864.
[3] Ibid., pp. 376, 1882.

Proverbs 19:21
Many are the plans [*machashabah*][4] in a man's heart,
but it is the LORD's purpose [*etsah* / counsel / determina-
tion][5] that prevails. (NIV1984)

For sure, we see this truth: *If we would seek God's counsel—what He
by His wisdom determines is best on a matter—we would have success.*
Only His ways stand! His ways are higher!

Psalm 33:10-11
The LORD foils the plans [*etsah* / "counsel" in KJV][6] of
the nations; he thwarts the purposes [*machashabah* /
plans][7] of the peoples. But the plans [*etsah* / counsel /
determinations][8] of the LORD stand firm forever, the
purposes [*machashabah* / plans][9] of his heart [*leb*][10]
through all generations. (NIV1984)

It is so helpful knowing the actual Hebrew words originally stated. A
distinction between "counsel" and "plans" is seen. The counsel and
plans of nations are being compared to the counsel and plans of God.
Although some have used this passage to say otherwise, this scripture
does not say that *only* God's plans are carried out. Instead, we see that,
although man may think he knows what is best and may make his own
plans, **only what God determines is best and only what God plans
will stand firm forever—not to be shaken**. God will thwart, and He
will see that no counsel or any plan rises above what He determines
best to happen.

Isaiah 14:24-27
The LORD of hosts hath sworn, saying, Surely, as I have
thought [*damah*],[11] so shall it come to pass: and as I

---

[4] Ibid., p. 1898.
[5] Ibid., pp. 312, 1940.
[6] Ibid.
[7] Ibid., pp. 367, 1898.
[8] Ibid., pp. 312, 1940.
[9] Ibid., pp. 1516, 1898.
[10] Ibid., pp. 672, 1888.
[11] Ibid., pp. 1516, 1840

have purposed [*ya'ats* / determined / decided],[12] so shall it stand: That I will break the Assyrian in my land, and upon my mountains tread him under foot: then shall his yoke depart from off them, and his burden depart from off their shoulders. "This is the purpose [*etsah* / counsel / determination / decision][13] that is purposed [*ya'ats* / determined / decided][14] upon the whole earth: and this is the hand that is stretched out upon all the nations. **For the LORD of hosts hath purposed [*ya'ats* / determined],[15] and who shall disannul it?** And his hand is stretched out, and who shall turn it back? (KJV)

God sovereignly executes judgments *just as He has planned them.* Truly, no man can annul—no man can thwart—what God decides to do. **Only God Himself can change His mind in order to thwart His decisions and plans.**[16]

Isaiah 46:10-11
[While getting Israel's attention so that they might remember who He is, the LORD says these words concerning His greatness and His sovereignty.] Declaring the end from the beginning, and from ancient times the things that are not yet done, saying, my counsel [*etsah* / determination][17] shall stand and I will do all my pleasure [*chephets*]:[18] Calling a ravenous bird from the east, the man that executeth my counsel [*etsah*][19] from a far country: yea, I have spoken it, I will also bring it to pass; I have purposed [*yatsar* / "to form, to fashion"][20] it, I will also do it. (KJV)

---

[12] Ibid., pp. 1181, 1875.
[13] Ibid., pp. 312, 1940.
[14] Ibid., pp. 1181, 1875.
[15] Ibid.
[16] See Jeremiah 26: 3 and 36:2-3 listed with *chashab* words in the chapter "The *Will* of God." Also, consider God's mercy upon Ninevah.
[17] Strong, *Strong's Complete Word Study and Concordance*, pp. 312, 1940.
[18] Ibid., pp. 1148, 1861.
[19] Ibid., pp. 312, 1940.
[20] Ibid., pp. 1181, 1876.

Isaiah 46:10-11 is powerful and important in what it reminds us! God ultimately does declare the end from the beginning. Every move of man must pass by Him—to be (Acts 17:28). Nothing sidesteps Him.

Understandably, the words in Isaiah 46:10 that say, "I will do all my pleasure [*chephets*]," may lead some to think God causes *all* His perfect and probable desires—all that would bring Him pleasure—to always be done. Such a take on Isaiah's words, however, would not be consistent with what many other words of Scripture also say (e.g., Isaiah 65:12; Isaiah 66:4; and Jeremiah 32:30-35). Proverbs 15:26, itself, says: "The thoughts of the wicked are an abomination [*tow'ebah* / "an abhorrence"][21] to the LORD: but the words of the pure are pleasant [*no'am* / "agreeableness, i.e. delight, suitableness . . ."][22] words" (KJV). Clearly, not everything that would bring God pleasure happens; some things are even abominable to Him!

Yet, as can be seen by this passage of Scripture, it is **only God's *determinations*—God's decisions—that stand**. God is sovereign. He alone rules! *If He wants* to intervene in the affairs of men, He will! *If He wants* to make something happen, we cannot stop Him. He does what He wants to do![23]

The following scriptures are also very clear in what they say. Likewise, they, too, can aid in understanding the likely intent of other words of Scripture that are sometimes seriously misunderstood. Note the use of the verb *kuwn* in the following:

Proverbs 12:3
A man is not established [*kuwn*][24] by wickedness, but the root of the righteous cannot be moved. (NKJV)

---

[21] Ibid., pp. 6, 1998.
[22] Ibid., pp. 1147, 1921.
[23] Significantly, concerning Isaiah 46 and God's rule from beginning until end, see also the chapter entitled "The Foreknowledge of God."
[24] Strong, *Strong's Complete Word Study and Concordance*, pp. 442, 1882.

Proverbs 12:19
The lip of truth shall be established [*kuwn*]^{25} for ever:
but a lying tongue is but for a moment. (KJV)

Proverbs 16:3
Commit thy works unto the LORD, and thy thoughts shall
be established [*kuwn*].^{26} (KJV)

Proverbs 20:18
Every purpose is established [*kuwn*]^{27} by counsel: and
with good advice make war. (KJV)

The previous four passages speak of the ones whom God establishes—
the ones whom God *makes to stand*. In contrast to the wicked *not* being
established, the righteous *are* established. They will not be moved!
Likewise, in contrast to ones who speak lies, lasting only for a moment,
the ones speaking truth are established forever. The ones who seek the
good counsel of the Lord—who want to do things God's way (leaning
not unto their own understanding)—these are the ones whose plans
God causes to succeed!

Although the following passages of scriptures have often been misin-
terpreted as supporting the thought that God causes *all* the good and *all*
the bad that happens (perhaps because of translations), the passages
should not be used that way. They should be seen in a way similar to
the scriptures just previously mentioned. At most, they should be interpreted as speaking of *God's last say in all that we consider and in all
that we do*. So then, alongside the additional verbal meanings given, as
well as surrounding context, consider again the scriptures that follow:

Proverbs 20:24
A man's steps are of the LORD; how then can a man understand his own way? (NKJV)

---

^{25} Ibid.
^{26} Ibid.
^{27} Ibid.

We may make our plans, but God is in ultimate control of whether we are free to take the steps. We do not know even whether we have another day. *It is up to God.* That is why, as James alludes in James 4:13-16, it is presumptuous and prideful to say such things as "today or tomorrow we will go to such and such a city, spend a year there, buy and sell, and make a profit" (James 4:13 NKJV). Instead, we should remember to say "if the Lord wills, we shall live and do this or that [submitting to and aligning ourselves to do His will]" (James 4:15 NKJV).

> Proverbs 16:9
> A man's heart plans his way, but the LORD directs [*kuwn* / makes firm / establishes][28] his steps. (NKJV)

> Jeremiah 10:23
> O LORD, I know the way of man is not in himself; it is not in man who walks to direct [*kuwn* / make stand firm / establish][29] his own steps. (NKJV)

> Psalm 40:1-2
> I waited patiently for the LORD; and He inclined to me, and heard my cry. He also brought me up out of a horrible pit, out of the miry clay, and set my feet upon a rock, and established [*kuwn*][30] my steps. (NKJV)

> Psalm 37:23
> The steps of a good man are ordered [*kuwn* / made to stand firm / established][31] by the LORD, and He delights in his way. (NKJV)

The Lord will not let the righteous be shaken! He *establishes* the righteous! Even as Psalm 37:24 (which follows the last scripture) declares: "Though he fall, he shall not be utterly cast down; for the LORD upholds him with His hand" (NKJV). For sure, one may make his own plans,

---

[28] Ibid., pp. 376, 1882.
[29] Ibid.
[30] Ibid., pp. 449, 1882.
[31] Ibid., pp. 1094, 1882.

but it is the Lord who establishes his steps—who makes them stand firm so they will not be shaken.

Finally, the following historic account gives good illustration concerning the ones whom God establishes and His timeline and guidelines for doing so:

> [Saul receives the following rebuke from the Lord, as delivered by Samuel.] "You have done foolishly. You have not kept the commandment of the LORD your God, which He commanded you. For now **the LORD would have established** [*kuwn*]³² **your kingdom over Israel forever. But now your kingdom shall not continue.** The LORD has sought for Himself a man after His own heart, and the LORD has commanded [*tsavah*]³³ him to be commander over His people, **because you have not kept what the LORD commanded you.**" (1 Samuel 13:13-14 NKJV)

Together, both verses of 1 Samuel 13:13-14 are significant in what they state. Although some things are established or appointed by God ahead of time, apart from anything we do, **many appointments of God and things He would establish are conditional to *our* responses.** According-ing to Samuel's words, Saul's throne would have been made to stand—would have been established "for all time"—*if he had obeyed.*

Because of their complexity and importance, discussions of the next few verses will follow in greater detail than previous verses.

---

³² Ibid., pp. 441, 1882.
³³ Ibid., pp. 294, 1953.

PSALM 139:16
Are All Our Days *Ordained*?

A look at Psalm 139:16 is very important because many think it gives proof that God causes *everything* that happens. Such thinking comes, in part, because several translations (e.g., NIV1984, NKJV, NASB) have translated part of Psalm 139:16 like either **"the days ordained for me"** or **"the days fashioned for me."** Various translations read as follows:

> Your eyes saw my unformed body. **All the days ordained for me** were written in your book before one of them came to be. (NIV1984)

> Your eyes saw my substance, being yet unformed. And in Your book they all were written, **the days fashioned for me**, when *as yet there were* none of them. (NKJV)

> Yours eyes have seen my unformed substance; and in Your book were all written **The days that were ordained *for me*,** when as yet there was not one of them. (NASB)

At the same time, according to the King James Version and Young's Literal Translation, the scripture so reads:

> Thine eyes did see my substance [*golem*],[34] yet being unperfect; and in thy book all *my members* were written, *which* **in continuance** [*yowm*][35] **were fashioned** [*yatsar*],[36] when *as yet there was* none of them. (KJV)

> Mine unformed substance Thine eyes saw, And on Thy book all of them are written, **The days they were formed**—And not one among them. (YLT)

---

[34] Goodrick and Kohlenberger, *The NIV Exhaustive Concordance*, pp. 1191, 1411; Wilson, *Wilson's Old Testament Word Studies*, p. 428.

[35] Goodrick and Kohlenberger, *The NIV Exhaustive Concordance*, pp. 262, 1468; Wilson, *Wilson's Old Testament Word Studies*, p. 95.

[36] Goodrick and Kohlenberger, *The NIV Exhaustive Concordance*, pp. 842, 1476; Wilson, *Wilson's Old Testament Word Studies*, p. 158.

Note: where *italics* are found in the above translations, the translated words were *not* found in the original Hebrew.[37] They were added by the translator. Significantly then, "my members" (KJV), "which" (KJV), "for me" (NIV1984, NKJV, and NASB), and "as yet there [was/were]" (KJV, NKJV, and NASB) do not appear to have been found in the Hebrew rendering. (The NIV1984 does not reference unlisted words with italics.) Moreover, because of the absence of these italicized words, it is also understandable how the different translations may have occurred.

Bible translations vary in their renderings. Even so, a careful look at the original Hebrew, as *is* found, proves very helpful in consideration of what very likely may have been the original intent of the passage. In particular, a look at the Hebrew words *yatsar* and *yowm*, as well as surrounding context, demonstrates the strength of both the King James Version and the Young's Literal Translation.

The Hebrew Word *Yatsar*

As has already been noted in a word discussion within the chapter "The *Will* of God," the Hebrew verb *yatsar*, meaning "to form, fashion, or shape, as a potter the clay,"[38] is translated in the 1984 New International Version (as well as in other translations) similar to "formed" or "fashioned" in most of the scriptures where it is found [39] (e.g., Genesis 2:7-8 and 2:19; Psalm 94:9 and 95:5; Isaiah 44:2 and 45:9). It seems right, therefore, that *yatsar* should also be strongly considered as "fashioned" or "formed," instead of "ordained," in the passage of Psalm 139.

The Hebrew Word *Yowm*

Then significantly, the Hebrew word *yowm* (translated as "days" in several translations) should also have special consideration. Although

---

[37] *New American Standard Bible—Updated Edition* (La Habra, CA: The Lockman Foundation, 1995), p. viii; *The Holy Bible, New King James Version* (Nashville, TN: Thomas Nelson Publishers, 1994), p. vii.

[38] Goodrick and Kohlenberger, *The NIV Exhaustive Concordance*, p. 1476; Wilson, *Wilson's Old Testament Word Studies*, p. 158.

[39] Goodrick and Kohlenberger, *The NIV Exhaustive Concordance*, p. 1476.

most often thought of as "day," this word sometimes is used for wider expression. Notably, *The New International Dictionary of New Testament Theology* explains the word as follows:

> The Hebrews had no word for time in the abstract, and similarly had no corresponding expressions for past, present and future . . . Of the various words used to express aspects of time by far the most frequent in Heb. is *yowm* . . . Often it is qualified by a genitival phrase, an infinitive, or a relative clause . . . Whereas in some of these instances *yowm* is a literal day, in others it appears to denote a concrete *time* **which may have extended for more than twenty-four hours, but which was nevertheless *characterized by a specific event*** [emphasis mine].[40]

Moreover, in agreement, *Wilson's Old Testament Word Studies* also supports the correctness of other types of translation. According to Wilson, *yowm* carries the following ideas: "a day, **continually**; *Heb.* all the days, all day, every day." Wilson defines further: ". . . it is frequently put for **time in general**, or for a long time; **a whole period under consideration**, as, in the day signifieth **in the time when**; in that day, at that time. Day is also put for **a particular season or time when any extraordinary event happens** . . . ."[41]

Lastly, the following scriptures demonstrate the aforementioned "time" meaning (e.g., "*day* of battle" and "*day* of Jerusalem") that the word *yowm* indeed may have: Psalm 137:7; Lamentations 1:12; 2:1; 2:21; Ezekiel 34:12; Hosea 10:14; and Zechariah 14:3.[42]

Context

Truly, "the *days fashioned*" is a literal translation of Psalm 139:16. Yet, at the same time, if *yatsar* is translated as "formed"/"fashioned" and

---

[40] Colin Brown, *The New International Dictionary of New Testament Theology—Vol. 2* (Grand Rapids, MI: The Zondervan Corporation, 1976), pp. 888 - 889.

[41] Wilson, *Wilson's Old Testament Word Studies*, pp. 95, 109.

[42] Brown, *The New International Dictionary of New Testament Theology*, p. 889; Wilson, *Old Testament Word Studies*, p. 109.

yowm is thought of as "a period [of time] under consideration," the context surrounding the words in Psalm 139:16 also would support the renderings of both the King James Version and Young's Literal Translation. Within these translations, contextual consideration is being given to *body parts being formed*.

Just as is understood by the King James Version and Young's Literal Translation, the verb *yatsar* and "not one among them" (YLT) clearly refers, by context, to the just previously mentioned *unformed body parts* (v. 16). In truth, the Hebrew word *golem*, which was translated as "substance" in verse 16, specifically *does* mean "anything rolled or wrapped together; **hence an unformed mass, substance, not yet wrought, the *parts* of which are not yet unfolded nor developed, spoken of the embryo [fetus]**"[43] (emphasis mine)! So, if one is referring to *unformed body parts*, the fashioning/forming of *unformed body parts*—when "not one among them"—is very likely the writer's intent.

Not only is the rendering of a "fashioning" contextually supported, but with an understanding of the expanded meaning of the word *yowm*, the King James Version distinguishes *yowm* as *the continuation of time* in which fashioning of the unformed embryo takes place. Hence, when put with the rest of verse 16, the translation renders the idea of God's seeing the unformed substance and writing in His book—"when as yet there was none of them"—all the parts, which "in continuance" were being fashioned.

To be sure, the King James Version fits context! And yet, slightly different from the rendering of the King James Version, the Young's Literal Translation, and even the New King James Version (if the added "for me" is removed), presents still another possible intent for the *yowm* and *yatsar* combination. Could the intent of *yowm* with *yatsar* have been "time *when* fashioned"? Just as there is "the day of anger" and "the day of battle" (see scriptures with the discussion of *yowm*), could the words "days fashioned" simply have been a qualifying of *the time the special event of fashioning took place*? Could "the days fashioned . . . , when as yet there were none of them" (NKJV / without added "for me") have been David's way of ending his focus on God's

---

[43] Wilson, *Wilson's Old Testament Word Studies*, p. 428.

169

complete knowledge of and involvement in his life—the time even before and during the formation of his body?

Indeed, one passage of Scripture, that of Jeremiah 11:23, demonstrates to us the real possibility of such a "time when" rendering. According to Young's Literal Translation and the New American Standard Bible the Jeremiah passage translates as follows:

> "And they have no remnant, For I bring evil unto the men of Anathoth, **the year of their inspection**." (YLT)

> "And a remnant will not be left to them, for I will bring disaster on the men of Anathoth—**the year of their punishment**." (NASB)

Notably, God's words of judgment are given with a "time when" statement. Likewise, the occurrence of these "time" words have a marked similarity with the way "*yowm yatsar*" occurs in Psalm 139:16.

Thus, in contrast to various translations of Psalm 139:16—which give renderings such as "the days ordained"—at least equal attention should be given to the King James Version and Young's Literal Translation. The latter translations surely are warranted by the meanings and typical usages given for the crucial words *yowm* and *yatsar*—and surrounding context supports these translations as well. Very likely, while continuing his expression of God's intimate knowledge—that nothing about himself ever had been hidden from God's sight—David simply was recounting how God had foreseen, had written in His book, and even had fashioned him, when as yet there were none of his body parts.

For certain, because of the varying ways the passage is translated, the words of Psalm 139:16 should be handled very carefully. In fact, if we are not careful in our interpretation, we also can come to some seriously wrong conclusions about our Maker. The "planning" and the responsibility for untimely abortions of innocent babies might be attributed to God. The planning and the responsibility for wicked schemes of murder might be attributed to God. Wrong conclusions can have very serious effects.

JOB 14:5

In close similarity to the misunderstanding that often arises from Psalm 139:16, with the words "the days ordained for me," Job 14:5 is also often misunderstood in its interpretation. Some believe the passage to mean one's days on earth are *decreed* from the very beginning. So, consider again the words that read:

> "Since his **days** [*yowm*][44] **are determined** [*charats*],[45] the number of his months is with you; You have appointed [*'asah* / "to make"][46] his limits, so that he cannot pass." (KJV)

At first glance, this scripture does appear to say that the *specific* length of one's days are determined by God. The verses before and following verse 5, however, give clue to something else which may have been intended. (See Job 13:25, 28 and Job 14:1-2, 7-12.)

When the words of verse 5 were spoken, Job was pleading his case before God. He was crying out to God, in all honesty, concerning what he perceived was His wrath toward him (Job 13:24-26; Job 14:13). Job did not understand! He wanted to know if he had sinned (Job 13:20-23), and he wanted to be restored!

Part of Job's plea towards God was an acknowledgement of the weakness and the frailty of not only himself, but of every man:

> "Man decays like a rotten thing, like a garment that is moth-eaten. Man who is born of woman is of few days and full of trouble. He comes forth like a flower and fades away; he flees like a shadow and does not continue. [Job, then, pleas with God . . .] And do You open Your eyes on such a one, and bring to judgment with Yourself? Who can bring a clean thing out of an unclean? No one!" (Job 13:28 – Job 14:4 NKJV)

---

[44] Strong, *Strong's Complete Word Study Concordance*, pp. 346, 1872.
[45] Ibid., pp. 366, 1864.
[46] Ibid., pp. 100, 1942.

It is following the above words, then, that he continues with the words found in verses 5 and 6:

> **"Since his days are determined, the number of his months is with You; You have appointed his limits, so that he cannot pass.** Look away from him that he may rest, till like a hired man he finishes his day." (Job 14:5-6 NKJV)

It was in consideration of man's weakness *and the brevity of man's days on earth* that Job presented his case for God's mercy and rest—"till like a hired man he finishes his day."

In truth, the days and months of a man are in God's hands, and they are numbered by the Lord. That is not to say, however, that man's days are *ordained*—that God has set specific lengths for each individual ahead of time, definitely to happen. Instead, there is other probable meaning that flows, contextually, with what Job has been saying, as well as with other words from Scripture.

Although most men do not live so long, notably, Genesis 6:3 speaks of *boundaries* God has determined for the length of man's days:

> And the LORD said, "My Spirit shall not strive with man forever, for he is indeed flesh; yet *his days shall be one hundred and twenty years.*" (NKJV, emphasis mine)

For certain, a man's days are measured by the Lord. His life on earth does not go on indefinitely. It is short and like a vapor (Psalm 39:4-5; 90:10, 12). Job was probably affirming this fact when he acknowledged God's appointment of *limits* over which man cannot pass.

Although, contextually, in Job 14:5, Job appears to have been speaking in regard to *the short span of time every man has on earth*, this truth of Job 14:5 should not be missed: God rules over the number of a man's days! "The number of [man's] months *is* with [God]" (Job 14:5, emphasis mine). It is up to God how long one may live; therefore, *if* God should determine for one to die, he will die.

David knew the rule of God over his times, and David was comforted by it. His words in Psalm 31:14-15 should, likewise, give great comfort to any who would trust in Him and follow His ways:

> But as for me, I trust in You, O LORD; I say, "You are my God." My times are in Your hand; deliver me from the hand of my enemies . . . . (NKJV)

Because our times are in His hands, we *can* have rest. We have no need to fear, for *God is greater* than everything. *If we look to Him and dwell in His shadow*, "no evil shall befall [us]" (Psalm 91:10). We will have the life He desires for us and the life that will bring Him great glory.

ISAIAH 45:7
Does God Create All Evil?

This scripture is confusing to many. By the way the King James Version translation is expressed, in particular, some think it supports the idea that God causes everything that happens—even *all* the evil. The King James Version so reads:

> I form the light, and create darkness: I make peace, and **create** [*bara'*][47] **evil** [*ra'*]:[48] I the LORD do all these things. (KJV)

Other translations, however, render Isaiah 45:7 a bit differently:

> I form the light and create darkness, I make peace and **create calamity**; I the LORD do all these things. (NKJV)

> I form the light and create darkness, I bring prosperity and **create disaster**: I, the LORD, do all these things. (NIV 1984)

---

[47] Ibid., pp. 318, 1828.
[48] Ibid., pp. 458, 1971.

> The One forming light and creating darkness, causing well-being and **creating calamity**; I am the LORD who does all these. (NASB)

Accurately, the word *ra'* can be thought of in the sense of "evil." There are many scriptures where "evil" is rendered for the word. Yet, because of the general inference when people hear the word "evil," it is helpful to get further meaning of the original word translated as such. The Hebrew word used for "evil" in Isaiah 45:7 is the adjective *ra'*. According to *Wilson's Old Testament Word Studies*, it brings the following idea: "evil, unfortunate, calamitous." Then, according to Wilson, the verb *ra'a'*, to which *ra'* is closely related, brings the following meaning: "to break, to break in pieces; *intrans.* to be evil, bad; from the idea of breaking, being broken and so made worthless; to be evil; to do evil; to deal ill with . . . ."[49]

At bare minimum, we *should* affirm that God has the last say in all. He not only brings and establishes peace, but our God will bring into being "bad" and "calamitous" events when He so determines best. That is part of who He is. Although He is good and loving and brings favor and peace to those who acknowledge Him, He is to be feared. He "break[s] in pieces"—He brings to judgment.[50]

Context is so important for rightly handling the words of God. By the chapters surrounding the words of Isaiah 45:7, it is apparent that God desired the Jewish people (and all the world) to know of His greatness—His reigning power—both in sending the good *and* in sending the bad that would happen to His people. He wanted men to know His ability to bring to pass *all* that He determines and foretells He will do. Just as He had decreed and just as He had foretold by His prophets, His people would indeed receive His judgment (*and* also His deliverance)—"that they [might] know from the rising of the sun to its setting that there is *none* besides [Him]" (Isaiah 45:6 NKJV, emphasis mine).[51]

---

[49] Wilson, *Wilson's Old Testament Word Studies*, p. 150.
[50] See Isaiah 3:11 and Isaiah 31:2, where God speaks of bringing *ra'*.
[51] For context, see Isaiah 40:23-24; 41:2-4, 18-20, 22-24; 42:23-24; 43:12-13; 44: 6-8, 24-28; 45:5-7; 45:20-21; and 46:9-11.

God is jealous that we know His rule over *all* that happens—"that there is none besides [Him]." He is also jealous that we know He allows nothing that cannot be turned to His glory. He alone is God and He alone *will* receive glory! Noticeably, verses Isaiah 45:8 and 22-25 also proclaim that, just as declared, He even would be the One to bring righteousness and salvation to all the ends of the earth!

For sure, the words of Isaiah 45:7 are very significant in what they speak. God, alone, *does* determine "peace" or "destruction." Just as Amos 3:6 affirms: "If there is calamity in a city, will not the LORD have done it?" Nonetheless, the broad conclusion that God causes *all* evil (i.e., the evil within men's hearts) simply is not warranted by what is said in this passage (nor in alignment with James 1:13). The words do not even say "*all* evil." For sure, we must tread very softly in the things we attribute to God.[52]

THE UN-DOING OF IMBALANCE

Hard-core Calvinists maintain that God causes *everything* that happens and that His will is *always* accomplished. One theologian has even asserted that "scripture nowhere" supports a man's ability to make decisions not *caused* by God. Yet, the following accounts of Scripture would contradict that assertion:

> 1 Samuel 15:10-11
> Now the word of the LORD came to Samuel, saying, "I greatly regret that I have set up Saul as king, for **he has turned back from following Me, and has not performed My commandments.**" And it grieved Samuel, and he cried out to the LORD all night. (NKJV)

Samuel "turned back from following [the Lord]." The Lord "regret[ted]." And the prophet Samuel "grieved." In light of all these responses, it becomes apparent: God's perfect desire/will is not always

---

[52] Significantly, concerning the truth that God *does* sometimes *use* the evil in men's hearts to carry out His schemes of judgment, see also the chapter "God's Sovereignty Over the Hearts of Men."

accomplished. (See also 1 Samuel 13:13-14 for the consequences of Saul's decisions.)

Further, words from *The Book of Jeremiah* also enlighten:

> Jeremiah 23:32
> Behold, I am against them that prophesy false dreams, saith the LORD, and do tell them, and cause my people to err by their lies, and by their lightness; **yet I sent** [*shalach*][53] **them not, nor commanded** [*tsavah*][54] **them**: therefore they shall not profit this people at all, saith the LORD. (KJV)

> Jeremiah 32:30-35
> "Because the children of Israel and the children of Judah have done only evil before Me from their youth. For the children of Israel have provoked Me only to anger with the work of their hands," says the LORD. . . . "And they have turned to Me the back, and not the face; though I taught them, rising up early and teaching them, yet they have not listened to receive instruction. But they set their abominations in the house which is called by My name, to defile it. And they built the high places of Baal which are in the Valley of the Son of Hinnom, to cause their sons and their daughters to pass through the fire to Molech, **which I did not command** [*tsavah*][55] **them, nor did it come to My mind** [*leb*][56] that they should do this abomination, to cause Judah to sin." (NKJV)

According to the words of Jeremiah, God did not send the false prophets, nor did He appoint (*tsavah*) them. Likewise, the Lord **did not "command" nor even imagine** that the children of Israel and the children of Judah would do the abominable acts that they did. These words

---

[53] Strong, *Strong's Complete Word Study Concordance*, pp. 1301, 1986.
[54] Ibid., pp. 295, 1953.
[55] Ibid.
[56] Ibid., pp. 979, 1888.

of the prophet Jeremiah show specifically: *God does not cause everything that happens, nor is His will always accomplished.*

IN CONCLUSION
With Respect to Who He Is

"The earth is the LORD's and the fullness thereof . . ." (Psalm 24:1 NKJV). He is King over all the earth! Today, the Lord would establish this truth in our hearts. He would be known in the greatness of who He is.

Truly, under His sovereign rule, everything that happens—only may happen because He has given *permission* for its occurrence (even *allowing* man's choices to stand). The Lord is greater than all! He lets stand and He establishes—"*upholding* all things by the word of His power" (Hebrews 1:3 NKJV, emphasis mine).

In His sovereignty, the Lord will do *all* His pleasure—all that He pleases to do. *If* He commands something to happen, it shall happen. Nothing can thwart that which He makes determination to do! Nonetheless, concerning His *determined* rule—His ways with mankind—it is clear: God does not command all things that happen, nor is His "perfect" will—that which has been put within our grasp—always accomplished. God has chosen, instead, to limit Himself and to engage in real relationships with men.

Chapter 6

Significant Scriptures Concerning God's Sovereignty—
Part 2:
Acknowledging *the Giver*

Truth dispels darkness. Truth brings down strongholds (Psalm 119:11). We are sanctified and cleansed "with the washing . . . by the word" (Ephesians 5:26)—*His* word of truth. Today, the Lord would establish His truth within our hearts—in order that we might be free.

In His sovereignty, the Lord does not *cause* all that happens. His most "perfect will" is not always accomplished.[1] Nonetheless, having said that, we would all do well to esteem Him in the greatness of who He is. He is *the Giver*. Consider the following account of His greatness:

OVER ALL

Psalm 103:19
The LORD has established His throne in heaven, and **His kingdom rules over all**. (NKJV)

Romans 13:1
For there is **no authority except from God, and the authorities that exist are appointed by God**. (NKJV)

John 19:11
Jesus answered, "You could have no power at all against Me **unless it had been given you from above**." (NKJV)

John 3:27
John answered [concerning the success of Jesus] and said, "A man can receive nothing **unless it has been given to him from heaven**." (NKJV)

---

[1] See 1 Samuel 13:13-14; 15:10-11; Jeremiah 23:32; 32:35; and "Significant Scriptures—Part 1."

1 Corinthians 7:17
But **as God has distributed to each one**, as the Lord has called each one, so let him walk. (NKJV)

Truly, nothing may happen *without* the Father's permission. He is the Giver—and He rules over all.

Over All Understanding

Without partiality, all men have received free wills (Psalm 33:15) in order that they might choose to know and to worship God. All men have been specially fashioned *"so that they [can] seek the Lord, in the hope that they might grope for Him and find Him"* (Acts 17:26-27). Even so, in all our pursuits, we must retain a fear of God—acknowledging His continued and higher place to grant us the "eyes to see." Just as Scripture affirms:

Job 38:36
"Who has put wisdom in the mind? Or **who has given** understanding to the heart?" (NKJV)

Proverbs 2:6
For the LORD gives wisdom; from His mouth come knowledge and understanding; (NKJV)

James 1:5
If any of you lacks wisdom, let him ask of God, **who gives to all liberally** and without reproach, and **it will be given** to him. (NKJV)

Romans 1:18-21, 28
For the wrath of God is revealed from heaven against all ungodliness and unrighteousness of men, who suppress the truth in unrighteousness, because **what may be known of God is manifest in them, for God has shown it to them**. . . . being understood by the things that are made, even His eternal power and Godhead, so that they are without excuse, because, although they

knew God, they did not glorify Him as God, nor were thankful, but became futile in their thoughts, and their foolish hearts were darkened. . . . And even as they did not like to retain God in their knowledge, **God gave them over** to a debased mind, to do the things which are not fitting; (NKJV)

Indeed, the Lord—the One of all wisdom—is the One who gives wisdom and understanding to the heart. *He* enlightens and *He* confounds.

Over Those Enlightened to Know the Savior

In truth, although there has been distortion with the Calvinist doctrine of *unconditional election*, the Father is the One, ultimately, who rules over the ones *given* to His Son. Not all are enlightened to know the identity of Jesus; therefore, knowing Christ, we *should* retain gratitude, not only for His work of redemption upon the cross, but also for *the revelation* that we received of Him as Savior. Consider the following words of Jesus:

John 6:37, 44, 65
"**All that the Father gives Me** will come to Me, and the one who comes to Me I will in no wise cast out." . . . "No one can come to Me **unless the Father who sent Me draws him;**" . . . "Therefore I have said to you that no one can come to Me **unless it has been granted to him by My Father.**" (NKJV)

Matthew 13:11-12
He answered and said to them, "Because **it has been given to you to know the mysteries** of the kingdom of heaven, but **to them it has not been given. For whoever has, to him more will be given**, and he will have abundance; but whoever does not have, even what he has will be taken away from him." (NKJV)

Matthew 21:43
"Therefore I say to you, the kingdom of God will be taken from you and **given to a nation bearing the fruits of it.**" (NKJV)

For sure, the one not bearing fruit with things God has given should fear—lest what he has be taken away. (Note Romans 1:18-32.) Likewise, we all should be careful, not only to hear, but to respond in obedience to things already given. Even so, although we should rightly fear God, we may also have rest and consolation—*for it is the Father's good will to give us the kingdom.* Just as it is written:

Luke 12:32
"Do not fear little flock; for it is **your Father's good pleasure to give you the kingdom.**" (NKJV)

James 1:17
Every good gift and **every perfect gift is from above**, and comes down from the Father of lights, with whom there is no variation or shadow of turning. (NKJV)

Assuredly, we may know His *great* desire for us, and yet, we should retain humility and gratitude toward the One from whom we have received all good gifts. He who glories should glory *only* in the Lord (1 Corinthians 1: 31; Jeremiah 9:23-24).

Over All Revelations and Positions of Ministry within the Body

Likewise, although we are surely responsible to use what is given in Christ, the Lord is the Giver of *all* revelations received and of any positions of ministry found within the body. Understanding this truth not only gives "honor to whom honor is due" (Romans 13:7), but it also brings us into a new freedom—a freedom from undue striving and undue envying of one another. The Lord has determined and *He* will bring to pass—*to the extent that we will faithfully commit our ways unto Him* (Psalm 37:5-6). Just as the following declares:

Galatians 1:11-12
But I make known to you, brethren, that the gospel which was preached by me is not according to man. For I neither received it from man, nor was I taught it, but **it came through the revelation** of Jesus Christ. (NKJV)

Romans 12:3-4
For I say, through the grace given to me, to everyone who is among you, not to think of himself more highly than he ought to think, but to think soberly, as **God has dealt to each one a measure of faith**. For as we have many members in one body, but all the members do not have the same function, so we, being many, are one body in Christ, and individually members of one another. (NKJV)

Ephesians 4:7-11
But to each one of us **grace was given** according to the measure of Christ's gift. Therefore He says: "When He ascended on high, He led captivity captive, and **gave gifts** to men." . . . And He Himself **gave some to be** apostles, some prophets, some evangelists, and some pastors and teachers, (NKJV)

1 Corinthians 3:5-7
Who then is Paul, and who is Apollos, but ministers through whom you believed, **as the Lord gave to each one**? I planted, Apollos watered, but **God gave the increase**. So then neither he who plants is anything, nor he who waters, but **God who gives the increase**. (NKJV)

1 Corinthians 4:1, 6-7
Let a man so consider us, as servants of Christ and **stewards of the mysteries of God**. . . . that none of you may be puffed up on behalf of one against another. For who makes you differ from another? **And what do you have that you did not receive?** Now if you did indeed receive it, why do you boast as if you have not received it? (NKJV)

1 Corinthians 12:11
But one and the same Spirit works all these things [the manifestations of the Spirit], **distributing to each one individually as He wills**. (NKJV)

1 Corinthians 12:18
But now **God has set the members**, each one of them, in the body just as He pleased. (NKJV)

2 Corinthians 10:13
But we will not boast of things without our measure, but **according to the measure of the rule which God hath distributed to us**, a measure to reach even unto you. (KJV)

Surely, there is no room for pride within the body of Christ. There is no room for pride as God's place is rightly esteemed.

Over the Weaknesses of Men

Notably, also, as the Giver, *God knows best*—and He will orchestrate even the weaknesses and "understanding" of men in order to fulfill His greater works within our lives.[2] In accordance with the *fullness* of His counsel, oftentimes, not only will God humble us and stretch us, personally, through our own weaknesses and lack of understanding, but He also will *use* our weaknesses for the benefit or testing of others. Understanding is good (Proverbs 2:2)! Yet, although the Lord liberally gives understanding to the hearts of those who will seek it (Proverbs 2:1-9; James 1:5), He also may choose to postpone.

---

[2] **Please note:** Neither weakness nor lack of understanding is synonymous with "sin"—for we are only accountable to what we have attained. Likewise, we may also stand confident—for, amidst the process of our "perfecting" and sanctification, God sees deeper into *the intentions* of our hearts. (See 2 Corinthians 4:7; Hebrews 4:15; 1 Samuel 16:7; Psalm 66:18; 1 John 3:21-22; 1 Corinthians 4:3-5; Philippians 3:12-16; and Luke 12:47-48.) Additionally, with respect to God's *orchestrations*, see "God's Sovereignty Over the Hearts of Men."

Who gives understanding? *God* gives understanding (Job 38:36). Although we are to seek understanding—although it is surely "a tree of life to those who take hold of [it]" (Proverbs 3:18 NKJV)—we, too, must wait on God for it . . . because God's timing is perfect. He works *all things* together for good. He works all things "in accordance with [His greater] counsel" (Romans 8:28; Ephesians 1:11). Just as Paul proclaimed:

> Oh the depth of the riches both of the wisdom and knowledge of God! How unsearchable are His judgments and his ways past finding out? "For who has known the mind of the LORD? Or who has become His counselor?" (Romans 11:33-34 NKJV)

Over All Our Trials

In like manner, in His sovereignty, the Lord is the Giver over all our trials. *All that touches our lives must first pass by the Father.* Just as others have understood and rested in this knowledge, so can we. Consider the truth of the following words:

John 18:11
"Shall I not drink the cup **which My Father has given Me**?" (NKJV)

Daniel 7:25
" ' . . . Then **the saints shall be given into his [the fourth beast's] hand** for a time and times and half a time.' " (NKJV)

1 Corinthians 10:13
No temptation has overtaken you except such as is common to man; but God is faithful, **who will not allow you to be tempted beyond what you are able**, but with the temptation will also make the way of escape, that you may be able to bear it. (NKJV)

Genesis 20:6
And God said to [King Abimelech] in a dream, "Yes, **I know that you did this in the integrity of your heart**. For I also withheld you from sinning against Me; **therefore I did not let you touch her**." (NKJV)

Indeed, we may have great assurance, as we understand God's role in that which may touch the lives of His children. As our Father, the Lord is faithfully watching over *all* that may touch our lives, only allowing that which may be fashioned for our good (Romans 8:28-29). He is the Giver over all our trials.[3]

Over All Nations and Governing Authorities

Significantly, although, as citizens, we are to responsibly use the things we have been given (even our freedoms to expose deeds of darkness and to support that which is godly), *we need not fret* concerning the nations—for the Lord is the Giver over all the nations. Consider the words of Paul:

> God, who made the world and everything in it, since He is Lord of heaven and earth, does not dwell in temples made with hands. Nor is He worshiped with men's hands, as though He needed anything, since He gives to all life, breath, and all things. And He has made from one blood every nation of men to dwell on all the face of the earth, and **has determined their preappointed times and the boundaries of their dwellings**, (Acts 17:24-26 NKJV)

To be sure, God allows men's choices, and those choices have very real effects upon governments. Yet, even as Acts 17 declares, He is the ultimate authority over whether those nations or governments will be permitted to exist (even over their boundaries and over their times). God is enthroned over the nations.

---

[3] Notably, trials will come and are *necessary* for the testing and development of our faith. See James 1:2-4 and 1 Peter 1:6-7.

The Lord remains greater! In the end, He will thwart the decisions of men—*if* those decisions will conflict with His purposes (Psalm 33:10-11).[4] He will have *only what He desires and chooses to allow.* To the greater purpose that His name is exalted and proclaimed in all the earth (see Romans 9:17), God is purposeful with regard to governing nations.

Over All Our Provision

Even as the apostle Paul understood, "in Him we live and move and have our being" (Acts 17:28). The Lord is *the source* over all our provision. Consider the following words from Scripture:

2 Peter 1:3
As **His divine power has given to us** all things that pertain to life and godliness, through the knowledge of Him . . . (NKJV)

Matthew 7:7
"Ask, and **it will be given to you**; seek, and you will find; knock, and it will be opened to you." (NKJV)

Matthew 10:19
"But when they deliver you up, do not worry about how or what you should speak. For **it will be given** to you in that hour what you should speak;" (NKJV)

Psalm 37:3-5
Trust in the LORD, and do good; dwell in the land, and feed on His faithfulness. Delight yourself also in the LORD, and **He shall give** you the desires of your heart. Commit your way to the LORD, trust also in Him, and **He shall bring it to pass.** (NKJV)

Hebrews 13:6
"**The Lord is my helper**; I will not fear. What can *man* do to me?" (NKJV, emphasis mine)

---

[4] See also the chapter entitled "God's Sovereignty Over the Hearts of Men."

Truly, in a right knowledge of our Lord as *Giver*, we need not fret. "Having done all," we may stand (Ephesians 6:13). Nonetheless, for all that He would provide for us—even for His "abundant provision of grace"—*we must agree* with the Lord in a continued posture of faith (Jonah 2:8; Romans 5:17; Hebrews 10:36).

Over All the "Kingdoms" of Men

Indeed, there is no authority greater than His authority—no authority, including our own. The authorities that exist—exist because they have been *given* by God. That which stands only stands because *He has allowed it.* Truly, only that which He chooses to do and the ways He chooses to do—may stand. Significantly, just as King Nebuchadnezzar learned the significance of God's place, we also can learn.

The Lesson of King Nebuchadnezzar

The most High rules in the kingdoms of men and **gives
it to whomever He chooses**. (Daniel 4:25-26 NKJV)

Nebuchadnezzar had to learn this truth the hard way. (See all of Daniel 4.) Thankfully, we can also learn from his mistakes. We do not have to experience the hardship he experienced. Nonetheless, if needed, the Lord knows how to bring down low.

We must keep our eyes *on Him* and not get into the prideful position into which Nebuchadnezzar fell. Nebuchadnezzar considered the good in his life as that which he, himself, had made (a looking to *man*). Consequently, he also was brought down low, losing control of his faculties.

To be sure, man's frame has not been fashioned to carry the load for good that happens to him—neither the good that may (or may not) have already happened to him, nor the good that may yet happen. As was with Nebuchadnezzar, it is also when we do not rightly acknowledge God that soundness of mind leaves. In the end, however, Nebuchadnezzar did gain an understanding—acknowledging that God rules over the kingdoms of men and that *He is the One who gives.*[5]

IN CONCLUSION
Reigning under His Rule

The words of Jesus—"come to Me, all you who labor and are heavy laden, and I will give you rest" (Matthew 11:28 NKJV)—were in the context of *a rest* Jesus had amidst His passion that men have life (see Matthew 11:20-30). Jesus knew the place His Father *ultimately* had in determining the ones who would "see" Him and the ones who would not. He understood and rested in His Father's *final* authority over all. In all things, we too may have rest. We too may rest as we hunger for God's kingdom among men.

It is important to *rightly* acknowledge the place of our Father. A failure to recognize and to accept His place as Giver not only undermines God's greatness, but it also leaves us unnecessarily vulnerable to much sin and conflict within ourselves.[6] Failure to acknowledge and to accept the Father as Giver, likewise, leaves us vulnerable to many of the enemy's lying schemes. Today, our Lord would set us free. Knowing the Giver brings peace and rest in Him.

Truly, the Lord is great—"upholding all things by the word of His power"—upholding all things by His own authority (Hebrews 1:3). A while back, the Lord spoke to my heart concerning a posture that would hinder our going forth in Him—"an *excessive* sense of responsibility and having our identity in another." To the contrary and essential to our freedom and rest is a true knowledge of the Lord as *Giver*.

---

[5] Concerning God's greatness over *all* the affairs of men, see also Isaiah 40:12 – 41:7.
[6] E.g., grumbling, discontentment, resentment, envying, pride, feelings of insignificance, perfectionism, anxiousness, "the fear of man," and contention with authority figures.

Chapter 7

God's Sovereignty Over the Hearts of Men

The Lord would not be blamed for the things He does not do. In His sovereignty, He has not "commanded" all things nor unconditionally predetermined any individuals unto hardness and wrath.[1] Notwithstanding, although it is an affront to God's name to attribute to Him acts of partiality or injustice towards men, foremost, we must recognize His greatness—His sovereign rule over even the hearts of men. Although the Lord has fashioned, individually, the hearts of all men—in order that *all* might have true heart-felt relationships with Him—He has remained always greater (1 John 3:20). Scripture makes this very clear:

> Psalm 103:19
> The LORD has established His throne in heaven, and **His kingdom rules over all.** (NKJV)

> 1 John 3:20
> For if our hearts condemn us, **God is greater than our heart**, and knows all things. (NKJV)

> Proverbs 21:1
> **The king's heart is in the hand of the LORD**, like the rivers of water; He turns it wherever He wishes. (NKJV)

Truly, He is the One with whom we have to do (Hebrews 4:13; Acts 17:27-28). We would all do well to retain a fear of Him and to acknowledge His rule over all.

---

[1] See 1 Samuel 13:13-14; 15:10-11; Jeremiah 23:32; 32:35; the chapters "Inconsistencies—Part 1" and Inconsistencies—Part 2; and the chapter "Significant Scriptures—Part 1."

HIS WATCHFUL EYE UPON THE HEARTS OF MEN

At the outset, and in light of God's rule upon the hearts of men, we should foremost recognize and appreciate the height of God's measure for righteousness. While man may look upon outward performance as the means for obtaining acceptance before his Maker, God, instead, looks deep upon the *intentions* of the heart. God is *a respecter of men's hearts*—and He renders accordingly. Consider God's greatness according to Scripture:

> 1 Samuel 16:7
> "For the LORD does not see as man sees; for man looks at the outward appearance, but **the LORD looks at the heart**." (NKJV)

> Psalm 33:13-15
> The LORD looks from heaven; He sees all the sons of men. From the place of His dwelling He looks on all the inhabitants of the earth; **He fashions their hearts individually; He considers all their works**. (NKJV)

> Psalm 44:20-21
> If we had forgotten the name of our God, or stretched out our hands to a foreign god, would not God search this out? For **He knows the secrets of the heart**. (NKJV)

> Proverbs 21:2
> Every way of a man is right in his own eyes, but **the LORD weighs the hearts**. (NKJV)

> Jeremiah 17:10
> **"I, the LORD, search the heart, I test the mind, even to give every man according to his ways**, according to the fruit of his doings." (NKJV)

For certain, man shall never measure up to God's perfection by his own doings—for God is *set apart* and there is none like Him (Isaiah 46:9). Instead, that which God esteems and that which He considers **holiness**

192

is *a heart totally surrendered to Him.* While man measures by the outward, God looks at the heart that is willfully committed to Him. (See Matthew 15:7-9; Psalm 37:5-6; and Jeremiah 29:13.)

Moreover, seeing into the hearts of men, God will also be *great to intervene* on our behalf. He will restrain a person or He will move a person *if* He so desires. Consider the account of God's restraint upon King Abimelech and the subsequent protection of Abraham's wife:

> And God said to [King Abimelech] in a dream, "Yes, **I know that you did this in the integrity of your heart**. For I also withheld you from sinning against Me; **therefore I did not let you touch her**." (Genesis 20:6 NKJV)

Likewise, *in spite of his own earlier distinct failings*, the apostle Paul understood God's greatness to see into the heart and to mercifully intervene. It was concerning his own rescue that he would even write to Timothy:

> And I thank Christ Jesus our Lord **who has enabled me, because He counted me faithful**, putting me into ministry, although I was formerly a blasphemer, a persecutor, and an insolent man; but **I obtained mercy because I did it ignorantly** in unbelief. And the grace of our Lord was exceedingly abundant, with faith and love which are in Christ Jesus. (1Timothy 1:12-14 NKJV)

Just as He did with the king and Sarah, and just as He did with the apostle Paul, God, likewise, faithfully guards over all those who are "pure in heart"—granting life and letting *nothing* touch them that can cause them lasting harm (Matthew 5:8; 1Timothy 1:12-13; Psalm 34:7; Psalm 91:9-12). With certainty, we may have a rest as we understand God's greatness on behalf of those whose hearts are "loyal to Him" (2 Chronicles 16:9). God watches over our hearts—and *He allows* that which may happen among men.

Truly, over all things, God will be exalted. According to His great mercy (Romans 2:4), and just as He did with the king and Paul, God will move within the heart of an individual *to grant* a change of mind. Not-

193

withstanding, if, according to His infinite knowledge, He is most glorified to the contrary, He also may move to harden.

THE KINDNESS AND THE SEVERITY OF THE LORD

To be sure, although *we* must choose to repent, although *we* have real responsibility to turn from our own ways and live (Ezekiel 18:31-21),[2] we also should soberly remember the Lord's place *to grant* repentance—even "eyes to see" (2 Timothy 2:25-26). He is the One who, in His kindness, must make the determination *to allow* conviction and *to bring to* a conviction of sin (Deuteronomy 29:4; Romans 2:4; Philippians 2:12-13). It was with such understanding of God's place that the apostle Paul would even speak the following warning:

> Or **do you show contempt for the riches of his kindness**, tolerance and patience, not realizing that **God's kindness leads you toward repentance**? But because of your stubbornness and your unrepentant heart you are storing up wrath against yourself for the day of God's wrath . . . . (Romans 2:4-5 NIV1984)

Thankfully, God is merciful—desiring mercy rather than sacrifice (Matthew 9:13). Nonetheless, for some, time may be up (see Isaiah 55: 6-7), and He may make a determination to harden instead. God's dealings with Israel, alone, make this point very clear. Consider the following:

> Deuteronomy 29:4
> [Concerning God's rule over the "wandering" children of Israel and *God's place* to grant understanding, Moses speaks . . .] Yet **the LORD has not given you a heart to perceive and eyes to see and ears to hear**, to this very day. (NKJV)

---

[2] See the chapter "Our Real Effect upon Our Salvation."

Isaiah 29:10-14
[Concerning God's determination to harden His people, consequential to their own stubbornness and defiance, Isaiah prophesies . . .] For **the LORD has poured out on you the spirit of deep sleep, and has closed your eyes,** namely, the prophets; and He has covered your heads, namely, the seers. . . . Therefore the LORD said: "**Inasmuch as these people** draw near with their mouths and honor Me with their lips, but **have removed their hearts far from me,** and their fear toward Me is taught by the commandment of men, therefore behold, I will again do a marvelous work among the people, a marvelous work and a wonder; for **the wisdom of their wise men shall perish, and the understanding of their prudent men shall be hidden.**" (NKJV)

Notably, according to Isaiah 29:13, **those blinded first had removed** *their own hearts* far from the Lord.

Isaiah 63:17
[Crying out concerning the judgment upon his people, Isaiah questions God (later to declare God's response and prophetic promise of restoration) . . .] "O LORD, **why have You made us stray from Your ways, and hardened our heart from Your fear?**" (NKJV)

Romans 11:7-23
[In reference to God's dealings with Israel, and in agreement with the words of Isaiah 29, the apostle Paul explains . . .] What then? Israel has not obtained what it seeks; but the elect have obtained it, and **the rest were blinded.** Just as it is written: "**God has given them a spirit of stupor, eyes that they should not see and ears that they should not hear,** to this very day." . . . **Because of unbelief they** [the once favored Israel] **were broken off,** and you stand by faith. Do not be haughty, but fear. For if God did not spare the natural branches, he may not spare you either. Therefore **consider the**

195

goodness [*chrestotes* / "kindness"][3] **and severity of God**: on those who fell, severity; but toward you, goodness, if you continue in His goodness. Otherwise you also will be cut off. And they also, *if they do not continue in unbelief* [emphasis mine],[4] will be grafted in, for God is able to graft them in again. (NKJV)

A Sovereign *Awakening*

Declaring to the Romans the work of God's judgment, Paul also proceeded to speak words of hope and perspective concerning God's sure future plan for the "elect" nation:

> For I do not desire, brethren, that you should be ignorant of this mystery, lest you should be wise in your own opinion, that **blindness in part has happened to Israel until the fullness of the Gentiles has come in**. And so all Israel [as an "elect" nation] shall be saved, as it is written [from Isaiah]: "**The Deliverer will come out of Zion, and he will turn away ungodliness from Jacob**; for this is My covenant with them, when I take away [even the judgment for] their sins." (Romans 11:25-27 NKJV)

In the fullness of time, the elect nation Israel *shall* obtain mercy (Romans 11:28-32; Jeremiah 31:29-37; Jeremiah 33:24-26)! She shall again shine glorious! No more shall the *whole* nation suffer for the sins of those ungodly. Instead, each individual shall die for his own sins (Jeremiah 31:29-30).

Just as Paul recognized, earlier prophets not only had prophesied the judgment of the children of Israel, but they also had foretold *God's*

---

[3] Ralph Earle, *Word Meanings in the New Testament* (Peabody, MA: Hendrickson Publishers, Inc., 1997), p. 198; James Strong, LL.D., S.T.D., *Strong's Complete Word Study Concordance* (Chattanooga, TN: AMG Publishers, 2004), pp. 593, 2179.
[4] **Significantly**, according to Romans 11:23 and John 10:37-38, *if* the blinded individuals of Israel would but believe and acknowledge the Father's clear workings, *they still could receive* enlightenment concerning Jesus and, thus, be grafted in again.

sovereign and merciful awakening of the hearts of His people in days to come. Not only would God harden, but also, more importantly, He would take initiative to restore. Just as Jeremiah and Ezekiel declared, respectively:

> "Behold, I will gather them out of all countries where I have driven them in My anger, in My fury, and in great wrath; I will cause them to dwell safely. They shall be My people, and I will be their God; then **I will give them one heart and one way, that they may fear Me forever**, for the good of them and their children after them. And I will make an everlasting covenant with them, that I will not turn away from doing them good; but **I will put my fear in their hearts so that they will not depart from Me. . . . I will cause their captives to return**." (Jeremiah 32:37- 44 NKJV)

> "Then **I will give them one heart, and I will put a new spirit within them, and take the stony heart out of the flesh, and give them a heart of flesh**, that they may walk in My judgments and do them; and they shall be My people, and I will be their God." (Ezekiel 11:19-20 NKJV)

God would restore! Significantly, nonetheless, although there would be a sovereign move of God to prepare the hearts of His people, there would also remain *individual* responsibility to desire His reign. Just after the promise as recorded above, God also spoke with respect to the intent of *individuals'* hearts: *"But as for those whose hearts follow the desire for their detestable things and their abominations*, I will recompense their deeds on their own heads" (Ezekiel 11:21 NKJV, emphasis mine).

Indeed, God will harden and He will awaken. In His sovereignty, He will move within the hearts of men to fulfill all that He determines to do. Yet, at the same time, *as individuals* before our Maker, we all have real ability to choose *the way we will* to go. Even today, as God is call-ing His people back unto Himself, some will—and some will not.[5]

WITH RESPECT TO THE "KING"

It was true with Pharaoh, and it was true with warring nations. It was true with the hardening of Israel, and it will also be true for others. In His sovereignty, not only must God make determination to allow a thing that happens (see "Significant Scriptures—Part 2"), but, taking initiative, God also may choose to move upon men's hearts *to make them* carry out His plans and judgments. Even as Solomon understood:

> **The king's heart is in the hand of the LORD**, like the rivers of water; He turns it wherever He wishes. (Prov-erbs 21:1 NKJV)

Truly, always, *if we will commit our ways to Him* (perhaps the first statement indicates *the king's* placing), the Lord will watch over to bring to pass His perfect desires for our lives (Psalm 37:5-6). He will work in us both the desire and the ability to do of His good pleasure—the thing that is *most* in accordance to the counsel of His will (Philippi-ans 2:13). Truly, this is a blessed hope. Yet, there may have been fur-ther meaning intended by the words of the writer.

Just as King Nebuchadnezzar came to understand (see "Significant Scriptures—Part 2"), perhaps King Solomon also was acknowledging *God's ultimate rule* over the "king" and all the influential decisions that he might make. Although the king still has choice (and *can* do contrary to God's desires, as did King Saul), God will watch over to turn the king's heart in the matters that He may determine. Consider the follow-ing accounts:

Exodus 4:21
And the LORD said to Moses, "When you go back to Egypt, see that you do all those wonders before Pharaoh

---

[5] See the article entitled "The 'Bringing Back' of a People" found within the chapter "Our Real Effect upon Our Salvation."

which I have put in your hand. **But I will harden his heart, so that he will not let the people go.**" (NKJV)

Exodus 7:3-5
"And **I will harden Pharaoh's heart**, and multiply My signs and My wonders in the land of Egypt. But Pharaoh will not heed you, **so that I may lay My hand on Egypt and bring My armies and My people, the children of Israel, out of the land of Egypt by great judgments. And the Egyptians shall know that I am the LORD** when I stretch out My hand on Egypt and bring out the children of Israel from among them." (NKJV)

Romans 9:17-18
For the Scripture says to the Pharaoh, "For this very purpose I have raised you up, **that I may show My power in you, and that My name may be declared in all the earth!" Therefore, He has mercy on whom He wills, and whom He wills He hardens.** (NKJV)

For sure, God was purposeful in the way He delivered His people. He was purposeful—in order that the Egyptians might know and all the earth might know that He alone is God (Exodus 7:5; Romans 9:17). In like manner, for the fulfillment of His determinations, God also moved upon the hearts of others:

Joshua 11:20
For it was *of the LORD* to harden their hearts [the peoples of other kingdoms], **that they should come against Israel in battle**, that He might utterly destroy them, and that they might receive no mercy, but **that He might destroy them** [the peoples of other kingdoms], as the LORD commanded Moses. (NKJV, emphasis mine)

To be sure, the Lord will raise up and He will bring down nations, just as He pleases. (See Acts 17:24-26 and Daniel 4:25-26.) Even as the following continues to make known, the Lord will be declared as God.

> Isaiah 10:5-6
> [Concerning Assyria's position as a "rod" to carry out God's punishment on a defiant Israel...] "Woe to Assyria, the rod of My anger and the staff in whose hand is My indignation. **I will send him against an ungodly nation, and against the people of My wrath I will give him charge . . .** " (NKJV)

Concerning Assyria and the works of *all* kingdoms, in truth, "a man can receive nothing unless it has been given to him from heaven" (John 3:27).[6] Yet, in particular, God was especially angry at Assyria (and so judged them) because of their haughtiness—thinking that, by their own strength, *they* had done it and, by their own wisdom, *they* had removed the boundaries of Israel. (See Isaiah 10:12-16, 33-34.) To be certain, although God does not command all things that happen (as He did with Assyria's invasion of Israel), nothing can happen unless God grants it to be so.

Particularly, and in view of Assyria's judgment, we would all do well to acknowledge God's rightful place. He watches over all the affairs of men, and *He* must choose to uphold a king's decision (Psalm 2:1-5; 33:10-13). Likewise, although God may use some nations and grant some nations to conquer, those nations still must maintain a right posture before God, lest they also fall into judgment.

In the Days to Come

Yesterday, God moved men's hearts for His purposes. Today, God moves men's hearts for His purposes. Likewise, tomorrow God also will do the same. Even as Ezekiel and the apostle John foretold, in the days to come, nations will be moved by the command of the Lord:

> Ezekiel 38:3-6
> 'Thus says the Lord GOD: "Behold, I am against you, O Gog, the prince of Rosh, Meshech, and Tubal. **I will turn you around, put hooks into your jaws, and lead**

---

[6] See also "Significant Scriptures—Part 2."

you out, with all your army, horses, and horsemen, all splendidly clothed, a great company with bucklers and shields, all of them handling swords. Persia, Ethiopia, and Libya are with them, all of them with shield and helmet; Gomer and all its troops; the house of Togarmah from the far north and all its troops—many people are with you." (NKJV)

Revelation 17:17
"For God has put it into their hearts to fulfill His purpose, to be of one mind, and to give their kingdom to the beast, until the words of God are fulfilled." (NKJV)

Indeed, God is well able to fulfill all His plans. "[He] is able to do exceedingly abundantly above all that we ask or think, *according to the power that works in us* [even within our hearts]" (Ephesians 3:20 NKJV, emphasis mine).

IN ACCORDANCE WITH THE COUNSEL OF HIS WILL

Him who works all things according to the counsel of His will, (Ephesians 1:11 NKJV)

A Just and Resourceful Creator

God is great. Nothing—not even our hearts—shall be greater than our God. So then, with regard to His workings even for plans of violence, is God also responsible for sin? Are all His ways truly just? Understanding the differences between God's judgments and personal sin, as well as noting words from Scripture, help to bring perspective. Although He will allow us to be tried by evil—although He will *give* us to be tried— *God does not make us* sin. He will not go there—to the compromise of His goodness and law. Just as the apostle James concluded:

Let no man say when he is tempted [to sin], I am tempted [to sin] of God: **for God cannot be tempted by evil, neither tempteth he [to sin] any man**: But every man is tempted, when he is drawn away of his own lust, and enticed. Then when lust hath conceived, it bringeth forth sin: and sin, when it is finished, bringeth forth death. Do not err, my beloved brethren. **Every good gift and every perfect gift is from above**, and cometh down from the Father of lights, with whom is **no variableness**, neither shadow of turning. (James 1:13-17 KJV)

God is always good. Significantly, although He will move upon men's hearts to carry out schemes of "breaking" upon others, God's workings are never to the enticement of personal or lustful sin. God's breakings and men's schemes of sin are two different things—even as, within God's law, *the "killing" of the innocent* and the legitimate *"killings" of war* are also two different things. Additionally, although the breakings from God may be difficult to receive, His breakings are also neither undeserved nor unproductive. To the contrary, and unlike that of men's sinful "evil," which "bringeth forth death" (v. 15), the breakings of God have intention for life and the "peaceable fruit of righteousness" (Hebrews 12:11). (See also Isaiah 26:10; Jeremiah 29:11; and Romans 8:28.)

God's ways with men are always just. Although He may use the evil in men's hearts to carry out His plans and His judgments—although He may even move men's hearts unto battle—*it is because of the wickedness* of those nations that they may be dispossessed or destroyed. (See Deuteronomy 9:1-5.) Just as Scripture clearly states:

He does not afflict willingly, nor grieve the children of men. To crush under one's feet all the prisoners of the earth, **to turn aside the justice due a man before the face of the Most High, or subvert a man in his cause—the LORD does not approve.** . . . Why should a living man complain, a man for the punishment of his sins? Let us search out and examine our ways, and turn back to the LORD. . . . **We have transgressed and rebelled; You have not pardoned.** (Lamentations 3:33-42 NKJV)

> **"I, the LORD, search the heart, I test the mind, even to give every man according to his ways,** according to the fruit of his doings." (Jeremiah 17:10 NKJV)

> Happy is the man who is always reverent, but **he who hardens his heart will fall into calamity.** (Proverbs 28:14 NKJV)

Significantly also, those individuals purposefully hardened and *used* by God, even for merciless acts of self-destruction, are *already* in hardened states (*as a result of* the deceitfulness of their own sins against God). Simply, in their own rebelliousness, our resourceful Creator wisely *keeps* them and *uses* them as instruments to carry out His plans.[7]

Indeed, nothing is wasted by God! All things are worked in conformity with *what He determines best to do* (Ephesians 1:11). The Lord makes the most of every opportunity, and *all His works* shall praise Him (Colossians 4:5; Psalm 146:10). Although the Lord detests the ways of the evildoer and although He surely will punish, through His foreknowledge, our Sovereign Lord will *use* the evildoer for the fulfillment of His plans. Then, in so working, *God sees to it that He is exalted even in the midst of the wickedness in men's hearts.* Just as the writer of Proverbs clearly states: "The LORD has made *all for Himself*, yes, even the wicked for the day of doom" (Proverbs 16:4 NKJV, emphasis mine).

IN CONCLUSION

In all, we should surely bow before the Lord—for He is the One "with whom we have to do" (Hebrews 4:13). We should be still and reverence ourselves before Him as we note His great rule over all.

Understanding God's authority is so important. Understanding that He will move within the heart of a king to fulfill all His desire (all that He determines to do) is not just another theology statement open for de-

---

[7] See "Inconsistencies—Part 2." Also, concerning God's like *resourcefulness* with Pharaoh and Israel, see the chapter "Another Look at Romans 9 –11."

bate, but *it is paramount in order that we might have faith* and overcome victoriously in our walk alongside the Lord. Furthermore, God has called His people to engage with Him and to do spiritual battle for His kingdom.[8] Yet, how can we do battle if we do not know the life-changing significance of our prayers? Even as Paul understood and even as he so instructed, in agreement with God, our prayers "for all men, for kings and all who are in authority" are certainly powerful to accomplish His will (1Timothy 2:1-2 NKJV).

Truly, in His sovereignty, the Lord may harden hearts—and He may move king's hearts for schemes of judgment; yet, to the contrary, and most like that of His merciful nature, the Lord will also hear our intercessions and our cries on behalf of another (Matthew 18:18; John 20:23). *As the Giver,* the Lord will move upon a sinner's heart—mercifully *granting* repentant "eyes to see"—because one righteous has cried out for mercy and has dared to stand in the gap. *Today, instead of doubters,* the Lord would call out for an army of compassionate intercessors—for friends who would *know* His greatness and His good intentions toward men—for friends who would agree with His heart of mercy and take multitudes for Him.

---

[8] See the chapter "The Place of Man's Authority."

Our Responsibility

Chapter 8

The Place of Man's Authority

Then God said, "Let Us make man in Our image, according to Our likeness; **let them have dominion** over the fish of the sea, over the birds of the air, and over the cattle, **over all the earth** and over every creeping thing that creeps on the earth." (Genesis 1:26 NKJV)

The heaven, even the heavens, are the LORD's; but **the earth He has given to the children of men**. (Psalm 115:16 NKJV)

God's kingdom rules over all (Psalm 103:19)! *He is greater* and He must allow![1] Yet, significantly, at creation, God delegated authority over the earth to man (Genesis 1:26-28; Psalm 115:16). Man, who was made in the image of God, was to join in relationship and agreement for things of the earth. At first, there was order and things were good. Sadly, however, *just as the earth had been delegated to man,* man relinquished it to Satan at the fall (2 Corinthians 4:4; Ephesians 2:2). Indeed, because of the sin of Adam, all creation has been subjected to "futility" and has suffered greatly (Romans 8:19-23). The beauty of God's creation has been enslaved to the enemy. That which God intended has been confused.

Notwithstanding these consequences, through Christ Jesus—and in alignment with God's greatness and His heart—we can, again, move in a place of triumph (2 Corinthians 2:14). Without Christ—and by God's allowance—man is under the dominion of Satan (Ephesians 2:1-3; Romans 6:16; Ephesians 6:12). *In Christ,* however, man is set free and sits with Him in heavenly places (Ephesians 1:18-23; 2:4-7; Colossians 1:13-14).

---

[1] See the chapters "Significant Scriptures—Part 1" and Significant Scriptures—Part 2."

TIMES OF RESTORATION

It's a new day! In Christ, old things are passed away—all things have been made new (2 Corinthians 5:17). Consider the power of the cross:

> **He has delivered us from the power of darkness and conveyed us into the kingdom of the Son of His love,** in whom we have redemption through His blood, the forgiveness of sins. . . . For it pleased the Father that in [Jesus] all the fullness should dwell, and **by Him to reconcile all things to Himself, by Him, whether things on earth or things in heaven, having made peace through the blood of His cross.** (Colossians 1:13-20 NKJV)

> **Having disarmed principalities and powers, He made a public spectacle of them, triumphing over them in it.** (Colossians 2:15 NKJV)

> **"When He ascended on high, He led captivity captive,** and gave gifts to men." (Ephesians 4:8 NKJV)

> "[Jesus Christ] whom heaven must receive **until the times of restoration of all things,** which God has spoken by the mouth of all His holy prophets since the world began." (Acts 3:21 NKJV)

> "He [Christ] is **able even to subdue all things to Himself.**" (Philippians 3:21 NKJV)

> Then comes the end, when He [Jesus] delivers the kingdom to God the Father, **when He puts an end to all rule and all authority and power.** For He must reign **till He has put all enemies under His feet.** The last enemy that will be destroyed is death. . . . Now when all things are made subject to Him, then the Son Himself will also be subject to Him who put all things under Him, that God may be all in all. (1 Corinthians 15:24-28 NKJV)

[In the end] "**The kingdoms of this world . . . become
the kingdoms of our Lord and of His Christ**, and He
shall reign forever and ever." (Revelation 11:15 NKJV)

Times of restoration are near—in Christ (Matthew 10:7; Acts 3:21; Colossians 1:19-22; Philippians 3:21)! Through the death of Christ Jesus,
the victory has been won! Now, however, "we do not yet see all things
put under him" (Hebrews 2:8 NKJV). Creation still *awaits* its full deliverance (Romans 8:19-22; Colossians 1:16-20).

The Place of Our Agreement

For the earnest expectation of the creation eagerly waits
for the revealing of the sons of God. (Romans 8:19
NKJV)

In the beginning, God delegated an authority over the earth to man. In
Christ, that position is restored. Consider afresh the words of Christ:

"**If two of you agree on earth** concerning anything that
they ask, it will be done for them by My Father in heav-
en. For where two or three are gathered together in My
name, I am there in the midst of them." (Matthew 18:19-
20 NKJV)

"Most assuredly, I say to you, **he who believes in Me,
the works that I do he will do also**; and greater works
than these he will do, because I go to My Father. And
whatever you ask in My name, that I will do, that the Father may be glorified in the Son." (John 14:12-13
NKJV)

"In this manner, therefore, pray: . . . **Your kingdom
come. Your will be done on earth as it is in heaven**."
(Matthew 6:9-10 NKJV)

"Assuredly, I say to you, **if you have faith and do not
doubt**, you will not only do what was done to the fig

209

tree, but also **if you say to this mountain**, 'Be removed and be cast into the sea,' **it will be done**. And whatever things you ask in prayer, believing, you will receive." (Matthew 21:21-22 NKJV)

"And **I will give you the keys of the kingdom of heaven**, and **whatever you bind on earth** will be bound in heaven, and **whatever you loose on earth** will be loosed in heaven." (Matthew 16:19 NKJV)

"Behold, I give you **the authority to trample on serpents and scorpions, and over all the power of the enemy**, and nothing shall by any means hurt you. Nevertheless do not rejoice in this, that the spirits are subject to you, but rather rejoice because your names are written in heaven." (Luke 10:19-20 NKJV)

God's kingdom rules over all! The enemy was defeated at the cross (Colossians 2:15; Philippians 3:21)! Notwithstanding these truths, *as stewards of the earth*, we must agree with the Lord for the thing He would do: "on earth as it is in heaven" (Matthew 6:10). We must come into an agreement with and appropriate His rule (Matthew 18:19-20; 1 John 5:14-15)!

Individually—in agreement with Christ—we become "loosed" from the domain of Satan! Not only so, but, *in alignment with God's will* and *"if [we] have faith and do not doubt"* (1 John 5:14-15; Matthew 21:21), we may again, through prayer, move in the place of our authority. Even mountains may be moved—if we have faith and do not doubt (Matthew 21:21). We can effect a release unto things of the earth (Ephesians 4:8).

IN CONCLUSION

God rules over all—He must give permission for a thing to occur! Notwithstanding, in His sovereignty, everything has *not* been predestined. Truly, as believers, we must be solid in this truth. We must be solid in order that we may fulfill our part—even to take our positions against the enemy (Ephesians 6:10-12; Matthew 21:21-22; Matthew 11:11-12).

Prophetically, God has given strong witness to the place of our authority. (For sure, God often will use an event to speak many different things to many different people.) *Just as* I had entered into my computer the words "The Place of Man's Authority," the earth began to shake. Virginia experienced a 5.8 magnitude earthquake. Yet—instead of fear—joyfully, at once, I felt the Lord had affirmed: **As we will know and take our positions in alignment with Him, things of the earth *will* move.** Moreover, and with great likeness, *just as* one of my daughters would rise up, one night, to take authority over her emotions unto the "the mind of Christ," Virginia experienced a 4.5!

In truth, Satan has been defeated. The victory has been won through Christ. Only now, we must take our places.[2]

---

[2] **Most significant to note**: Although, under the name of "God," some have distorted the place of spiritual warfare, in Christ Jesus, our engagement is *not* against men— "we wrestle not against flesh and blood" (Ephesians 6:12). To the contrary, ours is to be engagement *through prayer*. (See 2 Corinthians 10:3-5; Ephesians 6:12; and Ephesians 6:17-18.)

Chapter 9

Another Look at Romans 3:11
Is There *No One* Who Seeks God?

There is no one who understands, no one who seeks God. (Romans 3:11 NIV1984)

The argument some give—that man is so depraved without Jesus that he cannot even "desire" or "seek" to know God—often rests on Romans 3:11. All other passages where man is exhorted to seek and to respond to God are often dismissed as having nothing to do with salvation—just because of this passage of Scripture. Likewise, the notion that man has no responsibility in his coming to know God and that he, instead, is "irresistibly drawn"—because of a predestined decree—falls much upon the interpretation of Romans 3:11.

May we, however, take another look at the passage with the common interpretation: *"There is no one who understands, no one who seeks God"*? With a view to the normal connotation given to the English word "seek"—that of "looking for" or "going after"—might there be some other more accurate rendering of the Greek word in Romans that was translated as "seeks"?

THE GREEK WORD *EKZETEO*

Interestingly, the Greek word *ekzeteo* is the word rendered as "seeks" in Romans 3:11.[1] It shows up only seven times[2] in the New Testament (Romans 3:11; Luke 11:50, 51; Acts 15:17; Hebrews 11:6; Hebrews 12:17; 1 Peter 1:10). Yet, in contrast, the Greek word most commonly translated as "seek," *zeteo,* occurs 117 times.[3] (Please note: many times, *zeteo* is translated other than "seeks.") Some of the instances

---

[1] E. W. Bullinger, *A Critical Lexicon and Concordance to the English and Greek New Testament* (Grand Rapids, MI: Kregel Publications, 1999), pp. 679, xiii.
[2] Edward W. Goodrick and John R. Kohlenberger, *The NIV Exhaustive Concordance* (Grand Rapids, MI: Zondervan Publishing House, 1990), p. 1712.
[3] Ibid., pp. 1010-1712, 1728.

where *zeteo* appears in the New Testament are the following: Matthew 7:7, Revelation 9:6; Acts 17:27; Matthew 6:33, and John 7:18. *Zeteo* renders the meaning most commonly associated with "seeks"—that of "looking for," "investigating," "wanting," "asking for," "pursuing," and "trying to obtain."[4] *Ekzeteo*, however, appears quite different in intent and meaning.

Examine, for instance, Luke 11:50-51:

> That the blood of all the prophets, which was shed from the foundation of the world, **may be required** [*ekzeteo*] of this generation: From the blood of Abel unto the blood of Zacharias, which perished between the altar and the temple: verily, I say unto you, It **shall be required** [*ekzeteo*] of this generation. (KJV)

The thrust of the interpretation "require" is quite different from that of "seek" and "look for."

MANY WITNESSES TO THE SPECIAL MEANING OF *EKZETEO*

According to several witnesses there are, in fact, important differences between the meanings of the words *zeteo* and *ekzeteo*. Lexicons, the Septuagint, the meanings of Hebrew words (found in quoted Old Testament passages) that were rendered by *ekzeteo* in the New Testament, thesaurus and dictionary entries, and the contexts of New Testament scriptures in which the word *ekzeteo* occurs—all support the "other than 'seek' meaning" that *ekzeteo* may have.

Indeed, with agreement, Greek lexicons support the differences between *zeteo* and *ekzeteo*. For instance, Bullinger's *A Critical Lexicon and Concordance to the English and Greek New Testament* defines the more common word, *zeteo*, as follows: "to seek, seek after, look for,

---

[4] Warren C. Trenchard, *A Complete Vocabulary Guide to the New Testament* (Grand Rapids, MI: Zondervan Publishing House, 1998), p. 44.

strive to find . . . ."[5] Yet, in contrast, Bullinger states that, as well as meaning "to seek out, search out, inquire diligently, scrutinize," the verb *ekzeteo* **can mean "to require, i.e. to demand, avenge . . . "**[6] (emphasis mine). Similarly, Thayer and Smith's *The New Testament Greek Lexicon* describes meanings of *ekzeteo* as **"to demand back, require."**[7] Then, Arndt's and Gingrich's *A Greek-English Lexicon of the New Testament and other Early Christian Literature* acknowledges *ekzeteo* as meaning **"charge with, require of."**[8] Trenchard's *Complete Vocabulary Guide to the New Testament* attributes to *ekzeteo* the meaning "seek out, search for, **charge with**." [9] Finally, *Strong's Complete Word Study Concordance* renders meanings of *ekzeteo* as "demand" and "require."[10]

Next, as Bullinger's Lexicon points out, the Septuagint (a Greek translation of the Hebrew Old Testament available to the early church and often used by the writers of the New Testament)[11] also significantly gives authority to the "require" meaning that *ezketeo* may have. Notably, Hebrew verbs that render meaning like "require" often *are* represented in the Greek translation of the Old Testament by the word *ekzeteo*. Examples of such *ekzeteo* renderings are as follows: Genesis 9:5; Genesis 42:22; Ezekiel 3:18, 20; and 2 Samuel 4:11.[12]

---

[5] Bullinger, *A Critical Lexicon and Concordance to the English and Greek New Testament*, p. 678.

[6] Bullinger, *A Critical Lexicon and Concordance to the English and Greek New Testament*, p. 641.

[7] Thayer and Smith. *Greek Lexicon Entry for Ekzeteo. The KJV New Testament Greek Lexicon*. Available:
http://www.biblestudytools.net/Lexicons/Greek/grk.cgi?number+1567&version=kjv>
. [2001, June 14].

[8] William F. Arndt and F. Wilbur Gingrich, *A Greek-English-Lexicon of the New Testament and Other Early Christian Literature* (Chicago, IL: The University of Chicago Press, 1957), p. 239.

[9] Warren C. Trenchard, *A Complete Vocabulary Guide to the New Testament*, p. 44.

[10] James Strong, LL.D., S.T.D., *Strong's Complete Word Study Concordance* (Chattanooga, TN: AMG Publishers, 2004).

[11] *Great People of the Bible and How They Lived* (Pleasantville, NY: The Reader's Digest Association, Inc., 1974), pp. 253, 385.

[12] Bullinger, *A Critical Lexicon and Concordance to the English and Greek New Testament*, p. 641.

Then, equally significant, Hebrew words, corresponding to quoted material found within the New Testament, give good indication to the meanings that Greek words have. The Hebrew words *yarash* and *darash*, in particular, prove very helpful for understanding the meaning of *ekzeteo*. Consider, therefore, the following word discussions.

Ekzeteo and the Hebrew Word *Yarash*

An examination of Acts 15:17, where *ekzeteo* similarly is found—and which so reads "that the remnant of men may seek [*ekzeteo*] the Lord, and all the Gentiles who bear my name" (NIV 1984)—gives particularly helpful insight into the shade of meaning that *ekzeteo* has. Significantly, because Acts 15:16-17 states a quote from Amos 9:11-12, one might reasonably conclude that the Greek word *ekzeteo*—translated in the New Testament rendering as "may seek"—probably is also similar to the corresponding Hebrew verb in Amos that was rendered as "may possess."

In fact, the Hebrew verb translated as "possess," within Amos 9:12, is *yarash*.[13] With agreement, it is defined by Old Testament Hebrew scholar William Wilson as "to take into possession either by inheritance, gift, or violence, what belongs to others . . . ."[14] Similarly, according to Strong, this word is defined: "to take possession, to inherit, to dispossess, to drive out."[15] Then, as the *NIV Exhaustive Concordance* also demonstrates, often it is translated around the idea of "possessing" and "inheriting"[16] (e.g., Obadiah 17, 19, and 20; Nehemiah 9:22, 24, 25; and 1 Chronicles 28:8).[17] Markedly, the word *yarash* has meaning *other than* "to seek" and "to look for"! If, therefore, *yarash* reasonably helps to establish the meaning of *ekzeteo*, as is found within the passage of Acts 15:17, its meaning also may shed light on the special meaning that *ekzeteo* holds in other scriptures as well.

---

[13] Goodrick and Kohlenberger, *The NIV Exhaustive Concordance*, pp.894, 1478.
[14] William Wilson, *Wilson's Old Testament Word Studies* (Peabody, MA: Hendrickson Publishers, 1993), p. 319.
[15] Strong, *Strong's Complete Word Study Concordance*, p. 1878.
[16] Goodrick and Kohlenberger, *The NIV Exhaustive Concordance*, pp. 894, 1478.
[17] Wilson, *Wilson's Old Testament Word Studies*, p. 319.

Conclusively, according to the presumed relationship between *ekzeteo* and *yarash*, the new rendering of Acts 15:17 becomes the following: "that the remnant of men may ["possess"/ "inherit"] the Lord, and all the Gentiles who bear my name . . . ." (For sure, and concurrent with other scriptures, all who are "in Christ" do have an inheritance in the Lord!) Ultimately, as well, perhaps this rendering of Acts 15:17 also can lead to a better understanding of Romans 3:11.

Ekzeteo and the Hebrew Word *Darash*

Notably, Romans 3:11 is actually a part of a quote. The original rendering can be found in Psalm 53:2. In looking at the original Hebrew words found in Psalm 53:2, therefore, is there agreement between the verb *darash* (used in David's original writing) and the conclusions being drawn concerning a more likely intent of the Greek word *ekzeteo* (as used in the Romans quotation)? There should be agreement between the quote and the original.

Indeed, in the correlating passage of scripture in Psalm 53:2, "seeks" is derived from the Hebrew word *darash*.[18] With similarity to *ekzeteo*, *darash* often *does* appear to contain the intensity of "calling to account" and "insisting on." Clearly, according to Wilson, *darash* means "to seek, to search for; to inquire; **to demand, to require, to require or demand back**; hence to avenge, to punish."[19] Then significantly, and in agreement with the proposed "require" rendering of its paralleled Romans 3:11 Greek word, *darash* even is the verb used in the following Old Testament passages:[20]

> And surely your blood of your lives will I **require** [*darash*]; at the hand of every beast will I **require** [*darash*] it, and at the hand of man; at the hand of every man's brother will I **require** [*darash*] the life of man. (Genesis 9:5 KJV)

---

[18] Goodrick and Kohlenberger, *The NIV Exhaustive Concordance*, pp. 1010, 1420.
[19] Wilson, *Old Testament Word Studies*, pp. 351, 378.
[20] Goodrick and Kohlenberger, *The NIV Exhaustive Concordance*, pp. 273, 949, 1420.

> When thou shalt vow a vow unto the LORD thy God,
> thou shalt not slack to pay it: for the LORD thy God will
> surely **require** [*darash*] it of thee: and it would be sin in
> thee. (Deuteronomy 23:21 KJV)

> He has shown you, O man, what is good; and what does
> the LORD **require** [*darash*] of you but to do justly, to
> love mercy, and to walk humbly with your God? (Micah
> 6:8 NKJV)

Ekzeteo's corresponding Hebrew word, *darash*, surely has other meaning than just "to seek" and "to look for"! Also, further illustrations of *darash* can be found within the following: Psalm 9:12; Psalm 10:13, and 15; Psalm 24:6 (1st "seek"); 2 Chronicles 24:22; Genesis 9:5; 2 Chronicles 15:12; and Isaiah 1:17.[21]

The Thesaurus and Dictionary
Tying Meanings Together

In light of the scriptures examined in Luke 11, Acts 15, and Amos 9, which demonstrate "require" and "possess" as shades of meaning for *ekzeteo*, how do the new possibilities of meaning (given by both the scriptures and Lexicon meanings) all go together? In particular, how do they go together with the "charge with" definition of the word *ekzeteo*? Are we talking about the same word?

Roget's International Thesaurus proves very helpful in understanding the intent of English words used to express *ekzeteo*. It can be noted that the renderings of "charge with," from Arndt and Gingrich and from Trenchard, greatly do resemble the idea of "require" as found in Luke 11. According to the thesaurus, "charge" *is* a word that is given as a closely related meaning of "require."[22]

---

[21] Ibid., pp. 95, 171, 1010, 1420.
[22] *Roget's International Thesaurus*, (New York: Thomas Y. Crowell Company, 1962), pp. 1100, 551.

Webster's New World Dictionary of the American Language also is further help in understanding the intent of "charge" or "require." Two of the meanings given for "charge" are as follows: (1) "to put liability on (a person)" and (2) "to make liable for (a purchase, error, etc.)."[23] Particularly, in light of the contexts of Romans 3 and Luke 11:50-51, the "charge with" rendering of *ekzeteo* becomes more clear.

In addition, alongside the thesaurus's special entry of "charge," as a closely related word to "require," other words similarly are given (as words of closely related meaning). The words—"demand," "exact," "assess," "levy," and "impose"[24]—likewise become further help in understanding *the heart* of the word specially used in the New Testament on seven occasions. Their definitions or thesaurus word entries provide great help in getting a proper interpretation of *ekzeteo*. Only a few, however, are needed to see the emerging correlation.

"Exact," according to *Webster's New World Dictionary of the American Language*, renders some useful definitions. As an adjective, one meaning given for "exact" is "leaving no room for error, deviation, or doubt; precise; as put it on the exact spot." ("For all have sinned and come short of the glory of God" immediately comes to mind!) Then, as a verb, "exact" means (1)"to force payment of"; (2)"to demand and get by authority or force; insist on"; and (3)"to require; call for; make necessary."[25]

Interestingly, the entry for "impose" (a word related to "charge" in *Roget's International Thesaurus*) closely relates "impose" to these ideas: "put on or upon, lay on or upon, enjoin."[26] Among other helps given, "impose" continues to be stated with "levy," "exact," and "charge." Notably, as well, some closely related meanings to "impose" are also "affix," "fasten upon," and "lay hands on."[27] The idea of getting, hav-

---

[23] *Webster's New World Dictionary of the American* Language, *College Edition* (Cleveland and New York: The World Publishing Company, 1982), p. 246.
[24] *Roget's International Thesaurus*, p. 551.
[25] *Webster's New World Dictionary of the American Language*, College Edition, p. 505.
[26] *Roget's International Thesaurus*, pp. 741, 616.
[27] Ibid.

ing, and possessing comes to mind. (Remember the rendering of the verb in Acts 15:17 and Amos 9:12?)

Is there similarity between "require" and "oblige"/"obligate"? Although not obtained through the "charge" section of the thesaurus, in fact, under the word "require," "oblige" and "obligate" are also both given separately as closely related meanings.[28] Then, to "oblige," according to the thesaurus, means "necessitate, require, exact, demand, call for, say it must be done, take no denial."[29] (Continuously, there is repetition of words already noted.)

Clearly, *ekzeteo* is much different than *zeteo* (that of "looking for," "investigating," "wishing," "requesting," and "trying to obtain").[30] *Ekzeteo* "insists on," "hits the spot," "lays hold of," "possesses," "obligates," and "holds accountable for payment." *Ekzeteo* is a heavy word (whose depth, according to Hebrews 11:6, reveals the faith God both sees and rewards).

Surrounding Context

Always, one test for accuracy in the interpretation of Scripture must be as follows: Contextually, does the interpretation go along with the heart of what is being discussed? If, therefore, within Romans 3:11, *ekzeteo* can accurately render the meaning of "requiring," "holding accountable," and "obligating," that rendering *will* flow and make sense with the rest of what Paul has been saying.

Context is significant! Indeed, preceding the Romans 3:11 portion of Paul's letter, Paul is talking about what advantage, if any, the circumcised Jews "under the law" have over the uncircumcised Gentiles. He is holding the stance that, although it is certainly a privilege to have been entrusted with the "very words of God," *as far as righteousness before God goes,* Jews have no advantage. "All are under sin" (Romans 3:9). "There is no one righteous [before God], not even one" (Romans 3:10). Consider, for example, other words of Paul that preceded his statement about "seeking"—or, perhaps better stated, that preceded his statement

---

[28] Ibid., p. 1100.
[29] Ibid., p. 502.
[30] Trenchard, *A Complete Vocabulary Guide to the New Testament*, p. 44.

about "requiring," "holding accountable," and "obligating" God.

> For it is not those who hear the law who are righteous in God's sight, but it is those who obey the law who will be declared righteous. Indeed, when Gentiles, who do not have the law, do by nature **things _required_ by the law**, they are a law for themselves, even though they do not have the law, since they show that **the _requirements_ of the law** are written on their hearts, their consciences also bearing witness, and their thoughts now accusing, now even defending them. (Romans 2:13-15 NIV1984, emphasis mine)

> If those who are not circumcised keep **the law's _requirements_**, will they not be regarded as though they were circumcised? (Romans 2:26 NIV1984, emphasis mine)

Notice the reoccurring reference to "requirements" (at least with the way the translators of the NIV1984 paraphrased, according to context). Paul wants the reader to know that God's requirements _must be met_ in order to be "right" before Him and to have His favor. Paul is asserting that, _according to the law_, "doing" _all_ the various requirements—and not just "hearing" the requirements—is that which makes one righteous. Consequently, therefore, Paul asserts that "having heard the law" had given the Jews no advantage over the Gentiles as far as God's righteousness was concerned (see also James 2:10).

Never sinning is the requirement for righteousness _by the law_ ("works"). Paul concludes that "Jews and Gentiles alike are all under sin" because no one has ever _completely_ hit the mark. No one has met God's requirements, _under the law_, for being esteemed by God as "righteous." Hence, it is after a discourse concerning the law's requirements not being met, that Paul goes on to make the quote of Romans 3:11.

> There is no one righteous, not even one; there is no one who understands, **no one who seeks** [or, as I suggest,

"requires" by having reached the standard] **God**. (Romans 3:10-11 NIV1984)

In turn, from verses 12 to 18, Paul follows with ways that men have failed to meet God's righteous standards. He then recounts the verdict that "having the law" makes no difference for the Jews. All God's righteous requirements will never be able to be met "by observing the law; rather, through the law [men] become conscious of sin" (v. 20).

Next, immediately following the verdict that all alike are under sin, Paul tells us God's way of righteousness, whom it is for, and why He chose that way. Interestingly, it is at that point that Paul also declares:

> This righteousness from God comes through faith in Jesus Christ to all who believe. There is no difference, **for all have sinned and fall short of the glory of God**. (Romans 3:22-23 NIV1984)

Paul's statement about falling short of God's glory seems, in conclusion, to be a *reiteration* of the point that he made earlier in verses nine through eleven. "There is no difference." No one is righteous. **No one has hit the exact spot, "exacting" God's reward.** Contextually, therefore, it makes sense that, according to Romans 3:11, Paul might have simply begun his discourse with the declaration that no one "exacts," "requires," or "holds accountable" ("that He should repay") God.

Furthermore, the idea that no one has "obligated" God by meeting His righteous requirements similarly appears, *only a few verses later* (in Romans 4:2-5), as Paul addresses why the way of faith, and *not* that of "works," is the way that was chosen by God.

> If, in fact, Abraham was justified by works, he had something to boast about—but not before God. What does the Scripture say? "Abraham believed God, and it was credited to him as righteousness." Now **when a man works, his wages are not credited to him as a gift, but as an obligation**. However, to the man who does not work but trusts God who justifies the wicked, his faith is credited as righteousness. (NIV1984)

222

Accordingly, *if* one's own works had accomplished God's righteousness, *God would have been obligated* to pay back as a debt. Yet, the truth is: **There is no one charging anything to God's account—that He should repay**. The Lord chooses to credit righteousness as a gift, not as a debt—that no one may boast before Him! Even as Romans 11:34-35 proclaims:

> "Who has known the mind of the Lord? ["There is no one who understands" (Romans 3:11).] Or who has been his counselor? **Who has ever given to God, that God should repay him?**" ["No one requires, obligates, or holds accountable for payment—God" (Romans 3:11, paraphrase mine).] For from him and through him and to him are all things. To him be the glory forever! (NIV1984)

IN CONCLUSION

Hopefully, the reader now can see the most *probable* meaning of the Greek word *ekzeteo*, as originally was found in Romans 3:11. Hopefully also, the words of Romans 3:11 will cease to confuse and to undo all of the other scriptures that tell of God's equal provision of salvation for all men—and of the benefits of our own real choices and decisions to draw near toward Him (James 4:8).

Chapter 10

Our Real Effect upon Our Salvation

God is sovereign and He rules over all! His plans—the things He purposes *to do*—will prevail! *Whatever He determines to do* happens—and no one can thwart it (Psalm 103:19; Proverbs 19:21; Psalm 33:10-11)!

God's name will be proclaimed and exalted throughout all the earth! Every knee shall bow and every tongue shall confess that Jesus Christ is Lord—to the glory of the Father. He will have a people who love Him, who are holy and blameless, and who rise "to the praise of His glory." He will have a people whose hope of glory is only in Him.

For those who love God and will follow, it is concluded: "All things work together for [their] good," they are made to be "more than conquerors," and "no weapon formed against [them] shall prosper" (Romans 8:28, 37; Isaiah 54:17 NKJV). Even in persecution, that which the enemy may mean for harm, God will use for their good and for His glory. Truly, nothing shall harm the ones who will entrust their lives to Him.

God is so on the throne that every circumstance is under His careful scrutiny. The ones who love Him shall have all their needs met and be conformed into the image of His Son. These things are predestined by God.

In His sovereignty, however, not everything that God wills or desires happens. He *chooses* to limit Himself.[1] Even establishing the height of God's rule, together with the height of God's desire for all men, the prophet Ezekiel declared it powerfully:

> "Why will you die, O house of Israel? For I take no pleasure in the death of anyone, declares *the Sovereign* LORD. Repent and live!" (Ezekiel 18:31-32 NIV1984, emphasis mine)

---

[1] See the chapter "The *Will* of God" and the chapter "Significant Scriptures—Part 1."

Certainly, although our "Sovereign LORD" rules and does not take pleasure in the death of anyone, not all men always repent and do the things He desires. This scripture is so significant in what it says! Moreover, through the prophet Isaiah, the consequences of *our own* responses similarly are established:

> Thus says the LORD, your Redeemer, the Holy One of Israel: "I am the LORD your God, who teaches you to profit, who leads you by the way you should go. **Oh, that you had heeded My commandments! Then your peace would have been** like a river, and your righteousness like the waves of the sea. **Your descendants also would have been** like the sand, and the offspring of your body like the grains of sand; **his name would not have been** cut off nor destroyed from before Me." (Isaiah 48:17-19 NKJV)

Clearly, the Lord's desire was for the profit and the blessing of His people; nonetheless, His intent—that which He had foreseen for her—still was not fulfilled. Likewise, God's intent—the good that He has planned and foreseen for *each one of us*—also may not be fulfilled. The Lord is faithful to "lead [us] by the way [we] should go"—He will teach us "to profit." Yet, although the Lord's intent toward all men has been for good, our responses toward His initiatives shall have very real effects.

THE ISSUE OF *CHOICE*

It has been God's highest desire that we have relationship with Him—that we know Him and love Him—and that we enjoy Him fully (1 Timothy 2:4; 2 Peter 3:9). It has been God's desire that we love Him with all our heart, soul, mind, and strength (Deuteronomy 6:5; Mark 12:30). And yet, just as with any human relationship, it is not a heartfelt relationship that has no choice. Accordingly, *God has given us a choice—so that we might choose to love him.*

In truth, according to Romans 1:18-32, it is clear that, even by what has been made, God has reached out and revealed Himself unto *all* men—so that *all* have had an opportunity to fully know Him and to give Him due thanks (vv. 19-21). Because not all men know Him, it has not been His doing. To the contrary, *it is the ungodly* who have "[suppressed] the truth" (v. 18) and "exchanged the truth of God for a lie" (v. 25). It is the ungodly who are responsible—so that "men are without excuse" (v. 20).[2]

What about "Total Depravity"?

Calvinist Reformed TULIP teaching concludes that, before spiritual birth in Christ, *all* men are in states of "*total* depravity," and, thus, unable to even *want* to do God's will (unless "irresistibly drawn" to want Him). It also concludes that such a depravity and being "dead in sins" are one in the same. In truth, some individuals do have *wholly* depraved minds; notwithstanding, according to Scripture, the conditions under which individuals *are* so depraved appears to be quite different than that asserted within the Calvinist TULIP teaching. Such conditions of depravity, which *are* upon certain individuals, are not universally upon all without Christ.

Notably, according to Scripture, and in contrast to the Calvinist teaching of "total depravity," *the ones thus depraved have not begun that way.* Quite the contrary, as judgment for not esteeming the revelation that initially was given, those depraved have *become* depraved. They have been *given over* to depraved minds. (See Mark 4:24-25; Luke 8:18; and Romans 1:21-22, 24, 26, and 28.)

Additionally, although some unbelievers surely are at a point of serious depravity and have no desire for what is right, not all, without Christ, share the same description of heart. According to Scripture, those individuals who *are* in such states of depravity not only "know God's righteous decree that those who do such things deserve death"—and continue to do them—but they "also approve of those who practice them" (Romans 1:32 NKJV). These ones have *no desire* for what is right. **Yet, significantly,** as the writer of Romans also later would explain the powerlessness of the law for fulfilling God's righteousness—even with respect to his own condition apart from Christ—he did *not*

---

[2] See the greater discussion of Romans 1, entitled "Man's Refusal of Available Grace," within the chapter "Inconsistencies—Part 2."

share that same description of depravity. Quite the opposite, the writer had *a strong desire* to follow God's commands:

> We know that the law is spiritual; but I am unspiritual, sold as a slave to sin. I do not understand what I do. **For what I want [*thelo*] to do I do not do, but what I hate to do. . . . For I have the desire [*thelo*] to do what is good, but I cannot carry it out**. For what I do is not the good I want [*thelo*] to do; no, the evil I do not want [*thelo*] to do—that I keep on doing. . . . **For in my inner being I delight in God's law**; but I see another law at work in the members of my body, waging war against the law of my mind and making me a prisoner of the law of sin at work within my members. . . . So then, I myself in my mind am a slave to God's law, but in the sinful nature a slave to the law of sin. (Romans 7:14-15, 18, 22-23, and 25 NIV1984)[3]

As is with all men, before conversion, the apostle Paul was sold as a slave to sin (unlike the freedom in Christ referenced in Romans 6). Having said that, can it be seen that, although he continued to fail, he still had *a hunger and willingness* for God's righteousness—even before conversion from his state of spiritual death? (The Greek word *thelo* means, with certainty "to will, to wish, to desire.")[4] Just as 1 Timothy 1:13 explains, Paul had acted in ignorance in his original unbelief.

In truth, we "all have sinned and fall short of the glory of God" (Romans 3:23 NKJV). Without our lives hidden in Christ, we are all under condemnation because of the sin of the one man, Adam. We are dead in our sins, under the control of the sinful nature. We are *slaves* to sin, *powerless* to fulfill the righteous requirements of the law—no matter how much we may want to fulfill them (Romans 7:14-26). We are all in need of a savior; nonetheless, this does not mean all men are in conditions of *total* depravity—without an ability to hear or see, even upon

---

[3] Edward W. Goodrick and John R. Kohlenberger, *The NIV Exhaustive Concordance* (Grand Rapids, MI: Zondervan Publishing House, 1990), pp. 279, 1216, 1730.

[4] E.W. Bullinger, *A Critical Lexicon and Concordance to the English and Greek New Testament* (Grand Rapids, MI: Kregel Publications, 1999; orig. pub. 1908), pp. 904, 905, xiii.

their births. Likewise, men are not so bad off under the sinful nature that they cannot "hunger and thirst after righteousness" (Matthew 5:6) or seek God.[5]

What about These Scriptures?

Sadly, the following scriptures often have been cited to discount teaching that *our* choice and *our* willingness really are involved in whether we receive salvation through Jesus. For sure, when cited independent of context, these scriptures might appear to contradict the other words that tell of our responsibility to repent and to go God's way. So importantly, we shall examine the contexts in which the following passages occur.

Philippians 2:12-13

Therefore [*hoste* / "so as that"],[6] my beloved, as you have always obeyed, not as in my presence only, but now much more in my absence, work out [*katergazomai* / "effect, achieve"][7] your own salvation with fear and trembling; **for** [*gar* / "the fact is"][8] **it is God who works** [*energeo* / "to be effective, active, operative, to energize or be energized"][9] **in you both to will** [*thelo* / "to desire"][10] **and to do** [*energeo*][11] **for His good pleasure** [*eudokia* / "good pleasure"].[12] (NKJV)

---

[5] **Note:** Because of translations of Romans 3:11, some representatives of Calvinism would dismiss the notion of a *man's* ability to seek God, and, instead, suggest the premise of one's being "*irresistibly* drawn." See, therefore, the previous chapter "Another Look at Romans 3:11," where a more likely rendering of the Greek verb *ekzeteo* is discussed. Also, see "Inconsistencies—Part 2."

[6] Bullinger, *A Critical Lexicon and Concordance to the English and Greek New Testament*, pp. 871, xiii.

[7] Ibid., pp. 899, xiii.

[8] Ibid., pp. 296, xiii.

[9] Ibid., pp. 899, xiii.

[10] Ibid., pp. 884, xiii.

[11] Ibid., pp. 231, xiii.

[12] Ibid., pp. 589, xiii.

Indeed, the true and great significance of Paul's admonition can be established through an examination of context and the original words used. First and notably, the beginning of verse 12 uses the Greek word *hoste*, which means "so as that, marking the result . . . representing it as a necessary and logical consequence."[13] So, in consequence to Jesus' great sacrifice and His being "highly exalted" by the Father—so that "every knee should bow" and "every tongue should confess that [He] is Lord" (vv. 9-11)—Paul would remind the Philippians, in a fear of the Father, to effect their salvation through a continued obedience to *the Lord* Jesus Christ.

Furthermore, because verse 13 begins with the Greek word *gar*, which, according to Bullinger, means "the fact is, in fact . . . expressing the reason, cause, motive, principle, etc. of what has been previously said,"[14] the rest of verse 13 must follow to interject the principle by which maintaining a fear of God will occur. For certain, while noting God's *continued* place to grant us the "eyes to see" and the ability "to desire and to do" His will, we *shall* maintain a proper fear of God.

Truly, considering our Savior, we must never forget—and never let complacency set in. We must keep a holy regard for the work of Christ and, with it, a holy fear of God—who has now exalted Jesus to the place high above all other names.[15]

Isaiah 65:1

"I was sought [*darash* / "to tread or frequent"; "require"][16]by those who did not ask for Me; I was found by those who did not seek Me. I said, 'Here I am, here I am,' to a nation that was not called by My name.' " (NKJV)

---

[13] Ibid., pp. 871, xiii.

[14] Ibid., pp. 296, xiii.

[15] See Paul's words from Hebrews 10:26-31, the related discussions of Romans 2:4 within the chapter "Inconsistencies—Part 2," and the chapter "God's Sovereignty Over the Hearts of Men."

[16] James Strong, LL.D., S.T.D., *Strong's Complete Word Study Concordance* (Chattanooga, TN: AMG Publishers, 2004), pp. 1383, 1841.

What about seeking? Is there inconsistency, here, by the description—"who did not seek Me"? Again, there need not be—if taken with context and with what other words also clearly say. Just as God's words through Isaiah would continue to explain, although Israel had "sought," it was not God's way (v. 2)—for "she did not seek it [God's righteousness] by faith" (Romans 9:32).

Hence, even much like the context surrounding the upcoming Romans 9:16 scripture passage, the words of Isaiah speak concerning a shift in God's favor, from the highly regarded position that earlier had been exclusively upon Israel, unto a position of favor unto the nations (Psalm 22:27-28).[17] **Yet, most significantly**, the prophet Isaiah was speaking in regards to God's relationship toward *nations*, and *not* His relationship toward individuals.

Romans 9:16

So then it is not of him who wills [*thelo*],[18] nor of him who runs [*trecho* / "to run, hasten, hurry"][19] but of God who shows mercy. (NKJV)

Significantly, all of Romans 9 is in the context of why God's favor had seemingly departed from the people of Israel. Had God's word failed? Had He been unjust? Had God suddenly changed?

In response to those questions, Paul would demonstrate the consistency of God's ways and declare, by example of Esau and Jacob, the truth that God has always chosen with whom His name will dwell. Man has had nothing to do with it. Then, it is in response to the question of

---

[17] For a deeper consideration of context and of Israel's continued place on God's heart, see Romans 9:25-26, Romans 9:30-32, and the chapter "Another Look at Romans 9 –11." Also, for further examination of the special "exacting," "reaching," and "possessing" tone of *darash*—which, here, was simply rendered as "sought"—see the previous chapter "Another Look at Romans 3:11."

[18] Bullinger, *A Critical Lexicon and Concordance to the English and Greek New Testament*, pp. 884, xiii.

[19] Ibid., pp. 653, xiii.

God's justness, in choosing a righteousness apart from "the works of the law" (vv. 11-13, 30-32), that Paul would speak the words of Romans 9:16. Reminding the reader that God is God and He will "have mercy on whom [He will] have mercy" (v.15), Paul would proclaim the sobering truth:

> It does not matter what man wants. It does not matter how much effort and zeal there may be. *It will be God's way. It is up to God to whom He wants to show mercy.* (Paraphrase mine)

Although Israel sought hard and had a zeal for God (Romans 9:31-32; 10:1-3), the *way* God had chosen was a "righteousness that is of faith" (Romans 9:30), and not "the works of the law" (Romans 9:32). God would only show mercy *to those who would look to Him.* These, alone, would be His people. As Romans 9:16 declares: "It does not, therefore, depend on man's desire or effort [his works], but on God's mercy" (NIV 1984).[20]

<h2 style="text-align:center">John 15:16</h2>

> "You did not choose Me, but I chose you and appointed you that you should go and bear fruit, and that your fruit should remain, that whatever you ask the Father in My name He may give you." (NKJV)

First of all, it is noteworthy that the words of John 15:16 were words spoken privately between Jesus and eleven of His disciples on the night of the Passover meal. In fact, all the words of John 13 – 17 appear to have just been spoken to his closest disciples. In chapter 13, however, one change occurs. Judas is recorded as leaving.

Jesus' words about *His choice* are true. The disciples were chosen in more than one sense. They had been given eyes to see who Jesus is. The Father had enabled them to see. (Note: although the Father does

---

[20] See a more complete discussion of Romans 9 within the chapter entitled "Another Look at Romans 9 – 11."

not choose to reveal Jesus to everyone, that decision is not "unconditionally" predestined.)[21] Also, they had been honored by being personally selected to walk with Jesus from the beginning of His ministry so that they could be His special witnesses (see verse 27). The disciples were never to take their appointed positions in Him lightly. They were to hold their positions in great humility and gratitude.

Then, contextually, the words of John 15:16 seem to have been spoken not only as comfort, but as *special admonition* for the disciples. Significantly, Jesus had spoken the words to the disciples *after* His warnings to them about remaining in Him, bearing fruit, and remaining in His love. (See verses 1-14.) Specially, the disciples had been entrusted with much, and much would be required of them (John 15:15; Luke 12:48). The disciples had been appointed to bear fruit that would last.

Again, the fact that the disciples were chosen is nothing to dispute. It is only unclear whether Jesus was referring just to their appointed positions as His special witnesses or to the Father's choice in revealing the Son to them. Even so, the words of John 15:16 do not undo our very real responsibility and choice to have demonstrated a repentant heart first.

A Multitude of Witnesses
To the Significance of Choice

The Great Flood
Because of Men's Choices

Then the LORD saw that wickedness of man and was great in the earth, and that every intent of the thoughts of his heart was only evil continually. And the LORD was *sorry* that He had made man on the earth, and He was *grieved in His heart*. So the LORD said, "I will destroy man whom I created from the face of the earth, both man and beast, creeping thing and birds of the air, for I

---

[21] See also the chapter "Significant Scriptures—Part 2."

233

am sorry that I have made them." (Genesis 6:5-7 NKJV,
emphasis mine)

Genesis 6:5-7 is so significant in what it conveys about man's responsibility to choose. God was "sorry" and "grieved in His heart" that He
had made man upon the earth. Surely, God had not made a mistake in
His creation—for all His creation had been "good" (Genesis 1). Quite
the contrary, it was *the choices of man* that had caused Him grief—"for
all flesh had corrupted *their* way on the earth" (Genesis 6:12 NKJV,
emphasis mine).

Men's Real Effect to Change God's Mind
God's Response to Hezekiah's Plea

Accordingly, King Hezekiah cried out wholeheartedly—and God added
to him fifteen more years upon the earth:

> In those days Hezekiah was sick and near death. And
> Isaiah the prophet, the son of Amoz, went to him and
> said to him, "Thus says the LORD: 'Set your house in or-
> der, for you shall die and not live.' " Then Hezekiah
> turned his face toward the wall, and prayed to the LORD,
> . . . And Hezekiah wept bitterly. And the word of the
> LORD came to Isaiah, saying, "Go and tell Hezekiah,
> 'Thus says the LORD, the God of David your father: I
> have heard your prayer, I have seen your tears; surely **I
> will add to your days** fifteen years.' " (Isaiah 38:1-5
> NKJV)

To be sure, God is not limited by time, and, having foreknowledge, He
can see the end from the beginning. Likewise, always, whatever God
determines to do shall stand. Notwithstanding, as the account of Hezekiah demonstrates, we do have an effect and can change God's mind.
Even through the mouth of Jeremiah, the Lord declared the real effect
that men can have upon His plans:

> "The instant I speak concerning a nation and concerning
> a kingdom, to pluck up, to pull down, and to destroy it,

234

if that nation against whom I have spoken turns from its evil, I will relent of the disaster that I thought to bring upon it. And the instant I speak concerning a nation and concerning a kingdom, to build and to plant it, if it does evil in My sight, so that it does not obey My voice, then I will relent concerning the good with which I said I would benefit it." (Jeremiah 18:7-10 NKJV)

With God is genuine interaction. (See Jeremiah 19:5.) With God is true possibility.

"Perhaps everyone will listen and turn from his evil way, **that I may relent** concerning the calamity which I purpose to bring on them because of the evil of their doings." (Jeremiah 26:3 NKJV)

Even as within healthy human relationships, there is openness and flexibility in God's dealings with men. Moreover, the choices of men are significant. Even after God has devised a plan, that plan still may be forfeited because of men's choices. And yet, God can foresee . . .

Foremost, we must acknowledge the vastness of the dimensions of God! God is God and He is not like us! The mind of God is awesome and his ways are past finding out (Romans 11:33-34)! Yet, although He has foreknowledge,[22] He seems to limit Himself to engage in real relationship with men. Indeed, according to Scripture, God may even change His mind as a real result of men's actions.

Jesus—Our Ultimate Example

". . . My judgment is just **because I do not seek My own will but the will of the Father who sent Me.**" (John 5:30 NKJV, emphasis mine)

"Therefore My Father loves Me, because I lay down My life that I may take it again. **No one takes it from Me,**

---

[22] See the chapter "The Foreknowledge of God."

but I lay it down of Myself. I have power to lay it down, and I have power to take it again. This command I have received from My Father." (John 10:17-18 NKJV)

". . . Nevertheless, **not my will, but Yours**, be done." (Luke 22:42 NKJV)

Jesus had *choice.* Even with regard to His most significant work on the cross, Jesus had the choice to do God's will. He gave His life—they did not take it (Mark 14:62-64; John 10:17-18). Likewise, *even as Jesus chose* to lay down His life for us, we too—in following His example—must choose to lay down our lives for Him (Mark 8:34; John 10:4; John 13:15-17; 1 Peter 2:21).

The Necessity of Agreement

"Can two walk together, **unless they are agreed**?" (Amos 3:3 NKJV)

". . . **If two of you agree on earth** concerning anything that they ask, it will be done for them by My Father in heaven. For where two or three are gathered together in My name, I am there in the midst of them." (Matthew 18:19-20 NKJV)

"In this manner, therefore, pray: . . . Your kingdom come. Your will be done on earth as it is in heaven." (Matthew 6:9-10 NKJV)

The Lord has (for each one of us) a "good and acceptable and perfect will" (Romans 12:2)—and yet, although it is available, we still must embrace. Just as the disciples were taught to pray—"Your kingdom come . . . Your will be done"—this, too, is to be our constant prayer. We must agree with the Lord for the thing He would do.

For a fact, whatever plan the Lord has for us—will be received only as we have aligned ourselves with Him (Romans 12:2; James 1:5-7; James

4:3; Psalm 37:4-5; 1 John 5:14-15). In order first to begin a relationship with the Father through Jesus, there must be an agreement in faith with what was declared about His Son. (Although Jesus died on the cross to atone for the sins of the world, salvation only will be realized by those individuals who will *agree* in faith.) Likewise, in all our prayers, *if* we will agree with what God has said—both by desiring it and by having a faith in *His* ability to perform it—we shall surely have it. Truly, our God is relational—He moves on the basis of agreement. And for real agreement, there also must be choice.[23]

The Witness of Scripture

To be sure, *man* is the one responsible for whether he knows God's life or not.[24] The following scriptures continue the point:

John 7:17
"If anyone chooses [*thelo*] **to do God's will** [*thelema*], he will find out whether my teaching comes from God or whether I speak on my own."[25] (NIV1984)

Significantly, even as the Jews debated His identity, Jesus rested in a knowledge that those genuinely wanting to follow God would surely come to the truth and know Him for who He is.

Isaiah 56:3-5
Let no foreigner who has bound himself to the LORD say, "The LORD will surely exclude me from his people." And let not any eunuch complain, "I am only a dry tree." For this is what the LORD says: "To the eunuchs who keep my Sabbaths, **who choose** [*bachar* / "to choose, select, prefer"][26] **what pleases** [*chaphets*][27] **me** and hold

---

[23] Concerning the place of man's agreement, see also the chapter entitled "The Place of Man's Authority."

[24] See "Man's Refusal of Available Grace" in the chapter "Inconsistencies—Part 2."

[25] Goodrick and Kohlenberger, *The NIV Exhaustive Concordance*, pp. 197, 1255, 1730.

[26] Ibid., pp. 197, 1395; William Wilson, *Wilson's Old Testament Word Studies* (Peabody, MA: Hendrickson Publishers, 1993), p. 76.

fast to my covenant—to them I will give within my temple and its walls a memorial and a name better than sons and daughters; I will give them an everlasting name that will not be cut off." (NIV1984)

Deuteronomy 30:19-20
"This day I call heaven and earth as witnesses against you that **I have set before you life and death, blessings and curses. Now choose** [*bachar*][28] **life**, so that you and your children may live and that you may love the LORD your God, listen to his voice, and hold fast to him. For the LORD is your life, and he will give you many years in the land he swore to give to your fathers, Abraham, Isaac and Jacob." (NIV1984)

2 Chronicles 15:1-2
Now the Spirit of God came upon Azariah the son of Oded. And he went out to meet Asa, and said to him: "Hear me, Asa, and all Judah and Benjamin. **The LORD is with you while you are with Him. If you seek Him, He will be found by you; but if you forsake Him, He will forsake you.**" (NKJV)

Isaiah 65:12
"Therefore I will number you for the sword, and you shall all bow down to the slaughter; because, when I called, you did not answer; when I spoke, **you did not hear, but did evil before My eyes, and chose that in which I do not delight.**" (NKJV)

Isaiah 66:3-4
". . . **Just as they have chosen their own ways**, and their soul delights in their abominations, so will I choose their delusions, and bring their fears on them; because, when I called, no one answered. When I spoke, they did

---

[27] Goodrick and Kohlenberger, *The NIV Exhaustive Concordance*, pp. 889, 1455.
[28] Ibid., pp. 197, 1395.

not hear; but they did evil before My eyes, **and chose that in which I do not delight**." (NKJV)

Luke 13:34-35
"O Jerusalem, Jerusalem, you who kill the prophets and stone those sent to you, **how often I have longed** [*thelo*] to gather your children together, as a hen gathers her chicks under her wings, **but you were not willing** [*thelo*]."[29] (NIV1984)

For the life God would give, the verdict seems clear. *We* must be willing—*we* must choose.

GOD'S *DRAWING* AND OUR FAITH

In close relation to the *perseverance of the saints* teaching (which states that the elect are *made* to persevere in faith until the end), it is taught by Calvinist teaching that, because of "*total* depravity," even the faith one must have toward God for initial salvation is *made* to happen (Calvinist teaching of *irresistible grace*). In truth, according to Jesus' own words to the Jewish people who did not believe in Him (see John 6:37, 44, and 65), all are not given revelation of who Jesus is (in order that they might believe on Him for salvation). Only those "given" to Him by the Father may come to Him.[30] From other statements made by Jesus, however, *it is not right to conclude that those unable to see Jesus had been unable to respond to the Father and to have faith toward the Father first*. Consider the rest of Jesus' words concerning those given eyes to see the Son:

John 6:44-45
"No one can come to me unless the Father who sent me draws him, and I will raise him up at the last day. It is written in the Prophets: 'They will all be taught by God.' **Everyone who listens to the Father and learns from him comes to me**." (NIV1984)

---

[29] Ibid., pp. 680, 1730; pp. 1256, 1730.
[30] See "Significant Scriptures—Part 2."

John 7:17
**"If anyone wills to do His will, he shall know con-
cerning the doctrine**, whether it is from God or whether
I speak on My own authority." (NKJV)

John 10:37-38
"If I do not do the works of My Father, do not believe
Me; but if I do, **though you do not believe Me, believe
the works,** *that you may know and believe* ["that you
may know and continue to know" IGNT] **that the Father is in Me, and I in Him.**" (NKJV, emphasis mine)

Those given eyes to see who Jesus is (who, in the end, also will be presented unto the Bridegroom) appear to be ones who have responded
well to things already given by the Father—ones who have truly listened to the Father and decided to go His way. Just as Romans 1:18-32
states, *all have had* the revelation needed for responding to and calling
out to the Father.[31]

Quite significantly, within the words of John 10:37-38, Jesus spoke of
the reason some do not see Him, and of *the hope still remaining* for
those who do not. If only they would but acknowledge the Father's
workings in things that *can* be seen, they might receive further revelation *in order to believe* on the Son.

God is so great in His mercy! We should continue to pray that people
would fear God—so that they might receive His gift of grace.

What about Ephesians 2:8-9 and Hebrews 12:2?

What about Ephesians 2:8-9 and Hebrews 12:2? Although these scriptures are often cited to support the teaching that "faith," itself, is simply
given by God—or, conversely, not given by God—there is other very
likely meaning to these scriptures.

---

[31] See the discussion of Romans 1 within "Inconsistencies—Part 2."

Ephesians 2:8-9

> For by grace are ye saved through faith; and that not of
> yourselves: it is the gift of God: Not of works, lest any
> man should boast. (KJV)

Some believe this scripture specifically makes an issue of "faith," itself, not being (in any way) from us, but being a gift from God alone. From this scripture, it is also taken further, by some, that if faith is not seen simply as a gift of God, one is attributing *to man* a "work" for which man can boast. Although it is understandable how this passage of scripture might be so interpreted, other very likely meaning should be considered.

Context is important. As was Paul's great emphasis at other times in other letters, in this portion of Paul's writing, Paul's emphasis is that of *God's initiative*—God's great work of salvation through sending Jesus to die on the cross for our sins. Likewise, in similar fashion to other statements he had made (see Romans 3:27 – 4:16), Paul is making issue that this great salvation is all by God's grace and *not by any of our works* ("lest any man should boast").

Noting the context, then, the words that appear have other probable application. Instead of referring to "faith," **the demonstrative pronoun "that," can very easily be referring to the salvation** that, "by grace" is being received "through faith." Such a rendering would flow contextually. By the words—"and that not of ourselves: it is the gift of God"—could Paul not be, just as likely, expanding his thought concerning the *salvation* being extended to us by grace? Grace, itself, *is* often described as undeserved, unmerited favor. Grace *is* "not of [our]selves." It is an undeserved *"gift of God."*

Finally, contrary to the assertion some would make that faith (for which we do have responsibility) might be a "work" of ours for which *we* could boast, Romans 3:27 also says something quite different:

> **Where is boasting then? It is excluded.** By what law? of works? Nay: but **by the law of faith.** (KJV)

241

As the scripture says, faith is nothing of which to boast. *Faith is simply looking to God, abandoning one's self to God and His promises, and saying, "I rely totally on You."* There is none of *our* works; there is an abandonment of our works. Such is the posture of those who call out to Him.

Hebrews 12:2

Looking unto Jesus the author and finisher of our faith . . . (KJV)

By themselves, the words "Jesus the author and finisher of our faith" might seem to support the teaching that Jesus "makes" people have the faith to begin and to finish the course. Contextually, however, Paul is not making that assertion. Instead, as part of an encouragement to lay aside sin and to "run with patience the race" set before them, Paul encourages believers that, as they continue to look to Jesus (who struggled with their sin and conquered it by His blood), they also will continue to conquer sin in their lives and finish the race ("the faith").

For certain, the walk of the righteous *is* "from faith to faith" (Romans 1:17). It is one of "continuing in the faith" (Colossians 1:23). Just as one begins the faith by *looking to Jesus*, he must end that way— looking unto Jesus and following Him until the end. According to the rules (2 Timothy 2:5), this is the only way the race can be completed.

A RIGHT POSTURE
TO BE USHERED INTO THE PRESENCE OF THE KING

We cannot just barge in on a king. We must be *ushered* into his presence. We must be postured rightly in order to enter into his presence. Likewise, in order for men to be saved, hearts must be *prepared* for the way of the Lord:

> . . . **[Who] acts for the one who waits for Him**. You meet him who rejoices and does righteousness, **who remembers You in Your ways**. (Isaiah 64:4-5 NKJV)

"**I, the LORD, search the heart**, I test the mind, **even to give every man according to his ways** according to the fruit of his doings." (Jeremiah 17:10 NKJV)

The voice of one crying in the wilderness: "**Prepare the way of the LORD**; make straight in the desert a highway for our God." (Isaiah 40:3 NKJV)

The preparations of the heart belong to man, but the answer of the tongue is from the LORD. (Proverbs 16:1 NKJV)

To be prepared for the kingdom and in order to receive the life that is given *in Christ*—our hearts first must be found in alignment with the Father: fearing Him, seeking Him, and repenting of our ways. Agreeably, few Calvinists would dispute the necessity of these postures. Often they have disagreed, however, concerning our own real responsibility as to whether these postures shall occur. And yet, according to Scripture, it is very clear. *We* are the ones held accountable for these postures. We are the ones—and not God (Proverbs 16:1).[32]

Aligning Ourselves with Hearts that Will Listen

Significantly, as we will listen *to obey Him*, our Father will speak to us more: *"[Our] ears shall hear a word [even Jesus] behind [us], saying, 'This is the way, walk in it' "* (Isaiah 30:21 NKJV). It is so vital that we listen to respond when God speaks. The words of Jesus declare:

Luke 8:18
"Therefore **consider carefully how you listen. Whoever has will be given more**; whoever does not have, even what he thinks he has will be taken from him." (NIV 1984)

---

[32] For further consideration of man's real initiative toward the preparation of his heart, see also the following: Lamentations 3:40-41; 2 Chronicles 12:14; 19:3; 27:6; 30:18-20; and 1 Kings 8:39. Also, note the upcoming discussion entitled "The 'Bringing Back' of a People" and the chapters "Another Look at Romans 3:11" and "God's Sovereignty Over the Hearts of Men."

John 6:44-45
"No one can come to me unless the Father who sent me draws him, and I will raise him up at the last day. It is written in the Prophets: 'They will all be taught by God.' **Everyone who listens to the Father and learns from him comes to me.**" (NIV1984)

Truly, it is the Father who gives unto Jesus. He enables us to know who Jesus is and to believe on Him for our salvation; notwithstanding, the *conditional* prerequisite for coming to Jesus is *listening to and heeding* the Father.

Additionally, the following scriptures, concerning Israel's continued unwillingness, likewise give us warning of the importance to listen to obey:

Zechariah 7:11-13
"But **they refused to heed, shrugged their shoulders, and stopped their ears** so that they could not hear. Yes, **they made their hearts like flint, refusing to hear** the law and the words which the LORD of hosts had sent by His Spirit through the former prophets. Thus great wrath came from the LORD of hosts. Therefore it happened, that **just as He proclaimed, and they would not hear; so they called out and I would not listen,**" says the LORD of hosts. (NKJV)

Ezekiel 3:5-7
"You are not being sent to a people of obscure speech and difficult language, but to the house of Israel—not to many peoples of obscure speech and difficult language, whose words you cannot understand. Surely if I had sent you to them, they would have listened to you. **But the house of Israel is not willing to listen to you because they are not willing to listen to me,** for the whole house of Israel is hardened and obstinate." (NIV1984)

Luke 16:31
[From Jesus' parable of the rich man and Lazarus.] "He [Abraham] said to him, **'If they do not listen to Moses and the Prophets, they will not be convinced even if someone rises from the dead.'** " (NIV 1984)

Luke 13:34
"O Jerusalem, Jerusalem, the one who kills the prophets and stones those who are sent to her! **How often I wanted** to gather your children together, as a hen gathers her brood under her wings, **but you were not willing!**" (NKJV)

Matthew 21:43-45
[In conclusion to the parable of the tenants, which explained Israel's rendered judgment, Jesus spoke these words.] "Therefore I tell you that **the kingdom of God will be taken away from you and given to a people who will produce its fruit. . . .**" (NIV 1984)

Can it be seen that it was Israel's continued failure to respond that caused her blessings to be given to another? (See also Matthew 21:14-15, 21:23-45, and Luke 14:16-24.) God *willed* to reach out to Israel (Luke 13:34). The condition of Israel as a whole, however, was that of an unwillingness to listen. (**Notably**, as well, according to Ezekiel 3:6, the condition found upon all unredeemed is not necessarily one of being so depraved that they cannot want to listen.)

Aligning Ourselves with Hearts of Gratitude

Israel's Failed Response—Refusing Him Who Speaks

Although they knew God, they **did not glorify Him as God, nor were thankful**, . . . And even as they did not like to retain God in their knowledge, God gave them over to a debased mind . . . (Romans 1:21-28 NKJV)

245

See that you do not refuse Him who speaks. (Hebrews 12:25 NKJV)

In a relationship, if one does not feel appreciated or heard, the temptation may be that of not talking anymore. Although this is not the best thing for any growing relationship, there may be a time to stop talking if the other is ungrateful and does not want to listen. Then, when that person does not receive the words once taken for granted, he may become hungry for those words once again.

Similarly, the Lord's reaction to those who do not receive Him is one of *pulling back*. We have an example in the Lord's relationship with His people (Zechariah 7:11-13). According to the apostle Paul, until the fulfillment of the "times of the Gentiles," there has been *a pulling back* from Israel (Romans 11:25). God's redemptive intent, nonetheless, has been to provoke Israel to jealousy (Romans 11:11)—in order that they might become thankful and listen once again.

"[Jesus] came to His own, and His own did not receive Him" (John 1:11 NKJV). Significantly, it was in response to Israel's callousness and unwillingness (Luke 13:34-35) that Jesus also declared the judgment: "*. . . You shall not see Me until the time comes when you say, 'Blessed is He who comes in the name of the Lord'*" (Luke 13:35 NKJV).

Truly, we need thankful hearts. We should all fear and examine the manner in which we have received things given in God's communication of love toward us. Have we been appreciative?

Furthermore, the Lord will test us—even exposing pride—by how we respond to others whom He may put into our path. We must be watchful—because He just may be doing something, and it may not be *our* way. Because King Jesus did not come the way the children of Israel had expected, they did not receive Him. Even as Jesus spoke: "[They] did not know the time of [their] visitation" (Luke 19:44 NKJV). Jesus did not look the way they thought He should look, nor did He say the things they thought He should say. He had "nothing in his appearance that [they] should desire him" (Isaiah 53:2 NIV1984).

The apostle Paul gave us all good warning to heed. Accordingly, we should all fear, remaining careful never to refuse Him who speaks, but, instead, to listen with intent and thankful hearts.

Aligning Ourselves in the Fear of God
With a High Regard toward His Greatness

The fear of God is to know God's greatness—to know that *He is worthy*. The fear of God responds with intent to do what He commands. Then, to "whoever has . . . more will be given" (Mark 4:23-25 NKJV). Even as Scripture specifically declares:

Proverbs 9:10
The fear of the LORD is the beginning of wisdom . . . (NKJV)

Proverbs 19:23
The fear of the LORD leads to life, and he who has it will abide in satisfaction: he will not be visited with evil. (NKJV)

Psalm 33:18
Behold, **the eye of the LORD is on those who fear Him**, on those who hope on His mercy, to deliver their soul from death, and to keep them alive in famine. (NKJV)

Psalm 103:11-18
For as the heavens are high above the earth, **so great is His mercy toward those who fear Him**; . . . As a father pities his children, so the LORD pities his children, so **the LORD pities those who fear Him**. For He knows our frame; He remembers that we are dust. . . . But **the mercy of the LORD is from everlasting to everlasting on those who fear Him** . . . (NKJV)

247

Acts 10:34-35
"In truth I perceive that God does not show partiality. But in every nation **whoever fears Him and works righteousness is accepted by Him.**" (NKJV)

It is as we will regard *His greatness* that we may receive from God. There are counterfeits, but the wisdom of God—that which remains—will only be received in humility and contriteness. Just as He did in the past, the Lord would engage us now:

> "Have you entered the springs of the sea? Or have you walked in search of the depths? Have the gates of death been revealed to you? Or have you seen the doors of the shadow of death? Have you comprehended the breadth of the earth? Tell Me, if you know all this." (Job 38:16-18 NKJV)

> ". . . I dwell in a high and holy place, with him who has a contrite and humble spirit, **to revive the spirit of the humble, and to revive the heart of the contrite ones.**" (Isaiah 57:15 NKJV)

> ". . . And where is the place of My rest? . . . **But on this one I will look: on him who is poor and of a contrite spirit, and who trembles at My word.**" (Isaiah 66:1-2 NKJV)

Truly, a man's posture—one of rightly regarding God's greatness—will be that which "leads to life." The fear of the Lord *is* the beginning point. The "poor in spirit" will be firstly blessed—"for theirs is the kingdom of heaven" (Matthew 5:3 NKJV).

Aligning Ourselves with Hearts of Repentance That Would Desire to Go *His* Way

Note the significance of our repentance—of our decidedly turning toward God.

248

Proverbs 14:12
There is **a way that seems right to a man, but its end is the way of death**. (NKJV)

Proverbs 14:14
The **backslider in heart will be filled with his own ways**, but a good man will be satisfied from above. (NKJV)

Isaiah 55:7-8
Let the wicked forsake his way, and the unrighteous man his thoughts; **let him return to the LORD**, and He will have mercy on him; . . . **"For My thoughts are not your thoughts, nor are your ways My ways,"** says the LORD. (NKJV)

Matthew 10:38-39
"And he who does not take his cross and follow after me is not worthy of Me. He who finds his life will lose it, and **he who loses his life for My sake will find it**." (NKJV)

James 4:4-8
. . . Whoever therefore wants to be a friend of the world makes himself an enemy of God. . . . **Therefore submit to God.** Resist the devil and he will flee from you. **Draw near to God and He will draw near to you.** (NKJV)

Matthew 3:1-3
. . . **"Repent,** for the kingdom of heaven is at hand!" For this is he who was spoken of by the prophet Isaiah, saying: "The voice of one crying in the wilderness: **'Prepare the way of the Lord; make His paths straight.'** " (NKJV)

Luke 13:3
". . . [But] **unless you repent** you will all likewise perish." (NKJV)

Acts 2:37-38
"Men and brethren, **what shall we do**?" Then Peter said to them, "**Repent**, and let every one of you be baptized in the name of Jesus Christ for the remission of sins . . . ." (NKJV)

2 Corinthians 6:17
Therefore "**Come out from among them and be separate**, says the Lord. Do not touch what is unclean, **and I will receive you.**" (NKJV)

In truth, the ways *of man* bring death—they keep us from receiving from God. In order to be postured for the Lord, and to be received by Him, there must be a wholehearted turning (Luke 3:8)—away from the wisdom of man (1 Corinthians 1:17 – 2:14).

We must agree to change our ways; and yet, thankfully, even as Psalm 10:17 declares, although we must have true willingness, seeing into the intent of our hearts, *God will continue* the necessary work to prepare our hearts for Him (even in giving us Jesus). God takes that which is committed to Him, and He completes it. He strengthens the hearts of the "contrite" ones—the "humble" who would desire to know Him (Isaiah 57:15).

Are We Truly Willing—With Intention toward Doing His Will?

". . . My judgment is just **because I do not seek My own will but the will of the Father who sent Me.**" (John 5:30 NKJV)

"**If anyone wills to do His will, he shall know concerning the doctrine**, whether it is from God or whether I speak on My own authority." (John 7:17 NKJV)

"Not everyone who says to Me, 'Lord, Lord,' shall enter the kingdom of heaven, but **he who does the will of My Father in heaven.** . . . And then I will declare to them, 'I never knew you; depart from Me, you who practice lawlessness [who have disregard for doing His pleasure]." (Matthew 7:21-23 NKJV)

Noticeably, for real repentance, there must be a *true intent* in one's heart to follow the Lord. Moreover, although "the kingdom of heaven" is larger than just our salvation, to "enter the kingdom" certainly would include our salvation. Yet, significantly, according to Matthew 7:21, without a set heart *to do* the will of the Father—*that one shall not even enter in.*

A Call for All

Indeed, *we all* must be willing. *We all* must turn. Scripture establishes this truth very sure:

Acts 17:30
"Truly, these times of ignorance God overlooked, but now **commands all men** [*anthropos* / "an individual"][33] **everywhere** to repent." (NKJV)

God *commands* "all men everywhere" to repent. He "commands" because *all individuals can repent* and come into the life He gives. There has been, and is, an "acceptable time" when *all* have had the ability to repent (2 Corinthians 6:1-2; Hebrews 4:7).[34]

Isaiah 55:6-7
Seek the LORD **while He may be found**, call upon Him **while He is near**. Let the wicked forsake his way, and the unrighteous man his thoughts; Let him return to the LORD, and He will have mercy on Him; And to our God, for He will abundantly pardon. (NKJV)

Isaiah 55:6-7 is so powerful in its life-giving entreaty! The Lord "may be found" *if* men's hearts will go after Him! Then as well, **by the cor-**

---

[33] Strong, *Strong's Complete Word Study Concordance*, pp. 967, 2025.
[34] See the discussion entitled "Man's Refusal of Available Grace" in the chapter "Inconsistencies—Part 2."

relation of *timeliness* to *seeking*, there is a substantial acknowledgment of man's real responsibility, and *not* the doctrine of *irresistible grace*.

To be sure, the Lord's mercies are great! His provision abounds; nonetheless, according to Isaiah 55:6, there is *a time upon which He may not be found*. Even as Paul also affirmed:

> We then, as workers together with Him implore you not to receive the grace of God in vain. For He says: **"In an acceptable time I have heard you, and in the day of salvation I have helped you."** Behold, now is the accepted time, behold, now is the day of salvation. (2 Corinthians 6:1-3 NKJV)

There is an acceptable day of salvation *for all*. Knowing this, we should all fear Him and be very careful to respond.

Aligning Ourselves with a Wholehearted Search

Consider the authority of the Word:

> Jeremiah 29:13
> "And you will seek me and find Me, **when you search for Me with all your heart**." (NKJV)

This is the necessary posture for receiving all that the Lord would give—for He is a jealous God. This is the posture that brings release. We must seek Him and search for Him *with all our hearts*.

> Matthew 5:6
> "Blessed are those who **hunger and thirst for righteousness**, for they shall be filled." (NKJV)

> Psalm 145:17-20
> The LORD is righteous in all His ways, gracious in all His works. **The LORD is near to all who call upon Him, to all who call upon Him in truth.** He will fulfill

the desire of those who fear Him. He also will hear their cry and save them. The LORD preserves all who love Him, but all the wicked He will destroy. (NKJV)

Acts 17:26-27
"And He has made from one blood every nation of men to dwell on all the face of the earth, and has determined their preappointed times and the boundaries of their dwellings, **so that they should seek the Lord, in the hope that they might grope for Him and find Him,** *though He is not far from each one of us."* (NKJV, emphasis mine)

Is He our heart's desire? Is He truly the cry of our heart? Do we seek the Lord so as that we grope after Him? He is not far from any of us.

As it is, because our heavenly Father is relational, *He has fashioned and given us all, individually, hearts that can relate to Him* (Psalm 33:14-15). We are not mechanical. He has fashioned our hearts with both desire and choice in order that we might all have true heartfelt relationship with Him. Our "groping after Him" and our wholeheartedly searching for Him is that which displays our love for Him and meets the requirement held before men—the requirement of a wholehearted relationship (Deuteronomy 6:5; Matthew 22:37).

Finally, the following speaks very clearly concerning the eternal significance of our affections:

Romans 2:5-11
But in accordance with your hardness and your impenitent heart you are treasuring up for yourself wrath in the day of wrath and revelation of the righteous judgment of God, who 'will render to each one according to his deeds': **eternal life to those who by patient continuance in doing good seek for glory, honor, and immortality;** but **to those who are self-seeking and do not obey the truth, but obey unrighteousness—indignation and wrath, tribulation and anguish, on every soul of man who does evil**, of the Jew first and also of the Greek; but glory,

honor, and peace to everyone who works what is good, to the Jew first and also to the Greek. For there is **no partiality with God**. (NKJV)

John 5:44
"How can you believe, who receive honor from one another, and do not **seek the honor that comes from the only God**?" (NKJV)

Truly, *we* are responsible for our actions. The Lord has shown *no partiality*, but has rendered grace to everyone who would seek to do His will.

THE "BRINGING BACK" OF *A PEOPLE* TO THE GLORY AND PRAISE OF HIS NAME

"Behold, I will gather them out of all countries where I have driven them in My anger, in My fury, and in great wrath; I will cause them to dwell safely. They shall be My people, and I will be their God; then **I will give them one heart and one way, that they may fear Me forever**, for the good of them and their children after them. And I will make an everlasting covenant with them, that I will not turn away from doing them good; but **I will put my fear in their hearts so that they will not depart from Me**. . . . **I will cause their captives to return**." (Jeremiah 32:37-44 NKJV)

Not only has Romans 3:11 been misapplied by many (note the chapter "Another Look at Romans 3:11"), but other scriptures (e.g., Deuteronomy 30:6 and Jeremiah 32:37-44) have also been cited to justify the teaching that God *makes* those individuals (who are "unconditionally elected") fear Him, seek Him, and love Him with all their hearts. Consequently, by such renderings, any real responsibility of individuals also has been dismissed. It is asserted that, apart from God's own select initiative, the ones who love God never would have even sought to know Him.

Understandably, these scriptures, at first, can lead some to wrong conclusions concerning the real responsibilities of individuals. May I suggest, however, that the scriptures used for this point of view refer, instead, to God's dealings with *the covenant group* of people with whom He displays Himself to the world—the nation Israel and His spiritual seed, the church? *As a people*, God has promised to take us through whatever is needed—in order that we might fear Him and learn to serve only Him with all our hearts.

The prophets understood the judgments that would come upon Israel; and yet they would be for redemptive purposes. Even as the prophet Isaiah spoke:

> **When your judgments come upon the earth, the people of the world *learn righteousness*.** Though grace is shown to the wicked, they do not learn righteousness; even in a land of uprightness they go on doing evil and regard not the majesty of the LORD. (Isaiah 26:9-10 NIV1984, emphasis mine)

Historically, the Lord has been at work with His chosen people, Israel, in order that they, *as a nation*, might come into His place of glory and bear His name well. Likewise, even today, *as a people*—as the spiritual seed—He is sovereignly dealing with the church in order to bring us back to Himself. The Lord is establishing Jerusalem—even His "Bride" and His church—to be unto Him "a praise in the earth" (Isaiah 62:7)!

As individuals, we *all* have the responsibility to choose and to return to the Lord. (See Deuteronomy 30:1-6, Ezekiel 11:19-21, and Malachi 3:7.) Then, if we will return to Him, even making intercession *for all His people* (Isaiah 62:6-7), He has promised to "circumcise" our hearts—that we may love Him with all our heart and soul, and so that we may live (Deuteronomy 30:6). With certainty, the Lord meets us exponentially with that which we offer Him. (See also Jeremiah 30.) Today, the Spirit is calling for His people. He is yearning for a *victorious* people—"holy and without blemish" (Ephesians 5:27 NKJV)—a people to the praise of His name.

IN CONCLUSION

God is great to do on behalf of those *whose hearts are His* (2 Chronicles 16:9)! Although individuals do have real responsibility, the burden of an individual remains light. Our responsibility rests simply in our coming into agreement with *His ways*. Our responsibility rests only in our committing *our ways* unto the Lord and then trusting in His goodness and His ability to do. Even as the psalmist wrote:

> **Commit your way to the LORD, trust also in Him, and He shall bring it to pass.** He shall bring forth your righteousness as the light, and your justice as the noonday. (Psalm 37:5-6 NKJV)

God is the One in whom we should trust, and *not in ourselves*. In His covenantal goodness toward us, He will be faithful to go way beyond us—both to cleanse us and to perfect us—as we willfully surrender unto Him.

Chapter 11

Continuing in the Faith
With Eyes Fixed *on Him*

And you, who once were alienated and enemies in your mind by wicked works, yet now He has reconciled in the body of His flesh through death, to present you holy, and blameless, and above reproach in His sight—**if indeed you continue in the faith**, grounded and steadfast, and are not moved away from the hope of the gospel which you heard . . . (Colossians 1:21-23 NKJV)

CONTINUING IN *THE DOCTRINE* "IN THE FAITH WHICH WAS ONCE FOR ALL DELIVERED"

Having begun in Christ, it is so significant how we proceed. Scripture makes clear:

> **Take heed to yourself and to the doctrine. Continue in them,** for in doing this you will save both yourself and those who hear you. (1 Timothy 4:16 NKJV)

> **Guard** what was committed to your trust, **avoiding the profane and idle babblings and contradictions of what is falsely called knowledge—by professing it some have strayed concerning the faith.** (1Timothy 6:20-21 NKJV)

> Note those who cause divisions and offenses, **contrary to the doctrine which you learned, and avoid them.** (Romans 16:17 NKJV)

> **Contend earnestly for the faith which was once for all delivered to the saints.** (Jude 3 NKJV)

Holding fast the faithful word as he has been taught, that he may be able, **by sound doctrine, both to exhort and convict whose who contradict**. (Titus 1:9 NKJV)

I marvel that you are turning away so soon from Him who called you in the grace of Christ, to a different gospel, which is not another . . . **But even if we, or an angel from heaven, preach any other gospel to you than what we have preached to you, let him be accursed.** (Galatians 1:6-9 NKJV)

Brethren, if anyone among you wanders from the truth, and someone turns him back, let him know that he who turns a sinner from the error of his way will **save a soul from death and cover a multitude of sins**. (James 5:19-20 NKJV)

Whoever transgresses [goes ahead] and does not abide in the doctrine of Christ does not have God. **He who abides in the doctrine of Christ** has both the Father and the Son. (2 John 9 NKJV)

Therefore **let that abide in you which you heard from the beginning. If what you heard from the beginning abides in you**, you also will abide in the Son and in the Father. And this is the promise that He has promised us—eternal life. (1 John 2:24-25 NKJV)

Even as the Word declares, that which we heed is very important.

A Faith that Would Forsake All Others

When we were powerless, Christ died for us—*the gift of God* is eternal life through Jesus Christ our Lord (Romans 5:6; 6:23). To as many as receive Him, to them is given power to become the children of God (John 1:12). Through Christ's death, we are restored into glorious relationship (Romans 5:6-11; 2 Corinthians 5:14-21; 1 Peter 3:18; Colossians 1:19-23)! Even so, there remains a cost. Consider the following:

"And whoever does not bear his cross and come after Me cannot be My disciple. For which of you, intending to build a tower, does not **sit down first and count the cost**, whether he has enough to finish it . . . So likewise, **whoever of you does not forsake all that he has cannot be My disciple**." (Luke 14:27-33 NKJV)

"Again, the kingdom of heaven is like treasure hidden in a field, which a man found and hid; and for joy over it he goes and sells all that he has and buys that field. Again, the kingdom of heaven is like a merchant seeking beautiful pearls, who, **when he had found one pearl of great price, went and sold all that he had and bought it**." (Matthew 13:44-46 NKJV)

"He who loves father or mother more than Me is not worthy of Me. And he who loves son or daughter more than Me is not worthy of Me. **And he who does not take his cross and follow after Me is not worthy of Me. He who finds his life will lose it, and he who loses his life for My sake will find it**." (Matthew 10:37-39 NKJV)

"**No one can serve two masters**; for either he will hate the one and love the other, or else he will be loyal to the one and despise the other. You cannot serve God and mammon." (Matthew 6:24 NKJV)

But what things were gain to me, these I have counted loss for Christ. Yet indeed I also count all things loss for the excellence of the knowledge of Christ Jesus my Lord, for whom I have suffered the loss of all things, and count them as rubbish, that I may gain Christ. (Philippians 3:7-8 NKJV)

Is He worth it? Even as Paul, would we lay aside *all else*—in order that we might have Christ? There is a cost (Mark 10:17-27; Mark 8:34-37). *His* is a faith that has counted the cost and knows that *He is worth it*.

To Know *He Is*

I found myself doubting, one day, and I was greatly shaken. *God Is*. We must believe and not doubt (Hebrews 11:6; James 1:6-7). When the things of the world have become more real to us than God—there is a problem. A stepping over still is needed unto "things above" (Colossians 3:1-2).

To really know and *connect* with Christ (Matthew 7:23) . . . the Lord would bring us counsel. He is reaching out, but the things of the world—even "the cares of this world and the deceitfulness of riches" (Matthew 13:22-23 NKJV)—will shake our connection. To the contrary, we must aggressively disconnect from *the pull of the world*. An intentional separation is needed.

To be sure, the things of the world are having a serious effect upon our relationships with the Lord— they are no little matter. Not only can they crowd in, to choke and to confound the things the Lord would be doing through us, but they can affect even the core of our relationship.

Covetous Idolatry

What else do we *need* besides Him? When some other than Him is required—when there is covetousness—this, even, is to the Lord as "idolatry." The Lord would do in our lives—He would surely lavish our lives with His blessings—but first we must be content to have no other.

Indeed, covetousness is idolatry—and He will not be where there are idols (Colossians 3:5; 2 Corinthians 6:16; Isaiah 42:8). We must put to death, spiritually, all other dependencies and affections. (See, wholly, Colossians 3:1-10; 2 Corinthians 6:12-18; and Matthew 6:19-24.)

Betrothed unto Christ
A Coming *Into* Relationship

Similar to the engagement custom of Jesus' day, those who receive Christ enter into a legal relationship likened unto a "betrothal"—whose consummation still is to come. (See 2 Corinthians 11:2; Matthew 25:1-12; Philippians 3:12, 20-21; and Colossians 3:2-4.) It is in consideration of this special betrothal relationship that revelation also can be gleaned.

"Forsaking All Others, Cleaving Only Unto Him" With a Heart that Is Wholly His

Most naturally, in any man-woman relationship, the greatest desire is for the other's heart—and not for what the other can do. So it is in *relationship* with Christ. **The Bridegroom most wants our hearts—and that where He is, there we *would be* also** (John 17:24). For a fact, all the Lord requires from us is a wholly given heart (which will be demonstrated by our "willful" choices) and that we trust in *Him*. He is faithful—He will do the rest.

Consider anew, and with annotation as given, even the wisdom of Jesus' own words:

> "And because lawlessness will abound [that of *doing our own ways* and *being independent* of one another], the love of many will grow cold. But he who endures to the end will be saved." (Matthew 24:12-13 NKJV, annotation mine)

To be certain, for any growing and intimate relationship, instead of doing "our own thing," we must actively and continually position ourselves together with our beloved. Likewise, we must aggressively pursue *oneness* in our relationship with the Lord—with a willingness to lay aside anything that hinders love. The question is: *Would we lay aside all for the sake of our relationship, or is something else more important?*[1] In all, the Lord sees into our hearts. He sees the measure of our real agreement (an agreement that is in measure with the revelation received[2]).

---

[1] Note the rich man in Mark 10:17-27, and also see Philippians 3:7-11.
[2] See Luke 12:47-48.

The Bridegroom is coming back! He is coming back to take His Bride unto Himself! Surely, if any Bridegroom deserved His Bride's *full* affections, it is Christ.

A Faith that Overcomes the Dominion of Sin

> For whatever is born of God overcomes the world. And this is the victory that has overcome the world—our faith. (1 John 5:4 NKJV)

As followers of Christ, we have been called to "continue in the faith." Yet, importantly, the gospel, first delivered, not only speaks of a forgiveness of sins through the sacrifice of Christ (2 Corinthians 5:17-19; 2 Peter 1:9; 1 John 1:7-9), but it also speaks of a victory we now can have over the sin nature. *As we will reckon* the sin nature ("the old man") to have been crucified with Christ, we are set free to serve unto righteousness (Romans 6:5-7, 11-14; Galatians 5:24). We, however, must believe it! We must continue not only with faith for the cleansing of sins, but also with *"saving faith" toward the power of Christ—that He has overcome sin's dominion*! As Scripture affirms:

> **How shall we who died to sin live any longer in it?** Or do you not know that as many of us as were baptized into Christ Jesus were baptized into His death? Therefore **we were buried with Him through baptism into death, that just as Christ was raised from the dead by the glory of the Father, even so we also should walk in newness of life.** For if we have been united together in the likeness of His death, certainly we also shall be in the likeness of His resurrection, knowing this, that **our old man was crucified with Him, that the body of sin might be done away with, that we should no longer be slaves of sin. For he who has died has been freed from sin.** (Romans 6:1-7 NKJV)
>
> **For sin shall not have dominion over you,** for you are not under law but under grace. (Romans 6:14 NKJV)

Through Christ, the victory has been fully won—and yet, for certain, our faith will be tested. Sin still will try to rule us, taunting us to believe its continued control over our lives. Even so, in the midst of these struggles—no matter what we may see—we must retain steadfastness in the thing *God* has spoken (Habakkuk 2:4; Hebrews 11:1; 2 Corinthians 5:7). Through the power of Christ, we have been set free—so that we now can serve another![3]

A *Working Out* of Our Faith

We must *work out* our faith (Philippians 2:12). This responsibility, however, does not espouse *man's* works. Quite to the contrary, we continue in an overcoming faith in *His* conquered victory over sin (which is demonstrated, first, by our confession of and alignment with His victory, and then by our steps to obey). Overcoming faith places no confidence in man's own ability or in his own "perfect" performance (Jeremiah 17:5-8; Romans 8:3-4; Philippians 3:2-9, 12-14).

To be sure, ours is a righteousness "by faith" (Habakkuk 2:4; Galatians 3:11; Romans 9:30; Ephesians 2:8-9). We are to put no confidence in man or in what we may see. Notwithstanding, our steps will show the reality of our faith. "Faith without works is dead" (James 2:26 NKJV).

A Faith that Fulfills the Requirements of the Law
The Law's Fulfillment *through the Love of Christ*

A true Christian, indeed, is *a follower* of Jesus. If we truly love Him, we have intent to obey Him (John 14:15). Nonetheless, sadly, what some would teach is that the obedience He *requires* for believers is the performing of specified Torah laws (i.e., civil laws, ceremonial laws, feasts). Yet, quite to the contrary (see Colossians 2:16 – 3:3 and Romans 14:5-6) the only commandment Jesus specified for all is that we love the Lord with all our heart, soul, mind, and strength (giving Him all the days and moments of our lives) and love our neighbors as our-

---

[3] See fully, with context, Romans 6:3-4, 5-7, 14, 17-18, 20, and 22; Romans 7:4-6; and Romans 8:2-4.

selves (Matthew 22:36-40; John 15:10-17). Scripture specifies that "by this shall all men know that [we] are [His] disciples, if [we] have love one to another" (John 13:35 KJV)—*not by a focused "performance" of the Torah.*

Then in agreement with Christ, *to truly love* also is the command referred to by Paul, which "sums up" or "fulfills" the whole law (Romans 13: 9-10; Galatians 5: 13-14). Of course, alongside the specified command "to love with God's love," we also, being "led by the Spirit," are called to move with the Lord, moment by moment, and only to do the things that we see Him doing (Romans 8:1-4, 12-14; Galatians 5:16-18, 22-25). Oh, but what a joy it is—the freedom of being led by the Spirit!

For certain, Jesus did say—He came not "to destroy the law," but to "fulfill it" in a "surpassing" way—nonetheless, the interpretation given of **a *focused performance mode*** does **not align with Scripture**, as demonstrated clearly by the following:

> But some of the sect of the Pharisees who believed rose up, saying, "It is necessary to circumcise them, and to command them to keep **the law of Moses.**" Now **the apostles and elders came together to consider this matter.** . . . Then it pleased the apostles and elders, with the whole church, to send chosen men of their own company to Antioch. . . . "**[The apostles, elders, and brethren] wrote this letter by them**: . . . **Since we have heard that some who went out from us have troubled you with words, unsettling your souls, saying, 'You must be circumcised and keep the law'—to whom we gave no such commandment**—it seemed good to us, being assembled with one accord, to send chosen men to you . . . For it seemed good to the Holy Spirit, and to us, to lay upon you no greater burden than these necessary things: that you abstain from things offered to idols, from blood, from things strangled, and from sexual immorality. If you keep yourselves from these, you will do well." (Acts 15:5-29 NKJV)

Quite notably, in the above reference, and apart from addressing the Talmud, Paul specifically addressed the requirements being made by some—that believers "keep *the law of Moses.*"

> Therefore **the law was a tutor to bring us to Christ**, that we might be justified by faith. But after faith has come, **we are no longer under a tutor**. For you are all sons of God through faith in Christ Jesus. . . . Now I say that the heir, as long as he is a child, does not differ at all from a slave, though he is master of all, but is under guardians and stewards until the time appointed by the father. Even so we, when we were children, were in bondage under the elements of the world. But when the fullness of the time had come, God sent forth His Son, "born" of a woman, born under the law, to redeem those under the law, that we might receive the adoption as sons. . . . Therefore you are no longer a slave but a son, and if a son, then an heir of God through Christ. . . . But now after you have known God, or rather are known by God, **how is it that you turn again to the weak and beggarly elements, to which you desire again to be in bondage? You observe days and months and seasons and years.** I am afraid for you, lest I have labored in vain. (Galatians 3:24 – 4:11 NKJV)

> But now we have been **delivered from the law, having died to what we were held by, so that we should serve in the newness of the Spirit** and not in the oldness of the letter. (Romans 7:6 NKJV)

> And **you are complete in [Christ]** . . . [Having] wiped out the handwriting of requirements that was against us, which was contrary to us. And He has taken it out of the way, having nailed it to the cross. . . . **So let no one judge you in food or in drink or regarding a festival or a new moon or sabbaths, which are a shadow of things to come, but the substance is of Christ.** (Colossians 2:10-17 NKJV)

Tell me, you who desire to be under the law, do you not hear the law? For it is written that Abraham had two sons: the one by a bondwoman, the other by a freewoman. But he who was of the bondwoman was born according to the flesh, and he of the freewoman through promise, which things are symbolic. For these are the two covenants: the one from Mount Sinai which gives birth to bondage, which is Hagar—for this Hagar is Mount Sinai in Arabia, and corresponds to Jerusalem which now is, and is in bondage with her children—but the Jerusalem above is free, which is the mother of us all. . . . But as he who was born according to the flesh then persecuted him who was born according to the Spirit, even so it is now. Nevertheless what does the Scripture say? **"Cast out the bondwoman and her son, for the son of the bondwoman shall not be heir with the son of the freewoman."** So then, brethren, we are not children of the bondwoman but of the free. (Galatians 4:21-31 NKJV)

Stand fast therefore in the liberty by which Christ has made us free, and **do not be entangled again with a yoke of bondage**. Indeed I, Paul, say to you that if you become circumcised [as a means of "being made perfect"], Christ will profit you nothing. **And I testify again to every man who becomes circumcised** [as a means of "being made perfect"] **that he is a debtor to keep the whole law. You have become estranged from Christ, you who attempt to be justified by law; you have fallen from grace.** For we through the Spirit eagerly wait for the hope of righteousness by faith. **For in Christ Jesus neither circumcision nor uncircumcision avails anything, but faith working through love.** You ran well. Who hindered you from obeying the truth? This persuasion does not come from Him who calls you. (Galatians 5:1-8 NKJV)

Now **the purpose of the commandment is love** from a pure heart, from a good conscience, and from sincere faith, from which **some, having strayed, have turned aside to idle talk, desiring to be teachers of the law**, understanding neither what they say nor the things which they affirm. **But we know that the law is good if one uses it lawfully, knowing this: that the law is not made for a righteous person [in Christ]**, but for the lawless and insubordinate, for the ungodly and profane, for murderers of fathers and murderers of mothers, for manslayers, for fornicators, for sodomites, for kidnappers, for liars, for perjurers, and if there is any other thing that is contrary to sound doctrine, according to the glorious gospel of the blessed God which was committed to my trust. (1 Timothy 1:5-11 NKJV)

(For further consideration, see also, with context, the following: Hebrews 9:22-24; 10:1, 8-9; Colossians 2:9-17; Romans 10:4-9; 2 Corinthians 3:6-11; Hebrews 10:19-20; Romans 7:4-7; Galatians 2:19 – 3:12; 3:19-26; 4:1-11; 4:21 – 5:25; 6:12-16; Romans 2:25-29; 1 Corinthians 10:23-31; Romans 14; Galatians 2:3-16; and Philippians 3:2-11.)

To be sure, the law has its right and significant place (1 Timothy 1:9-10). According to the apostle Paul, "[we] would not have known sin except through the law" (Romans 7:7 NKJV); the law puts us to death and leads us to Christ (Romans 7:7-12; Galatians 3:19-25). Additionally, according to Paul, the requirements of the law are significant in that they provide copies of things in the heavens and shadows of things that are to come (Hebrews 9:22-24; 10:1, 8-9; Colossians 2:16-17). The commandments stand as a *minimum* standard of righteousness and one teaching others to break *the heart* of a command will be called "least" in the kingdom of heaven. (See Matthew 5:19-22, 27-28, 31-32, and 33-37.) Nonetheless, we must remember that *the law is not the end— Christ Is. The law finds its substance and fulfillment in Christ* (Colossians 2:17; Romans 10:4; Galatians 5).

In Christ, we are called to a *surpassing* righteousness (Matthew 5:17-48; Galatians 5:19-23; 1 John 2:6); even so, *His* is not the righteousness of a "written code" (Colossians 2:14 NIV 1984)—it is *His law upon our hearts* (Romans 2:26-29; Colossians 2:14-17; Jeremiah 31:33; Hebrews

267

8:6-13; Galatians 5:13-25; Colossians 2:20 – 3:4). Not only do we now have greater access to the heart of the Father, through the "new and living way" afforded by relationship with Christ (Hebrew 10:19-20), but, through an *abiding* relationship with Jesus (John 15:4-6; Colossians 3:3), the Holy Spirit will direct us in all our comings and goings—unto God's ongoing and specific counsel for all the moments of our lives (John 5:19; Acts 10:38; 1 John 2:6; John 14:16-17, 26; 16:13; Galatians 5:16-18, 24-25; Acts 17:28; Proverbs 14:12; Proverbs 3:5-7). Indeed, the law is fulfilled in Christ, the law's righteousness is surpassed in Christ, and the law of the Lord is established in Christ! Through a wholehearted commitment to Him and a faith in *His* ability to work in and out of us *His* righteousness, He will establish us to love Him with all our heart, soul, mind, and strength (Mark 12:30)—and to obey Him wherever He leads (Matthew 5:18-48; Romans 3:31; Deuteronomy 30:10-14; Romans 9:30 – 10:11; Psalm 37:5-6, 39-40; 1 Peter 4:11)!

Yet again, and most significantly, *the law is fulfilled in the truest demonstration of God's love*—that of laying down one's own life for others; esteeming others' interests more highly than one's own; and looking not only to one's own interests, but also to the interests of others (Romans 5:6-8; 2 Corinthians 5:17-21; Matthew 22:36-40; Romans 13:9-10; Galatians 5:13-14; John 15:13; Philippians 2:3-5). **Just as Jesus'** *sacrificial and substitutionary love* **would fulfill the just requirements of the law, so shall ours**—as we will follow in His example and hide ourselves in Him (1 Peter 3:18; 1 John 2:6; Colossians 3:3).

CONTINUING IN *RELATIONSHIP* WITH A FAITH THAT PERSEVERES

Giving all diligence, **add to your faith** virtue, to virtue knowledge, to knowledge self-control, to self-control **perseverance**, to perseverance godliness, to godliness brotherly kindness, and to brotherly kindness love. . . . For he who lacks these things is shortsighted, even to blindness, and has forgotten that he was cleansed from his old sins. (2 Peter 1:5-9 NKJV)

And we desire that each one of you show the same diligence to the full assurance of hope until the end, that you do not become sluggish, but **imitate those who through faith and patience inherit the promises.** (Hebrews 6:11-12 NKJV)

For **you have need of endurance**, so that after you have done the will of God, you may receive the promise: ". . . Now the just shall live by faith; but if anyone draws back My soul has no pleasure in him." But we are not of those who draw back to perdition, but of those who believe to the saving of the soul. (Hebrews 10:36-39 NKJV)

As Scripture declares, *we* must persevere—*we* must keep on. Sadly, however, there are some who would contest it.

A More Balanced "P" for TULIP

Contained within the TULIP of Calvinist teaching is a teaching called *perseverance of the saints*, which, according to one source, asserts: "All who are chosen by God, redeemed by Christ, and given faith by the Spirit are eternally saved . . . kept in faith by the power of Almighty God and thus persevere to the end."[4] For certain, there is important truth *within* the "P" of TULIP. Only, imbalance has occurred when *our part* is removed.

His Part *to Perfect*

One day, as an encouragement for me to endure through trial, the Lord spoke to me the following: "You can't take others where you haven't been yourself." Thankfully, through all our trials, Jesus can take us— He can give strength to endure—because He *has* been there Himself! He understands—and will be a source of salvation to those who *desire* to obey Him (Hebrews 4:15-16; Hebrews 5:2, 7-9).

---

[4] David N. Steele and Thomas Curtis, *Romans: An Interpretive Outline* (Phillipsburg, NJ: Presbyterian and Reformed Publishing Co., 1967), pp. 144-146.

Jesus is our solid foundation. He is the First and the Last. Our eyes must be stayed *on Him*. Scripture makes clear:

> Looking unto Jesus, **the author and finisher of our faith** . . . (Hebrews 12:2 NKJV)

> For I am not ashamed of **the gospel of Christ, for it is the power of God to salvation for everyone who believes**, for the Jew first and also for the Greek. For **in it the righteousness of God is revealed from faith to faith; as it is written, "The just shall live by faith."** (Romans 1:17-18 NKJV)

> This only I want to learn from you: Did you receive the Spirit by the works of the law, or by the hearing of faith? Are you so foolish? **Having begun in the Spirit, are you now being made perfect by the flesh?** (Galatians 3:2-3 NKJV)

> Thus says the LORD: "**Cursed is the man who trusts in man and makes flesh his strength**, whose heart departs from the LORD." (Jeremiah 17:5 NKJV)

> For we are the circumcision, who worship God in the Spirit, rejoice in Christ Jesus, and have **no confidence in the flesh**, (Philippians 3:3 NKJV)

> **The LORD will perfect that which concerns me**; your mercy, O LORD, endures forever . . . (Psalm 138:8 NKJV)

> Commit your way to the LORD, trust also in Him, and **He shall bring it to pass. He shall bring forth your righteousness as the light, and your justice as the noonday.** (Psalm 37:5-6 NKJV)

> I know whom I have believed and am persuaded that **He is able to keep what I have committed to Him until that Day**. (2 Timothy 1:12 NKJV)

Being confident of this very thing, that **He who has begun a good work in you will complete it** until the day of Jesus Christ; (Philippians 1:6 NKJV)

Particularly, although Paul knew the Lord's call for His people to live out holy and unblemished lives before Him, he was very careful, by his words, never to lead anyone away from a total confidence *only in Jesus*. The apostle Paul put "no confidence in the flesh," and he admonished others to live similarly.

Even as the apostle Paul would encourage, corporately, the ones whose hearts he knew (see all of Philippians 1:3-7): *those truly given to Christ will make it*! Those *in Christ* and remaining in Him may have confidence—and must have confidence—in *His* keeping power (2 Timothy 1:12). We must retain a posture of faith *toward Him*—and not ourselves—all the way.

He who began a good work in us will complete it! Notwithstanding, we must remain actively *in agreement with the Lord* for the thing that He would do.[5]

Our Part *to Abide*

Foremost, the apostles would encourage a steadfast faith *in Christ*. (See Galatians 3:1-7, Romans 8:37-39, and Philippians 1:6.) Yet, although the apostles' hearts were always to encourage, the apostles, likewise, exhorted the early church of their own continued responsibility before God. Consider the words of the following:

Strengthening the souls of the disciples, exhorting them **to continue in the faith**, and saying, "We must through many tribulations enter the kingdom of God." (Acts 14:22 NKJV)

---

[5] A side note: Even in the processing of these writings, I must "continue in the faith" that "He who began a good work . . . shall complete it." I must stay in the mode where I believe He is meeting me. *As long as I engage with the Lord*, to stay along His path, I can have confidence that He will have what He desires—because He is bigger than me.

271

And you, who once were alienated and enemies in your mind by wicked works, yet now He has reconciled in the body of His flesh through death, to present you holy, and blameless, and above reproach in His sight—**if indeed you continue in the faith**, grounded and steadfast, and are not moved away from the hope of the gospel which you heard . . . (Colossians 1:21-23 NKJV)

Therefore, **holy brethren, partakers of the heavenly calling**, consider the Apostle and High Priest of our confession, Christ Jesus . . . **Beware, brethren**, lest there be in any of you an evil heart of unbelief in departing from the living God; . . . For we **have become partakers of Christ if we hold the beginning of our confidence steadfast to the end**. (Hebrews 3:1, 12-14 NKJV)

Therefore, since a promise remains of entering His rest, **let us fear lest any of you seem to have come short of it**. (Hebrews 4:1 NKJV)

Pursue peace with all people, and holiness, without which no one will see the Lord: **looking carefully lest anyone fall short of the grace of God**; lest any root of bitterness springing up cause trouble, and by this many become defiled; lest there be any fornicator or profane person like Esau, who for one morsel of food sold his birthright. For you know that afterward, when he wanted to inherit the blessing, he was rejected, for he found no place for repentance, though he sought it diligently with tears. (Hebrew 12:14-17 NKJV)

Therefore let him who thinks he stands **take heed lest he fall**. (1 Corinthians 10:12 NKJV)

Therefore, my beloved, as you have always obeyed, not as in my presence only, but now much more in my absence, **work out your own salvation with fear and trembling;** . . . **holding fast the word of life**, so that I may rejoice in the day of Christ that I have not run in vain or labored in vain. (Philippians 2:12-16 NKJV)

Significant to note: In his entreaty to the Philippians, what consequence might Paul have been referring to—in that he would have "labored in vain"?

You therefore, beloved, since you know this beforehand, **beware lest you also fall from your own steadfastness, being led away with the error of the wicked**; but grow in the grace and knowledge of our Lord and Savior Jesus Christ. To Him be the glory both now and forever. Amen. (2 Peter 3:17-18 NKJV)

Therefore, brethren, **be even more diligent to make your call and election sure**, for if you do these things [noted in verses 5-7] you will never stumble; for so an entrance will be supplied to you abundantly into the everlasting kingdom of our Lord and Savior Jesus Christ. For this reason **I will not be negligent to remind you always of these things, though you know and are established in the present truth**. Yes, I think it is right, as long as I am in this tent, to stir you up by reminding you, (2 Peter 1:10-13 NKJV)[6]

Most significantly, Jesus highlighted our need to continue to follow, declaring such as the following words:

"And **he who does not take his cross and follow after Me is not worthy of Me**." (Matthew 10:38 NKJV)

"You are already clean because of the word which I have spoken to you. **Abide in Me**, and I in you. . . . **If**

---

[6]See the discussion of 2 Peter 3:9, within the chapter "Inconsistencies—Part 2," and also the chapter entitled "Discrepancies in Various TULIP Teachings: Revelation from 2 Peter 2."

> anyone does not abide in Me, he [seemingly *an individual*, and not just his works] is cast out as a branch and is withered; and they gather them and throw them into the fire, and they are burned." (John 15:3-6 NKJV)

> "But he who endures to the end shall be saved." (Matthew 24:13 NKJV)

Then as well, within just the 24th and 25th chapters of Matthew, Jesus gave many descriptions of either "servants" or "virgins" who, not being found ready, either would miss the coming of the "Bridegroom" or be cast into "outer darkness."

Just as Jesus and the apostles understood and taught, *we* must continue "in the faith" and in our agreement with Him. This is *our* responsibility.

A Continuation of "Will"
With a Holy Regard for Christ

> "Nevertheless not My will, but Yours, be done." (Luke 22:42 NKJV)

" 'It is finished' " (John 19:30). **Fixing our eyes upon the work of Christ and being wholly given to Him *from the heart* ensures our salvation.** Indeed, we must have faith in the finished work of Jesus and *His* keeping power, no matter what we may see. Yet again, it is important that our lives *remain* willfully committed unto Him. Just as our Savior warned:

> "And that servant who knew his master's will, and did not prepare himself or **do according to his will**, shall be beaten with many stripes." (Luke 12:47 NKJV)

> "Enter by the narrow gate; for wide is the gate and broad is the way that leads to destruction, and there are many who go in by it. Because narrow is the gate and difficult is the way which leads to life and there are few who find it. . . . **Not everyone who says to Me 'Lord, Lord,'**

274

shall enter the kingdom of heaven but he who does the will of My Father in heaven." (Matthew 7:13-14, 21 NKJV)

Notably, the gifting is not the measure of who one is before God (prophesy, miracles, healings, etc.). We should not be deceived. The measure is in those who have *real relational connection* with Christ— in those who, by pattern, are living their lives *to do* the will of the Father (Matthew 7:21-23). Even the apostle Paul understood this, and, having preached, aimed not to be disqualified (1 Corinthians 9:27).

Continue with consideration of the following:

"But **when a righteous man turns away from his righteousness and commits iniquity**, and does according to all the abominations that the wicked man does, shall he live? **All the righteousness which he has done shall not be remembered; because of the unfaithfulness** of which he is guilty and the sin which he has committed, because of them he shall die." (Ezekiel 18:24 NKJV)

"When I say to the righteous that he shall surely live, **but he trusts in his own righteousness and commits iniquity, none of his righteous works shall be remembered**; but because of the iniquity that he has committed, he shall die." (Ezekiel 33:13 NKJV)

Even as the prophet Ezekiel declared, the righteousness of the righteous—whose "righteousness" was always to be "by faith" (Genesis 15:6; Habakkuk 2:4)—shall no longer save him in the day that he turns away from God (Ezekiel 18:24-32; 33:12-16).

Therefore, *holy brethren, partakers of the heavenly calling*, consider the Apostle and High Priest of our confession, Christ Jesus, . . . **Beware, brethren, lest there be in any of you an evil heart of unbelief in departing**

from the living God; but exhort one another daily, while it called "Today," lest any of you be hardened through the deceitfulness of sin. For **we have become partakers of Christ *if* we hold the beginning of our confidence steadfast to the end**, while it is said: "Today, if you will hear His voice, **do not harden your hearts** as in the rebellion." (Hebrews 3:1, 12-15 NKJV, emphasis mine)

Quite notably, in the above exhortation, the ones to whom Paul was speaking were "brethren" who had become "partakers of the heavenly calling." Only, having begun in Christ, they needed to continue, taking careful heed to their hearts.

"Therefore whoever confesses Me before men, him I will also confess before My Father who is in heaven. **But whoever denies Me before men, him I will also deny before My Father who is in heaven.**" (Matthew 10:32-33 NKJV)

This is a faithful saying: For if we died with Him, we shall also live with Him. **If we endure, we shall also reign with Him. If we deny Him, He also will deny us.** (2 Timothy 2:11-12 NKJV)

For it is impossible for **those who were once enlightened, and have tasted the heavenly gift, and have become partakers of the Holy Spirit, and have tasted the good word of God and the powers of the age to come**, if they fall away, to renew them again to repentance, since **they crucify again for themselves** the Son of God, and put Him to an open shame. (Hebrews 6:4-6 NKJV)

For if, **after they have escaped the pollutions of the world through the knowledge of the Lord and Savior Jesus Christ**, they are again entangled in them and overcome, **the latter end is worse for them than the**

beginning. For it **would have been better for them not to have known the way of righteousness**, than having known it to turn from the holy commandment delivered to them. (2 Peter 2:20-21 NKJV)[7]

For if we sin willfully after we have received the knowledge of the truth, **there no longer remains a sacrifice for sins, but a certain fearful expectation of judgment, and fiery indignation which will devour the adversaries**. Anyone who has rejected Moses' law dies without mercy on the testimony of two or three witnesses. Of how much worse punishment, do you suppose, will he be thought worthy who has trampled the Son of God underfoot, **counted the blood of the covenant by which he was sanctified a common thing, and insulted the Spirit of grace**? For we know Him who said, "Vengeance is Mine, I will repay," says the Lord. And again, "The Lord will judge His people." It is a fearful thing to fall into the hands of the living God. . . . But we are not of those who draw back to perdition, but of those who believe to the saving of the soul. (Hebrews 10:26-31, 39 NKJV)

Significant to note: *willful* sins are the issue (Hebrews 10:26). God does not expect perfect performance. He sees our hearts—He understands our frame (1 Samuel 16:7; Psalm 33:13-15; Acts 15:8; Matthew 26:41). Only, *our wills/our hearts* must retain the posture: "I delight to do Your will" (Psalm 40:8; Psalm 37:4-6; Matthew 6:10).

By Pattern of Earthly Relationships
Grounds for Divorce

The apostle Paul gave a parallel between the union of a man and woman in marriage and that of the union of Christ and the church (Ephesians 5:22-33). Through that parallel, not only can insight be gained

---

[7] For a more in depth discussion, see the chapter entitled "Discrepancies of Various TULIP Teachings: Revelation from 2 Peter 2."

concerning right postures, both between husbands and wives and between the church and Christ, but insight also can be gained as to *grounds* for divorce.

Adulterous Fornication

> "Whosoever shall put away his wife, **except it be for fornication**, and shall marry another, committeth adultery . . ." (Matthew 19:9 KJV)

In pattern with Jewish marriage customs of Jesus' day, the church presently is betrothed to Christ. Although, legally, she already is the Bride of Christ, she has yet to walk with Him in white or to have her marriage consummated (Philippians 3:12, 20-21; Colossians 3:2-4). Firstly, therefore, with regard to the betrothal custom, consider these words of Christ:

> "And to the angel of the church in Sardis write, '. . . I know your works, that you have a name that you are alive, but you are dead. **Be watchful, and strengthen the things which remain**, that are ready to die, for I have not found your works perfect before God. **Remember therefore how you have received and heard; hold fast and repent.** Therefore if you will not watch, I will come upon you as a thief, and you will not know what hour I will come upon you. **You have a few names even in Sardis who have not defiled their garments; and they shall walk with Me in white, for they are worthy. He who overcomes shall be clothed in white garments, and I will not blot out his name from the Book of Life**; but I will confess his name before My Father and before His angels. He who has an ear, let him hear what the Spirit says to the churches." (Revelation 3:1-6 NKJV)

To walk with Him "in white" . . . Have we been intimate with another—have we loved the world? We soil our garments as we love the world. Just as the following expounds:

278

Do not love the world or the things in the world. **If anyone loves the world, the love of the Father is not in him.** For all that is in the world—the lust of the flesh, the lust of the eyes, and the pride of life—is not of the Father but is of the world. And the world is passing away, and the lust of it; but he who does the will of God abides forever. (1 John 2:15-17 NKJV)

For many walk, of whom I have told you often, and now tell you even weeping, that they are the **enemies of the cross of Christ: whose end is destruction, whose god is their belly, and whose glory is in their shame—who set their mind on earthly things.** (Philippians 3:18-19 NKJV)

Adulterers and adulteresses! Do you not know that friendship with the world is enmity with God? **Whoever therefore wants to be a friend of the world makes himself an enemy of God.** (James 4:4 NKJV)

Not to put away the wife "except for fornication" . . . According to Scripture, both in betrothal and in marriage, adultery is grounds for divorce. Similarly, its equivalence in the spiritual—that of *cleaving to the world*—seems also to be grounds to "put away."

As God Sees It

Concerning the sin of adultery, "man looks at the outward appearance, but **the LORD looks at the heart**" (1 Samuel 16:7 NKJV). "Whoever looks at [another] to lust for [him or her] has already committed **adultery . . . in his heart**" (Matthew 5:28 NKJV). Thus, in pattern, and with regard to our covenant relationship with the Lord, it is "a friend of the world" (James 4:4)—one who lusts after the things of the world—who becomes an adulterer and an enemy of God (see James 4:4-10 and 1 John 2:15-17).

Moreover, the Lord's response to Israel's outright adultery and Judah's "casual harlotry" also is very revealing.

> "So it came to pass, **through her casual harlotry**, that she defiled the land and **committed adultery** with stones and trees. And yet for all this her treacherous sister Judah has not turned to Me with her whole heart, but in pretense," says the LORD. Then the LORD said to me, "Backsliding Israel has shown herself more righteous than treacherous Judah." (Jeremiah 3:9-11 NKJV)

"Casual harlotry" is, to the Lord, the same as adultery—even worse (and at that, grounds for divorce). The Lord hates pretense. Perhaps, in it, the Lord detects the attitude for what it is— an attitude that does not esteem Him for who He is (as if one can "get one over" on God). Yet, in Revelation 3:15-16, Jesus' heart is seen: "I could wish you were cold or hot . . . because you are lukewarm, and neither cold nor hot, I will vomit you out of My mouth" (NKJV).

The Lord is coming back for a people "holy and without blemish" (Ephesians 5:27 NKJV)—whose hearts are set on Him. He would have all of us—all of our hearts. We should not deceive ourselves, therefore, ever presuming for anything less.

An *Unbelieving* One Who Would Desire to Leave

Then, according to the apostle Paul, if an "unbelieving" spouse *wants* to leave, this, also, is grounds for divorce (1 Corinthians 7:12-15). Notably, although believing couples are called to stay together (1 Corinthians 7:10-12), there are different guidelines in the case of *unbelieving* spouses. If an unbelieving spouse is *willing* to stay, the believing spouse should not divorce—for the unbelieving one is "sanctified" and made "holy" in that relationship (see 1 Corinthians 7:13-14). Yet, if an unbelieving spouse wants to leave, the believing spouse is freed from the marriage covenant—he is "not under bondage [to the covenant] in such cases" (1 Corinthians 7:15 NKJV). Seemingly, here, very applicable parallels also can be seen between one's covenant with a spouse and one's covenant with Christ.

With similarity to the case of an *unbelieving* spouse, even though, perhaps, there may be a weakness in the flesh (Matthew 26:41; Romans

280

15:1), we still are "made holy" *in Christ*—being "set apart" and in a special place. Just as a believing spouse is counseled to remain with the spouse *who desires to stay* in relationship, the Lord also will keep relationship with those individuals *who desire to stay* in relationship with Him. (He sees the intent of our hearts!) The one who will stay continues to be "made holy" through his relationship *in Christ*.

Just as the Lord is long-suffering to marriage partners on behalf of a believing spouse (1 Corinthians 7:14), the Lord also is long-suffering to us on behalf of our *connection* to Christ. Importantly, however, **we must *will* to stay connected to our Redeemer**. Just as the unbelieving is "made holy," as long as he *wants* to stay, the Lord, likewise, will continue His favor toward us, as long as we desire to stay.

Grounds for Divorce

Scripturally, both in the *natural* and in the *spiritual*, there are striking similarities between the scenarios where divorce is permitted—the scenarios of *adultery* or of an *unbelieving spouse desiring to leave* with the scenarios of one *willfully sinning* or of one *willfully turning away from* God. Just as is in marriage, if one *wills* to "adulterously" sin with the world after having come into a relationship with the Lord (see Hebrews 10:26), or if one falls into an evil and unbelieving heart and *wants* to depart (see Hebrews 3:12), that one may freely be released from the relationship. These are grounds for divorce.

The Lord hates divorce. Divorce has never been His desire—it never was (Matthew 19:8). He has not "determined best"[8] separations—"that any should perish" (2 Peter 3:9 NKJV). Just as mercy always "triumphs over judgment" (James 2:13), the Lord would beckon, "Return!" (Jeremiah 3 – 4; Ezekiel 18; Ezekiel 33; 2 Peter 3:9). **Notwithstanding the greatness of His love, divorce will be permitted because of *hardness of heart*** (Matthew 19:8). Today, therefore, if we can hear His voice, we would do well not to harden our hearts (Hebrews 3:15).

---

[8]See a full discussion of 2 Peter 3:9 within the chapter "Inconsistencies . . . Part 2."

What about These Scriptures?

Scripture seems so clear in its warning—one can fall from his secure position. Often, however, it is because of the following that many still would discount it.

Hebrews 13:5

"I will never leave you nor forsake you." (NKJV)

Would He ever leave us or forsake us? To those *whose hearts are His*, truly, He would not. Recklessly, however, the words of Hebrews 13:5 often have been used to support the teaching that, once truly having come into a "saving knowledge of Christ," one never can lose his salvation. Context is so important—God's promise was *conditional*!

Contextually, in Hebrews 13:5 (and also in Deuteronomy 31:6-8 and Joshua 1:5), the promise of God was spoken to remind us of *His faithfulness*. Indeed, He will take care of His own. He will give us all we need. He will be there for us. So, in His hands, why should we fear *man*? "What can man do to [us]?" (Hebrews 13:6 NKJV, verse following noted scripture). Rightly, we need not fear man. We should, however, retain a fear of God.

As it is, and quite significantly, earlier references to the words of God's promise give us details concerning the *conditions* of His promise:

> **The LORD is with you while you are with Him.** If you seek Him, He will be found by you, but **if you forsake Him, He will forsake you.**" (2 Chronicles 15:2 NKJV)

> "As for you, my son Solomon, know the God of your father, and serve Him with a loyal heart and with a willing mind; for the LORD searches all hearts and understands all the intent of the thoughts. **If you seek him, He will be found by you; but if you forsake Him, He will cast you off forever.**" (1 Chronicles 28:9 NKJV)

2 Timothy 2:13

If we are faithless, He remains faithful; He cannot deny Himself. (NKJV)

Taken by themselves, the above words have been used by some to discount the real significance of our continuing in faith. Yet, even with respect to the words immediately before and after this passage, there is other very likely intent. Paul would remind that, although *it still takes two in any relationship*—and we *can* deny Him (v. 12)—the Lord is always *the Faithful*. He does not change. "He cannot deny Himself."

In other words, if there is a lack of trust, the fault lies not on the Lord— for He will always do what He says. "If we are faithless, He remains faithful."

Romans 11:29

For the gifts and the calling of God are irrevocable. (NKJV)

Agreeably, apart from other scriptures, Romans 11:29 appears to make the case for the thought "once saved, always saved." For certain, God *will* do what He has spoken. *If He has spoken it, He will fulfill it.* (See also Numbers 23:19.) Contextually, however, with his statement, the apostle Paul is not speaking concerning the conditions for the salvation of individuals. To the contrary, he is bringing reminder of the unconditional nature of God's promise *toward Israel*. **The gift and calling *toward Israel* is irrevocable.** God's spoken promise to bring back Israel shall surely happen. Concerning election, *as a nation*, "they [remain] beloved for the sake of the fathers" (Romans 11:28 NKJV, verse preceding noted verse).

John 6:39-40

And this is the Father's will [*thelema*] which hath sent me; that of all which he hath given me I should lose nothing, but should raise it up again at the last day. And this is the will [*thelema*] of him that sent me, that every

283

one which seeth the Son, and believeth on him, may have everlasting life: and I will raise him up at the last day. (KJV)[9]

Although some may think the above words of Jesus discount the possibility of one's losing his salvation, one also should note that Jesus differentiated between God's desires (which may or may not happen) and God's decreed determinations (which do happen) by use of the word *thelema*. *Thelema* expresses "desire" and not "plans"[10] (see the chapter "The *Will* of God"). God "desires [*thelo* / verb form of *thelema*][11] all men to be saved and to come to the knowledge of the truth" (1 Timothy 2:4 NKJV), but we know that all do not. Similarly, although God does not will/desire that any should be lost, this does not mean that all the Father gives to Jesus will make it to the end.

There is security, knowing that Jesus came to do the Father's will. *Because it is God's will* **that any believing on Jesus be raised in the last day, Jesus will do it for those** *remaining* **in Him (for those who keep on believing).** He can be counted on to give the bread that will last forever. Notably, it was in the context of the plea "evermore give us this bread" (v. 34 KJV) that Jesus spoke the words of John 6:35-40—words telling both of the desire of the Father and of the Son's faithfulness to do.

1 Corinthians 3:15

If anyone's work is burned, he will suffer loss; but he himself will be saved, yet so as through fire. (1 Corinthians 3:15 NKJV)

Some believe the *only* retribution that awaits the "sinner"—who truly

---

[9] James Strong, LL.D., S.T.D., *Strong's Complete Word Study Concordance* (Chattanooga, TN: AMG Publishers, 2004), pp. 1690, 2086.

[10] E. W. Bullinger, *A Critical Lexicon and Concordance to the English and Greek New Testament* (Grand Rapids, MI: Kregel Publications, 1999; orig. pub. 1908), p. 883.

[11] Ibid., p. 884; Strong, *Strong's Complete Word Study Concordance*, pp. 1690, 2086, 2087.

has known Jesus—is his works being burned up, citing the words of 1 Corinthians 3:15. Yet, consider again the whole of context:

> **Now he who plants and he who waters are one, and each one will receive his own reward according to his own labor.** (9) **For [*gar* / "the fact is"]**[12] **we are God's fellow workers; you are God's field, you are God's building.** (10) According to the grace of God which was given to me, as a wise master builder I have laid the foundation, and another builds on it. But let each one take heed how he builds on it. (11) For [*gar* / "the fact is"]**[13] **no other foundation can anyone lay than that which is laid, which is Jesus Christ.** (12) Now if anyone builds on the foundation with gold, silver, precious stones, wood, hay, straw, (13) each one's work will become clear; for the Day will declare it because it will be revealed by fire; and the fire will test each one's work, of what sort it is. (14) If anyone's work which he has built on it endures, he will receive a reward. (15) If anyone's work is burned, he will suffer loss; but he himself will be saved, yet so as through fire. (16) Do you not know that you are the temple of God and that the Spirit of God dwells in you? (17) **If anyone defiles the temple of God, God will destroy him. For the temple of God is holy, which temple you are.** (1 Corinthians 3:8-17 NKJV)

Notably, in consideration of context, **Paul's words were *not in reference towards ones in rebellion before God*, but only in reference towards those who would presume to build upon the church—"God's building."** In both verses 9 and 11, by use of the Greek word *gar*, the statements expound upon the verses immediately preceding.[14] Then, even with the words that follow, from verses 16 to 17 and onward, there is also a continuation of such context. Significantly, as well, within the context of his statement in verse 15, the apostle Paul had made

---

[12] Bullinger, *A Critical Lexicon and Concordance to the English and Greek New Testament*, pp. 296, 298, xiii.
[13] Ibid.
[14] Ibid.

allowance that, **in all the burnings of "works," the foundation** *still had remained* **Christ** (v. 11).[15]

Finally, with respect to types of *burnings*—and a distinction between "works" and "individuals"—consider, as well, Jesus' words in the following:

> "You are **already clean** because of the word which I have spoken to you. **Abide in Me**, and I in you. . . . **If anyone does not abide in Me, he** [seemingly, **an individual**, and not just his works] **is cast out as a branch** and is withered; and they gather them and throw them into the fire, and **they are burned**." (John 15:3-6 NKJV)

To be sure, in certain cases, only works shall be burned—and yet, in others, according to John 15:6, the end may be more severe.

A *Very Fine* Line

There is such a very fine line to walk when talking about one's ability to lose his salvation. In the fear of God, we must never take away from the completeness of what Jesus did by looking wrongly unto our works. Nonetheless, according to Scripture, our works will prove the reality of the thing that is in our hearts (James 2:14-26; 1 Peter 1:6-7).

The Lord has given us a walk to walk out in His power. If we trust in Him—if we have truly given our lives over to Him—we *will* aim to do the things He tells us to do. Our heart's intent *will be* to do His will, being displayed by our *willful* choices. Indeed, even most who would call themselves "Calvinists" agree that the truly saved follower of Jesus Christ will aim to walk out a life unto Jesus Christ; only, they have disagreed that one who has truly known the Lord's salvation—having been cleansed "from his past sins" (2 Peter 1:9-11 NIV1984)—is one

---

[15] With respect to false teachers who would go to *an extreme*, even denying the One who bought them, again, please note the chapter "Discrepancies of Various TULIP Teachings: Revelation from 2 Peter 2."

still able to lose his eternal security. Then, others believe such consideration is simply irrelevant and unnecessary. Yet, because the Bible does note, with distinctiveness, such a remaining possibility, might it not be just the life-giving word that can cause some to repent?

IN CONCLUSION

Above all, we must remember God's mercy. His tender mercies—they "fail not"—they are "new every morning" (Lamentations 3:22-23 NKJV). The Lord is near. Today can be a new day. "The LORD is near to the brokenhearted" (Psalm 34:18 NASB). He is always near "in the day that [one] turns" (Ezekiel 33:12 NKJV).

In all, we must fear God—doing nothing that takes away from the greatness of what was done for us by Jesus (Philippians 2:9-12). Notwithstanding, are we really looking to Jesus? Is He really our hope? Our confidence will show forth one way or another by our works. The work of legalism demonstrates a failure to look only to the righteousness that is "by faith" *in Jesus*. Hence, such a walk becomes a "[falling] from grace" (Galatians 5:4). Likewise, the one who sins *willfully*, after "a knowledge of the truth" (Hebrews 10:26), demonstrates a failure to really repent. We should examine ourselves to see if we truly are in the faith (2 Corinthians 13:5).

The balance . . . The one who continues to look to Jesus—who will not, in an adulterous way, give himself over to a love of the world (James 4:4-5; 1 John 2:15)—the Lord will present blameless (1 Corinthians 1:8). He who began a good work will be faithful to complete it (Philippians 1:6).

To be certain, we must keep our eyes on the Lord, with a faith in *His* ability to keep those whose hearts are His (the ones who have wholly surrendered their lives unto Him). All the way, it must be a walk of faith *in Him* and not in our own works or in our own abilities to perfectly do. *He* must remain our confidence for that which *He* will do. It is *in Him* and *through Him* all the way.

287

Truly, He will keep. "The LORD will perfect that which concerns [us]" (Psalm 138:8 NKJV); nonetheless, **He will not keep those who *will not* to continue in Him**. It is *our* responsibility to remain in Him— with eyes that are totally His (Matthew 6:21-24; Hebrews 12:2). Even though Satan would try to discourage and to steal away what we have in Christ, *we* must not grow weary. We must fight the fight of faith (1 Timothy 6:12), receiving the promise by enduring until the end.

Satan knows the equal significance of both foundations—the foundations of *His keeping power* and of *our responsibility to remain aligned with Him*. It is not surprising, therefore, that he would build distortions to undermine and to confuse these foundations.

> Now to Him *who is able* to keep you from stumbling, and to present you faultless before the presence of His glory with exceeding joy, to God our Savior, who alone is wise, be glory and majesty, dominion and power, both now and forever. Amen. (Jude 24-25 NKJV, emphasis mine)

An Election

According to

Foreknowledge

Chapter 12

Who Are the *Elect*?

Simply said, the "elect," the ones God chooses, are *those who fear Him—who look to Him and not unto their own works*. Psalm 33:10-22 speaks of God's sovereignty and the ones He chooses for His inheritance.

> The LORD brings the counsel of the nations to nothing; He makes the plans of the peoples of no effect. **The counsel of the LORD stands forever, the plans of His heart to all generations. Blessed is the nation whose God is the LORD,** *the people He has chosen as His own inheritance.* The LORD looks from heaven; He sees all the sons of men. From the place of His dwelling He looks on all the inhabitants of the earth; He fashions their hearts individually; He considers all their works. No king is saved by the multitude of an army; a mighty man is not delivered by great strength. A horse is a vain hope for safety; neither shall it deliver any by its great strength. **Behold, the eye of the LORD is on those who fear Him, on those who hope in His mercy, to deliver their soul from death, and to keep them alive in famine**. Our soul waits for the LORD; He is our help and our shield. For our heart shall rejoice in Him, because **we have trusted in his holy name. Let Your mercy, O LORD, be upon us, just as we hope in You.** (NKJV, emphasis mine)

Similarly, in Malachi 3:16-18, we see the ones whom God has put in remembrance.

> Then those who feared the LORD spoke to one another, and the LORD listened and heard them; so **a book of remembrance was written before Him for those who fear the LORD and who meditate on His name. "They shall be Mine,"** says the LORD of hosts, **"On the day**

that I make them My jewels. And I will spare them as a man spares his own son who serves him." Then you shall again discern between the righteous and the wicked, between one who serves God and one who does not serve Him. (NKJV)

"Election" is an important truth to know. It speaks of God's sovereignty and of our need to reverence Him and to look to Him alone. Likewise, election is spoken about in both the Old Testament and the New Testament. In its proper interpretation, the truth of election is very good. It brings the fear of God. It brings peace and faith. And *God alone* is exalted. In the following, even Moses affirmed the importance of God's choice:

> "But you shall seek **the place where the LORD your God chooses**, out of all the tribes, to put his name for His dwelling place; and there you shall go." (Deuteronomy 12:5 NKJV)

> "You shall rejoice before the LORD your God, you and your son and your daughter, your male servant and your female servant, the Levite who is within your gates, the stranger and the fatherless and the widow who are among you, at **the place where the LORD your God chooses** to make His name abide." (Deuteronomy 16:11 NKJV)

In truth, God does not move our way; He moves *His* way. And He, alone, *does* choose whom His people will be—*the place where His name will dwell* (Deuteronomy 12:4-5; 16:11).

HIS CHOICE

To be certain, lest our hearts be exalted before God, we would all do well to note God's continued place. He is the One "with whom we have to do" (Hebrews 4:13). He is the One "in [whom] we live and move and have our being" (Acts 17:28). *It is the Lord* who sees and gives. Just as the psalmist understood and declared, we also should note:

The LORD looks from heaven; He sees all the sons of men. From the place of His dwelling He looks on all the inhabitants of the earth; **He fashions their hearts individually; He considers all their works**. (Psalm 33:13-15 NKJV)

If we had forgotten the name of our God, or stretched out our hands to a foreign god, would not God search this out? For **He knows the secrets of the heart**. (Psalm 44:21-22 NKJV)

The Lord—who has fashioned each one's heart, individually—looks down to consider *the ways* of each one whom He has made. Then, giving an account of himself before God, each one will receive according to what he has done. Has he walked humbly before his God?

His Giving

John the Baptist recognized: "A man can receive nothing **unless it has been given** to him from heaven" (John 3:27 NKJV). Likewise, Jesus understood: "No one can come to Me **unless it has been granted** to him by My Father" (John 6:65 NKJV). Similarly, King Nebuchadnezzar also learned: "The most High rules in the kingdoms of men and **gives it to whomever He chooses**" (Daniel 4:25-26 NKJV).

"Where is boasting then?" (Romans 3:27). "And what do [we] have that [we] did not receive?" (1 Corinthians 4:7). "The most High rules," and He, *who considers our hearts* (1 Samuel 16:7), chooses the ones to whom He will reveal Himself. Just as Romans 9:16 reminds:

So then it is not of him [man] who wills, nor of him who runs, but of God who shows mercy. (NKJV)

293

In truth, no matter how much a man may *want* to attain—no matter how much he may *strive* with his own good works—righteousness remains *of Him who looks into the hearts of men.*[1]

IN CONCLUSION—A RESPECTER OF HEARTS TOWARD HIM

The Lord chooses. He "knows those [whose hearts] are *His*" (2 Timothy 2:19). And those He chooses, He will sustain.

We are *as His people*—because we are the ones to whom the Lord has chosen to show mercy. Indeed, nothing we could ever have done would warrant us entrance into the kingdom of God *because He is so much higher than us.* Apart from Christ, none of us has ever, nor could ever meet His righteous requirements (Romans 3:23). Nonetheless, **God has chosen each one of us because He has seen—even displayed by our *intentional* actions—*hearts* that would truly desire to know and to follow Him**.

For a time, the *natural* "elect" nation of Israel has been broken off, and others have been grafted in. Yet, even as Paul noted, there is no place for boasting (Romans 11:17-22). To the contrary, we would all do well to align ourselves with *God's greatness*—fearing and humbling ourselves before Him—for these are the ones on whom He will look to deliver and to demonstrate His *continued* favor.

God's requirements for man are consistent:

> He has shown you, O man, what is good; and *what does the LORD require of you* but to do justly, to love mercy, and to walk humbly with your God? (Micah 6:8 NKJV, emphasis mine)

---

[1] See the discussions on Israel's failure, as well as discussions on Israel's continued place as an "elect" nation, within the chapters entitled "Another Look at Romans 9 – 11" and "God's Sovereignty Over the Hearts of Men."

This is the basis on which God chooses. His ways have not altered. He is the Lord and He changes not (Malachi 3:6).

Chapter 13

The Foreknowledge of God

With respect to *God's greatness*, consider the following:

> " '**Known to God from eternity** are all His works.' "
> (Acts 15:18 NKJV)

> O LORD, **You have searched me and known me**. You know my sitting down and my rising up; You understand my thought from afar off. You comprehend my path and my lying down, and are acquainted with all my ways. For there is not a word on my tongue, but behold, O LORD, You know it altogether. **You have hedged me behind and before**, and laid Your hand upon me. Such knowledge is too wonderful for me; it is high, I cannot attain it. (Psalm 139:1-6 NKJV)

> "Present your case," says the LORD. "Bring forth your strong reasons," says the King of Jacob. **"Let them bring forth and show us what will happen; let them show the former things, what they were, that we may consider them, and know the latter end of them; or declare to us things to come. Show the things that are to come hereafter, that we may know that you are gods . . ."** (Isaiah 41:21-23 NKJV)

> **"Indeed before the day was, I am He**; and there is no one who can deliver out of My hand; I work, and who will reverse it?" (Isaiah 43:13 NKJV)

> "Tell and bring forth your case; yes, let them take counsel together. **Who has declared this from ancient time? Who has told it from ancient time? Who has told it from that time? Have not I, the LORD?** And there is no other God besides Me, a just God and a Savior; there is none besides Me. Look to Me, and be saved,

all you ends of the earth! For I am God, and there is no other." (Isaiah 45:21-22 NKJV)

For whom He foreknew, He also predestined to be conformed to the image of His Son, that He might be the firstborn among many brethren. (Romans 8:29 NKJV)

[Elect] according to the foreknowledge of God the Father, in sanctification of the Spirit, for obedience and sprinkling of the blood of Jesus Christ . . . (1 Peter 1:2 NKJV)

God has foreknowledge. *He is able* to know ahead of time the ones who will love Him—the ones who will be His. He is able to know the beginning from the end. Yet, as is concluded by some, this part of who God is need not mean that He purposefully plans—before their births and apart from any conditions—the ones who will "irresistibly" be drawn unto Him and the ones who will not.[1] Again, God's sovereign will is that none would perish and that all would come to repentance (Ezekiel 18:31-32; 2 Peter 3:9).

IN CONSIDERATION OF GOD'S FOREKNOWLEDGE

A Most Intimate Knowledge

Notably, it was because of foreknowledge that God could speak of Abraham's heritage. He knew that Abraham, by his own choices, would respond to Him by commanding his family to obey Him. According to the words of the Lord found in Genesis 18:19,[2] it was on the basis of His foreknowledge—*because He knew that Abraham would command his family after him*—that He even could make His promise of greatness unto Abraham:

---

[1] For a proper interpretation of the words "foreknow" and "foreknowledge," see Appendix B, entitled "'Foreknow' and 'Foreknowledge'—Their Most Literal Meanings."

[2] Significantly, see the chapter "Another Look at Various Scriptures" for further discussion of Genesis 18:19 and notable discrepancies between various translations.

"For I **know** him, **that** he will command his children and his household after him, and they shall keep the way of the LORD, to do justice and judgment; that the LORD may bring upon Abraham that which he hath spoken of him." (KJV)

In like manner, it was also because of His foreknowledge that God could choose and separate unto Himself—even before their births—both the prophet Jeremiah and the man He would call "Paul":

> "**Before I formed you in the womb I knew you**, before you were born I set you apart; I appointed you as a prophet to the nations." (Jeremiah 1:5 NIV 1984)

> But when it pleased God, who separated me from my mother's womb and called me through His grace, to reveal His Son in me, that I might preach Him among the Gentiles . . . (Galatians 1:15-16 NKJV)

Moreover, perhaps it was because of foreknowledge—knowing that Pharaoh would *not* listen—that God also would choose to harden Pharaoh's heart and to move him for greater purposes (Exodus 4:21; 7:3-5; Romans 9:17-18).[3]

Having foreknowledge, the Lord could see, ahead of time, into the hearts and lives of Abraham, Jeremiah, and Paul—and He could see into the life of Pharaoh. He was "acquainted with all [their] ways" (Psalm 139:3 NKJV). Likewise, because of foreknowledge, the Lord also can see into the hearts and lives of all whom He has made (see Psalm 33:13-15). He can see into the lives of all men, individually, and He "knows those who are His" (2 Timothy 2:19 NKJV).

Prophetic Foresight

Specially, it is also because of God's infinite knowledge that prophetic

---

[3] For further discussion of the Lord's dealings within men's hearts, see the chapters "God's Sovereignty Over the Hearts of Men" and "Another Look at Romans 9 –11."

words can go forth. Because of His ability to "foresee," God can move prophets, not only to encourage us (see Acts 16:31), but also to prepare and to forewarn concerning future events. Significantly, an account in Acts 21 clearly demonstrates the foreknowledge of God with its prophetic application:

> And as we stayed many days, a certain prophet named Agabus came down from Judea. When he had come to us, he took Paul's belt, bound his own hands and feet, and said, "Thus says the Holy Spirit, 'So shall the Jews at Jerusalem bind the man who owns this belt, and deliver him into the hands of the Gentiles.' " Now when we heard these things, both we and those from that place pleaded with him not to go up to Jerusalem. Then Paul answered, "What do you mean by weeping and breaking my heart? For I am ready not only to be bound, but also to die at Jerusalem for the name of the Lord Jesus." So when he would not be persuaded, we ceased, saying, "The will of the Lord be done." (Acts 21:10-14 NKJV)

Just as the words of Acts 21 display, *because of God's foreknowledge*, the prophet could forewarn concerning the upcoming sufferings of the apostle Paul. Paul could be prepared for the hardships he would endure *if* he should continue toward Jerusalem. Notably, as it happened, the apostle Paul did resolve to journey there anyway—even in spite of sufferings—and also was sent out with a declaration of agreement: "The will [*thelema* / "desire"] of the Lord be done" (Acts 21:14).

The Significance of Acts 21:14

So then, if the will of the Lord was done by Paul's journeying to Jerusalem, does this also mean the Lord was behind and responsible for all the persecution that, in accordance with the prophecy, *did* come unto Paul? If the Lord's desire was done, does it mean the Lord took delight in and (by the inference some have given to God's ability to "foreknow") even *caused* the individuals to persecute Paul? Sadly, because of the connection between Paul's journey and foretold persecution and *the will of the Lord being done*, some have suggested God's "desire" for all evil and, also, it being "in character" with Him both to desire and to predestine any evil found in individuals' hearts.

For certain, because of His ability to see the end from the beginning, God can foresee all the evil that may happen. Even so, just because He foresees an evil event, it is not conclusive that He *caused* the incident or that it was His perfect intent (note Jeremiah 32:35). Having fore-knowledge, God simply may choose to *use* the evil that men will do—in order to carry out greater plans.

Paul understood God's ways—*it is* sometimes His desire that we go through various trials. Likewise, Peter understood God's rule over trials: "For it is better, if it is the will of God, to suffer for doing good than for doing evil" (1 Peter 3:17 NKJV). Abiding in Christ, we should know the greatness of His control over our lives: Nothing will touch us without His desire that it touch us *for a greater purpose*—even to try us and to make us more like His Son—that which *is* to His greater glory (1 Peter 1:6-7; James 1:2-4).

Things Predestined

Importantly, just because something is revealed through prophesy, it is not necessarily a predestined decree. At other times, however, it may be. As scriptures affirm:

> "Thus says the LORD, the King of Israel, and his Re-deemer, the LORD of hosts: 'I am the First and I am the Last; besides Me there is no God. **And who can pro-claim as I do? Then let him declare it and set it in order for Me, since I appointed the ancient people. And the things that are coming and shall come, let them show these to them. Do not fear, nor be afraid; have I not told you from that time, and declared it?** You are My witnesses. Is there a God besides Me? In-deed there is no other Rock; I know not one.' " (Isaiah 44:6-10 NKJV)

> **"Declaring the end from the beginning, and from an-cient times the things that are not yet done, saying,**

301

> **my counsel shall stand** and I will do all my pleasure: calling a ravenous bird from the east, the man that exe-cuteth my counsel from a far country: **yea, I have spo-ken it, I will also bring it to pass; I have purposed it, I will also do it**." (Isaiah 46:10-11 KJV)

> "For truly against Your holy Servant Jesus, whom You anointed, both Herod and Pontius Pilate, with the Gen-tiles and the people of Israel, were gathered together **to do whatever Your hand and Your purpose deter-mined before to be done**." (Acts 4:27-28 NKJV)

In truth, although God does *not* command all that happens,[4] the above words speak concerning the *sureness* of the things God *does* command to happen. Moreover, God declares beforehand so that, when it comes, we may know *He is God* and that He is like no other (Isaiah 45:21-22; Isaiah 48 – 49).

God watches over all. Indeed, *because of His infinite foreknowledge of men's actions*, some things have been commanded as a "let there be" that, as yet, still may not have happened. Notwithstanding, because God has spoken—and because His determinations shall stand—the day of their fulfillment will come.

Finally, consider, as well, the words of the following:

> All who dwell on the earth will worship him [the beast], whose names have not been written **in the Book of Life of the Lamb slain from the foundation of the world**. (Revelation 13:8 NKJV)

> And those who dwell on the earth will marvel, whose names are not written **in the Book of Life from the foundation of the world**, when they see the beast that was, and is not, and yet is. (Revelation 17:8 NKJV)

---

[4] See 1 Samuel 13:13-14; 15:10-11; Jeremiah 23:32; 32:35; and the chapter "Signifi-cant Scriptures—Part 1."

To be certain, in His foreknowledge, from the foundation of the world, the Father both saw and predestined the substitutionary sacrifice of His Son (who is the Passover Lamb)! Likewise, the Father can foresee the steadfastness of the ones who will remain written in the Lamb's Book of Life![5] (**See** Revelation 3:5 footnote below.) These words of Revelations need not cause confusion—if we accept the co-existing truths that are upon God's foundation.

THE FOREKNOWLEDGE OF GOD *AND* OUR RESPONSIBILITY
THE *SEAL* UPON GOD'S FOUNDATION

Consider the universe—how it goes on and on is beyond our capacity to comprehend. And yet, although we cannot fathom its infinite vastness—although we cannot grasp such with our human minds—the universe is real just the same. Likewise, although we may not fully comprehend it, these two also exist simultaneously—the foreknowledge of God and our own very real responsibility. Just as the apostle Paul would affirm:

> The solid foundation of God stands, having this seal: **"The Lord knows those who are His,"** and, **"Let everyone who names the name of Christ depart from iniquity."** (2 Timothy 2:19 NKJV)

Truly, although God is greater than all and can see all things, we still have very real responsibility. Even Jesus took note of the foreknowledge of God—with *man's* responsibility:

> "The Son of Man indeed **goes just as it is written of Him, but woe to that man by whom He is betrayed!** It would have been good for that man if he had never been born." (Mark 14:21 NKJV)

---

[5] **Note**: Lest the words of Revelation 17:8 be considered as support for Calvinist TULIP teaching, according to Revelation 3:5, individuals' names also can be "blot[ted] . . . out of the Book of Life."

Likewise, with respect to his own life, the apostle Paul also demonstrated an understanding of God's high place, alongside man's responsibility:

> But when it pleased **God, who separated me from my mother's womb** and called me through His grace to reveal His son in me, that I might preach Him . . . (Galatians 1:15-16 NKJV)

> But **I discipline my body and bring it into subjection, lest, when I have preached to others, I myself should become disqualified**. (1 Corinthians 9:27 NKJV)

Quite notably, in his words to the Galatians, Paul acknowledged God's greatness and care over all his life. Paraphrased further, one might read Paul's words: *"God was with me all along, having plans for me and seeing what I would become."* Yet, in his other statement, Paul spoke equally of the care that he took—lest, having preached, he should fail and be "disqualified" (1 Corinthians 9:27). Thus, very significant to note: Paul's understanding of God's greatness and foreknowledge in no way diminished his serious regard for his own responsibility.

IN CONCLUSION—HIS *INCOMPREHENSIBLE* GREATNESS

Although the truth of God's foreknowledge need not confuse the truth of our very real responsibility, some have failed to comprehend their co-existence. The Lord understands the limitations of our flesh; nevertheless, as God's creation, we must humble ourselves to remember His greatness: *God is not like us, and He has abilities that we do not share.*

Furthermore, in the fear of God, we must also be careful never to go "beyond what is written" (1 Corinthians 4:6), attributing things to God just because, by our own experiences, we may not have been able to understand their working. The truth is—we will never comprehend God's greatness! "His greatness is unsearchable" (Psalm 145:3 NKJV) and "His understanding is infinite" (Psalm 147:5 NKJV)! Only ours is not.

To be sure, nothing bypasses God, and nothing catches Him by surprise. Knowing all things, He can know beforehand what we shall become. Just as the psalmist recognized and expressed the greatness of God's infinite knowledge, we, too, should declare: *"Such knowledge is too wonderful for me; it is high, I cannot attain it"* (Psalm 139:6 NKJV).

CONFUSING SCRIPTURES

Chapter 14

Another Look at Ephesians 1

PREFACE

The first chapter of Ephesians is often cited as a text that supports the interpretation of election—that specific *individuals* are unconditionally predestined to receive Jesus before they are even born. Yet, may we take another look, going verse by verse, to see if there might be another meaning? Firstly, however, let us even consider a sampling of other scriptures that might help shed meaning to Paul's words.

> Acts 2:23
> [Peter, addressing the Pentecost crowd and describing the life and work of the man, Jesus.] "This man was handed over to you **by God's set purpose** [*boule*][1] **and foreknowledge**." (NIV 1984)

> Romans 1:2
> [Paul, speaking about the gospel for which he had been set apart by God.] **The gospel he promised beforehand** through his prophets in the Holy Scriptures regarding his Son . . ." (NIV 1984)

> 2 Timothy 1:9-10
> [Paul, speaking of God's eternal purpose in Jesus that was made manifest by the appearing of Jesus.] Who hath saved us, and called us with an holy calling, not according to our works, but according to **his own purpose and grace, which was given us in Christ Jesus before the world began, but is now made manifest by the appearing of our Saviour Jesus Christ**, who hath abol-

---

[1] E.W. Bullinger, *A Critical Lexicon and Concordance to the English and Greek New Testament* (Grand Rapids, MI: Kregel Publications, 1999; orig. pub. 1908), pp. 189, xiii.

ished death, and hath brought life and immortality to light through the gospel. (KJV)

1 Peter 1:18-21
For you know that it was not with perishable things such as silver or gold that you were redeemed from the empty way of life handed down to you from your forefathers, but with the precious blood of **Christ, a lamb without blemish or defect. He was chosen** [*proginosko* / "having been foreknown"][2] **before the creation of the world**, but was revealed in these last times for your sake. **Through him** you believe in God, who raised him from the dead and glorified him, and so your faith and hope are **in God**. (NIV1984)

God has always been on the throne and in control. The apostles knew that. From this sampling of scriptures, it can be seen that the apostles often addressed the fact that God, knowing man's sin, had planned and purposed ahead of time—even before the foundation of the world—to send a savior to redeem him from his sin.[3]

In addition, consider the following scriptures, where Paul makes mention of the wisdom of God ordained before the world—the mystery God had hidden for ages and had just revealed to the church:

1 Corinthians 2:6-8
[Paul, speaking of the wisdom of God—who is Jesus (1 Corinthians 1:30).] Howbeit we speak wisdom among them that are perfect: yet not the wisdom of the world, nor of the princes of this world, that come to nought: **But we speak the wisdom of God in a mystery, even the hidden wisdom, which God ordained before the**

---

[2] Ibid., pp. 302, xiii; *The Zondervan Parallel New Testament in Greek and English*, 8th ed. (New York: Zondervan Publishing House, 1982), p. 687.

[3] Please note: Although, in His foreknowledge, God planned to send mankind a savior, we need not conclude that God planned man's sin. God can see the end from the beginning—He is not limited by time. It was in that foreknowledge, *seeing that man would sin*, that He planned to send a savior.

world unto our glory: Which none of the princes of this world knew: for had they known it, they would not have crucified the Lord of glory. (KJV)

Colossians 1:25-27
[Paul, addressing the church, to whom he had become a servant.] I have become its servant by the commission God gave me to present to you the word of God in its fullness—**the mystery that has been kept hidden for ages and generations**, but is now disclosed to the saints. To them [the saints] God has chosen to make known among the Gentiles [the nations] the glorious riches of **this mystery, which is Christ in you, the hope of glory.** (NIV 1984)

Ephesians 3:2-12
Surely you have heard about the administration of God's grace that was given to me for you, that is, **the mystery made known to me by revelation**, *as I have already written briefly.* [Is he referring maybe to what he had previously written, found in Ephesians 1?] In reading this, then you will be able to understand my insight into **the mystery of Christ**, which was not made known to men in other generations as it has now been revealed by the Spirit to God's holy apostles and prophets. **This mystery is that through the gospel the Gentiles are heirs together with Israel, members together of one body, and sharers together in the promise *in Christ Jesus.*** . . . [This] grace was given me: to preach to the Gentiles the unsearchable riches of Christ, and to make plain to everyone the administration of **this mystery, which for ages past was kept hidden in God**, who created all things. His intent was that now, through the church, the manifold wisdom of God should be made known to the rulers and authorities in the heavenly realms, **according to the eternal purpose** [*prothesis*][4]

---

[4] Bullinger, *A Critical Lexicon and Concordance to the English and Greek New Testament*, pp. 614, xiii.

311

which he accomplished in Christ Jesus our Lord. In him and through faith in him we may approach God with freedom and confidence. (NIV1984, emphasis mine)

God had always had a special plan for how mankind would be restored to Himself following the fall: **"Christ in [us]"** (Colossians 1:27). He had planned that it would be *His* work and not man's work. Furthermore, as Ephesians 3:6 points out, God had purposed throughout all ages to have a people of all nations—and not just Israel—who would trust in Christ's work.[5] Yet, the plan of God to have a people "in Him," a mystery, had been kept hidden through the ages. That mystery was only then, upon Jesus' completed work, being disclosed to the church. Paul was excited about this revelation and he had to share it!

Throughout the New Testament, we also see other references made in terms of us being "in Christ" or "in Him." Also, phrases such as "by Him" and "through Him" are used. Phrases like these are all referring to the only hope and provision for life we have—Jesus Christ. Indeed, we must "be found in him, not having a righteousness of [our] own . . . but that which is through faith in Christ—the righteousness that comes from God and is by faith" (Philippians 3:9 NIV1984).

EPHESIANS 1

The previous scripture which was referred to, in Colossians 1:25-27, is only a part of a rich letter written by Paul. Before looking at Ephesians 1, therefore, may I suggest that the entire first chapter of Colossians be reviewed? Much of what Paul was impressed to share with the church of Colosse, in his opening remarks, seems quite similar to the introduction in his letter to the church of Ephesus. Likewise, because similar themes of *God's greatness* and *the sure hope of the believer* can also be found in Romans 8, that chapter is also helpful for understanding context.[6]

---

[5] Similarly, as can be seen in the chapter "Another Look at Romans 9 – 11," Paul also addressed the Romans concerning this *new* defining of whom God's people would be.
[6] See a discussion of Romans 8 within the chapter "Another Look at Various Scriptures."

Then significantly, as the first chapter of Ephesians is read, keep in mind the patterns of apostolic emphasis that have been noted. Keep in mind references to God's purpose, appointed beforehand, even before creation, *to have Christ become our substitutionary sacrifice.* When the verb "predestined" (*proorizo* / "determine, decree or ordain before-hand")[7] appears, ask the question "predestined what?". Also, watch for "in Christ" type references.

The Text of Ephesians 1:1-23

Paul, an apostle of Christ Jesus by the will [*thelema*][8] of God, to the saints in Ephesus, the faithful **in Christ Jesus**: (2) Grace and peace to you from God our Father and the Lord Jesus Christ. (3) Praise be to the God and Father of our Lord Jesus Christ, who has blessed us in the heavenly realms with every spiritual blessing **in Christ**. (4) For [*kathos* / "according as, even as . . ."][9] he chose us **in him** before the creation of the world to be holy and blameless in his sight. In love (5) he predestined [*proorizo*][10] us to be adopted as his sons **through Jesus Christ**, in accordance with his pleasure and will [*thelema*][11]—(6) to the praise of his glorious grace, which he has freely given us **in the One he loves**. (7) **In him** we have redemption **through his blood**, the forgiveness of sins, in accordance with the riches of God's grace (8) that he lavished on us with all wisdom and understanding. (9) And he made known to us the mystery of his will [*thelema*][12] according to his good pleasure, which he purposed [*protithemi*][13] **in Christ**, (10) to be put into effect when the times will have reached their fulfillment—to

---

[7] Bullinger, *A Critical Lexicon and Concordance to the English and Greek New Testament*, pp. 597, xiii.
[8] Ibid., pp. 883, xiii.
[9] Ibid., pp. 24, xiii.
[10] Ibid., pp. 597, xiii.
[11] Ibid., pp. 883, xiii.
[12] Ibid., pp. 883, xiii.
[13] Ibid., pp. 614, xiii.

bring all things in heaven and on earth together under one head, even Christ [*en auto* / **"in him"**].[14] (11) **In him** we were also chosen [*kleroo*[15] / "chosen as inheritance"/"have obtained an inheritance" (IGNT and KJV)[16]], having been predestined [*proorizo*][17] according to the plan [*prothesis*][18] of him who works out everything in conformity with the purpose [*boule*][19] of his will, (12) in order that we, who were the first to hope **in Christ**, might be for the praise of his glory. (13) And you also were included **in Christ** when you heard the word of truth, the gospel of your salvation. Having believed, you were marked **in him** with a seal, the promised Holy Spirit, (14) who is a deposit guaranteeing our inheritance [*kleronomia*][20] until the redemption of those who are God's possession—to the praise of his glory. (15) For this reason, ever since I heard about *your faith* **in the Lord Jesus** and *your love for all the saints,* (16) I have not stopped giving thanks for you, remembering you in my prayers. (17) I keep asking that the God of our Lord Jesus Christ, the glorious Father, may give you the Spirit of wisdom and revelation, so that you may know him better. (18) I pray also that the eyes of your heart may be enlightened in order that you may know the hope to which he has called you, the riches of his glorious inheritance [*kleronomia*][21] in the saints, (19) and his incomparably great power for us who believe. That power is like the working of his mighty strength, (20) which he exerted in Christ when he raised him from the dead and seated him at his right hand in the heavenly realms, (21) far above all

---

[14] Ibid., pp. 375-376, xiii; *The Zondervan Parallel New Testament in Greek and English*, 8th ed. (New York; The Zondervan Corporation, 1982), p. 563.

[15] Bullinger, *A Critical Lexicon and Concordance to the English and Greek New Testament*, pp. 413, xiii.

[16] *The Zondervan Parallel New Testament in Greek and English*, pp. 562-563.

[17] Bullinger, *A Critical Lexicon and Concordance to the English and Greek New Testament*, pp. 597, xiii.

[18] Ibid., pp. 614, xiii.

[19] Ibid., pp. 189, xiii.

[20] Ibid., pp. 413, xiii.

[21] Ibid.

rule and authority, power and dominion, and every title that can be given, not only in the present age but also in the one to come. (22) And God placed all things under his feet and appointed him to be head over everything for the church, (23) which is his body, the fullness of him who fills everything in every way. (NIV1984, emphasis mine)

Upon reading, certain things can be noted right away. Noticeably, there are fourteen "in Christ" type references. The emphasis is certainly **on what we have *in Jesus*.** The emphasis is *not* **on man.**

Also, we can see specifics concerning the ones *about whom* Paul is speaking. In verses 3 through 12, Paul is speaking about what has been given to *the whole church, corporately.* (Note that he speaks over and over with the pronouns "us" and "we.") Beginning with verse 13, Paul *then* turns and speaks specifically to those of the church in Ephesus. (Notice the change of person to second person "you.")

Significantly, as well, within Paul's greeting in verse 1, we also see a distinctive and *conditional* qualification of the ones to whom Paul is referring. The "we" and the "you" are all *"faithful in Christ Jesus."*

Another Look at Paul's Intent

Finally, and in contrast to certain interpretations, consider, anew, the meaning of this first chapter, verse by verse.

(1-2) Paul is addressing the letter to the church in Ephesus—to those "in Him" who are "saints" and "faithful" in Christ. (Note: *Pistos*, the Greek word translated as "faithful," also can be translated as "trusting, believing.")[22] Quite notably, in so doing, Paul likewise gives to us important qualification. Next, following Paul's greeting, he blesses them.

---

[22] Ibid., pp. 272, xiii.

(3) God is so good! We are so blessed! "In Christ," He has blessed us (all the faithful / all the believers "in Him") with every spiritual blessing in the heavenlies! This verse sets the tone and gives context to the verses that follow.

Next, Paul begins to outlay some of the spiritual blessings to which he is referring.

(4) He has given all these blessings to us (His church) now, according as (*kathos*) He had planned to do (because of foreknowledge) from the foundation of the world. His plan, purposed before the creation of the world, was that He would have a people, chosen because of their faith "in Him," who would be set apart and blameless before Him. As he had planned, it has happened! No longer are we separated from God and under the condemnation of sin. We have been brought near to God, free from accusation. To God's glory, let it also be known that His work to redeem us had been settled from the beginning!

(5) In love, He also predestined—purposed ahead of time—to adopt us as sons to Himself—and that "through Jesus Christ." (**This is not speaking of a predestination of particular "individuals"—nor of a predestination apart from choices that are made—** but of *a predestination to an adoption as "sons" for those who would put their hope "in Him."*) All of this was done because it pleased Him and it was what He wanted—His will (His desire).

(6) This is all to the praise of His glorious grace! These undeserved blessings, apart from works, but all by faith in His work, are to His glory! (His works praise Him!) God has freely given us this grace (this unmerited favor) "in the One He loves."

(7) Blessings continue. It is "in Him" (the One He loves—Jesus) that we have redemption through His blood—the forgiveness of our sins.

(8) The riches of God's grace (favor) were poured out on us by God, with all wisdom and intelligence. God knew what He was doing. His way is perfect.

(9) God made known to us the mystery of what His will has been. The mystery had been hidden for ages. Now it is revealed. Paul also reminds us that what God purposed—what God planned in Christ—was what brought Him great pleasure.

(10) Here is the mystery: At just the right time, "when the times will have reached their fulfillment," He planned to bring restoration to what had happened since the sin of Adam. He would bring *all things* in heaven and earth together under the headship of Christ (see Ephesians 2:11-22). Things would be brought together "in Him" (as the end of the verse says by *en auto* in the Greek). The complete fulfillment of God's plan is yet to come—coming in the end, when Jesus returns, with a glorious revelation of the "sons of God," even to all creation. (See Romans 8:18-23 and Colossians 1:15-20.)

(11) Blessings continue. "In Him," we not only have redemption and forgiveness of sins, but we also were made His heirs (**note** the paragraph following). The fact that God chose those "in Him" to be heirs is something He planned ahead of time, in accordance with what He determined best to do. He predestined, planned beforehand, that those redeemed and "in Him" would receive His rich inheritance (some to be received now and some to be received in the age to come). Paul also reminds us that God works out everything to see that His purposes are fulfilled. Nothing shall thwart His purposes.

(**Significantly**, the Greek translation of the word, which the NIV1984 translates as "chosen," renders more fully "chosen as inheritance."[23] According to Bullinger's Lexicon, the meaning of *kleroo*, the word the NIV1984 translated for "chosen," is "to acquire by lot, to obtain, possess."[24] Note even the root similarity to the Greek word *kleronomia*, which is translated as "inheritance" in verses 14 and 18.)

(12) Perhaps, to better understand the intent of this passage, it is first helpful to note that "the first to hope," as translated in the NIV1984, might also be translated "hoped before." The Greek from which it is translated is *proelpizo*, meaning "hope first."[25] The verb is a combination of *pro* (meaning "before") and *elpizo* (meaning "to expect, to hope").[26] Even the KJV translates the word as "first trusted." So, again, the fruit of God's purpose is that we, who hoped before "in Christ," should be to the praise of *His* glory. If our hope is *in Christ*, we *shall* be to the praise of His glory.

(13) Paul now turns to address the church in Ephesus, declaring such as the following: *You*, individually, were included "in Him." *You* not only heard the word of truth—the gospel of salvation—but you also believed "in Him." Because of this, *you* were sealed with the Holy Spirit who had been promised.

(14) Paul continues to affirm the inheritance all have received in Christ. Even the Holy Spirit, whom the Ephesians had received, is a deposit—guaranteeing that which we shall receive. Because of the Holy Spirit's continued presence in our lives, we can know that we are heirs. We can look forward to all that we shall re-

---

[23] *The Zondervan Parallel New Testament in Greek and English*, p. 573.
[24] Bullinger, *A Critical Lexicon and Concordance to the English and Greek New Testament*, pp. 413, xiii.
[25] Ibid., pp. 823, xiii.
[26] Ibid.

ceive. And all of this is "to the praise of His glory." (Paul's words, here, of the future glory to be revealed at "the redemption of those who are God's" are very similar to his words found in Romans 8:14-23.)

(15-16) There is a knowing, in Paul's heart, of the true faith of the Ephesians (very similar to his knowing of the Thessalonians' faith). Because Paul knows of the faith of those in Ephesus—seeing the evidence of the Holy Spirit and their love for all the saints—he is thankful for them and wants them to know of his prayers for them.

Lastly, in the following verses, we get a feel for Paul's heartthrob—what is probably the motivation behind the introductory words contained in the first chapter of his letter to the Ephesians and, similarly, behind many of his words found in Romans 8.

(17-19) Paul shares with these saints of Ephesus special things for which he prays for them. He prays that they would know God more fully. He prays that they would know the hope of His calling and the riches of His inheritance in the saints. He prays that the church of Ephesus would know the greatness of God's power to those who believe.

(20-22) Paul describes what God's power is like. God exerted His power in Christ when He raised Him from the dead and seated Him at His right hand in the heavenlies. Jesus has been raised so high that He is above and over all things—all rule and powers and every name both now and in the future.

(23-24) Paul continues to highlight the place the Father has given to Jesus. He has placed all things under Jesus' feet. He is the head of the church, His body. Paul alludes to the place that the church has *in Him*. The church is the "fullness" of Him.

IN CONCLUSION

Can it be seen that the emphasis of the beginning of Paul's letter to the Ephesians is *not* the unconditional election of individuals? The emphasis is an acknowledgement of the work God has done *for the church*, and the abundant blessings He has poured out upon all His people—*in Christ Jesus*. For He chose us, not by our works, but by *His* works alone—"to the praise of His glorious grace." Paul desired God to receive *all* the glory (vv. 6, 7, 12, and 14), not only for the work performed for individuals, but for the fulfillment of a work—even for *all* mankind—that had been purposed throughout the ages.

"Predestination" *is* a word found in the Bible—and, used correctly, it is not to be shunned. God *has* always been on the throne. He has never been defeated by Satan. He, in His foreknowledge, had always had a plan for the redemption of His creation (see Colossians 1:19-20), even from the foundation of the world. Just like the other apostles, in his letter to the Ephesians, Paul would glorify God for His eternal plan—and for all His purposes that He causes to be.[27]

---

[27] See the chapter "The *Will* of God" for a greater understanding of words used that specifically denote determinations and plans that God has made.

Chapter 15

Another Look at Romans 9 – 11

Within Romans 9 – 11, much is written concerning the important truth of God's "election of grace" (Romans 9:11; 11:5; 11:7). Yet, sadly, even though the intent of Paul's writings on election was to explain God's eternal purpose to have a people chosen by grace—*and never by man's works*—many of his words have been seriously misconstrued as support for the Calvinist doctrine of *unconditional election*. In light of this, therefore, and in order to understand more accurately the truth of election, let us examine several statements found within these chapters.

THE NOTION OF AN *UNCONDITIONAL HATRED*

Some have argued the doctrine of *unconditional election* just on the basis of Paul's words, found in Romans 9:10-13, which speak:

> When Rebecca also had conceived by one man, even by our father Isaac (11) **(for the children not yet being born, nor having done any good or evil, that the purpose of God according to election might stand, not of works but of Him who calls**), (12) it was said to her, "The older shall serve the younger." (13) As it is written, **"Jacob I have loved, but Esau I have hated [*miseo*]¹."** (NKJV)

Accordingly, by some, "election" is argued as being "unconditional" because of Paul's words that Jacob, "not yet being born, nor having done any evil," was selected over Esau. Furthermore, as an argument for "unconditional wrath," it is often noted that Esau, likewise, was "hated." Understandably, there can be confusion. May I suggest, however, that there is other likely intent for Paul's words?

---

¹ James Strong, LL.D., S.T.D., *Strong's Complete Word Study Concordance* (Chattanooga, TN: AMG Publishers, 2004), pp. 635, 2115.

First, with respect to God's *loving* ways, the connotation given to the word "hate" should not be the connotation normally given in the English language. This becomes evident from the following scripture, where the same Greek word is used:

> If anyone comes to Me and does not **hate** [*miseo*][2] his father and mother, wife and children, brothers and sisters, yes, and his own life also, he cannot be My disciple. (Luke 14:26 NKJV)

Surely, there must be other meaning. Surely, we are not called to hate our loved ones and our own selves. Likewise, God probably did not unconditionally hate Esau, in our own manner of speaking. Perhaps more accurately rendered: **God chose to demonstrate *less favor* toward Esau than to Jacob.** Indeed, accurately, according to Bullinger's Lexicon, not only can the word used convey the meaning "to hate," but the word also may express the idea: "to love less, not to love, to slight."[3]

Contextually, as the statements in verses 10-13 appear, Paul was explaining *God's continuing choice* with whom His people would be. He was illustrating the truth, concerning election, that God's ways had not changed, and His word had not failed (v. 6). The promise of Abraham's seed had been maintained throughout many junctures (vv. 6-13)—each involving God's selection. Not only would Paul declare God's faithfulness to His promises, by selecting through the seed of Christ, but he would also declare, with verse 11, the significance of the fact that God's purpose, **God's chosen and *elect* way, has always been contrary to man's works**—so that none may boast. (See also Romans 3:27; 4:2-5; 1 Corinthians 1:26-31; and Ephesians 2:8-9.)

PAUL'S RESPONSE TO THOSE WHO WOULD ACCUSE GOD

Furthermore, not only has Romans 9:10-13 often been misrepresented as a support for "unconditional election," but other verses of chapter 9

---

[2] Ibid.
[3] E.W. Bullinger, *A Critical Lexicon and Concordance to the English and Greek New Testament* (Grand Rapids, MI: Kregel Publications, 1999; orig. pub. 1908), p. 354.

have been misrepresented as well. It was following his prior statements about the unconditional selection of Jacob over Esau (as the line through which the nation of Israel would proceed) that Paul proceeded to make statements that have been the subject of equal confusion. Consider anew the following:

> What shall we say then? Is there unrighteousness with God? Certainly not! (15) For He says to Moses, **"I will have mercy on whomever I will have mercy, and I will have compassion on whomever I will have compassion."** (16) **So then it is not of him who wills, nor of him who runs, but of God who shows mercy. . . .** (18) **Therefore He has mercy on whom He wills, and whom He wills he hardens.** (19) **You will say to me then, "Why does He still find fault? For who has resisted His will** [*boulema* / "deliberate intention, that which is purposed, designed, planned or intended"[4]]**?"** (20) But indeed, O man, who are you to reply against God? Will the things formed say to him who formed it, "Why have you made me like this?" (21) **Does not the potter have power over the clay, from the same lump to make one vessel for honor and another for dishonor?** (Romans 9:14-21 NKJV)

Notably, it was in anticipation of men's reactions to his previous statements that Paul responded, in kind, with the statements of verses 14-16, and then later, following an interjection, with the words of verses 18-21. Paul took great issue with men's arrogance towards God, and so should we. Would we accuse God? Does He have to answer to us? Truly, God is God, and, just as God had spoken to Moses, He will show kindness to whomever He wants (as He had done in selecting the lineage of Jacob—the controversial action of God for which Paul was making a defense). None of us ever deserve His mercy.

Additionally, the statements of verses 16, 18, and 19 also often have been cited, together, as continued support for the predetermined and "unconditional election" of individuals unto either wrath or salvation.

---

[4] Ibid., p. 883; Strong, *Strong's Complete Word Study Concordance*, pp. 1690, 2044.

According to verses 16 and 18, men are viewed as having *no redress or choice* concerning the things that might happen eternally. Moreover, without an application of the *specific* Greek word used for the word "will," the statement in verse 19 becomes seeming support as well. The words "who can resist God's will?" are interpreted as *proof* concerning one's inability to affect his own salvation—for God's will (often wrongly rendered as "desire," in this verse, instead of the more accurate rendering as "deliberate intentions") will always happen, never to be resisted. Yet, with a better understanding of the original Greek word used (see "The *Will* of God"), as well as the surrounding context, other likely intent for Paul's statements becomes increasingly clear.[5]

To be sure, God will do what He wants to do—what He *determines*. He will do things *His* way. **No matter how much one may desire or strive to do so, no one can resist His *determinations*—the things He has planned to do.** Nonetheless, as is claimed by some, Paul was *not* referring to an unconditional selection of *individuals* unto salvation by the statements that he made.

As noted earlier, Paul was, instead, referring to God's fairness and consistency in having chosen a way other than man's works (for which man might boast) and in having craftily rendered *due judgment* upon a rebellious people. Through his bold, often misunderstood statements (see 2 Peter 3:16), Paul was responding to what he perceived peoples' reactions would be to an idea that **God will do things *His* way—apart from our "say so" or strivings**. God's predetermined plans *to choose* a people, apart from their own works, and His predetermined plan *to keep* for greater purposes and, afterwards, *to remove* rebellious Israel from her prior position of prominence and favor—just might ruffle a few feathers.

THE HARDENING OF PHARAOH'S HEART

Continuing his theme that God's word had not failed (v. 6), Paul then interjects, amidst the previous two sets of verses noted, further state-

---

[5] **Important**: See the chapter "The *Will* of God" for a discussion of the *specific* meanings of words that have sometimes just been translated as "will." Also, see the chapter "Significant Scriptures—Part 1."

ments that have been cited as support for "unconditional election." Bringing to mind the *consistency* of God's ways, Paul writes the strong and often misrepresented words of verses 17-18:

> For the Scripture says to the Pharaoh, "For this very purpose I have raised you up, that I may show My power in you, and that My name may be declared in all the earth!" **Therefore, He has mercy on whom He wills, and whom He wills He hardens.** (NKJV)

In truth, God's ways had not changed, nor had His word failed. Just as God had dealt with Pharaoh, God had dealt with Israel. Just as God had chosen to harden Pharaoh, God had chosen to harden Israel.

Significantly, even as God had spoken concerning His dealings with Pharaoh, Paul understood: "that [His] name may be declared in all the earth . . . He has mercy on whom He wills, and whom He wills He hardens" (v. 17). Truly, God's utmost purpose is that He be known in the greatness of who He is. We should never forget—*it is all about Him and His glory.*

Grievously, however, with response to God's hardening of Pharaoh's heart, some have argued a case of God's *total* responsibility as to whether one faces judgment or comes to know life in Christ. By the precedent of Pharaoh's hardening, some have argued it being, thus, in character with God, not to allow individuals *even an opportunity* to hear and to be saved. Indeed, there *was* a point at which *God* hardened Pharaoh's heart—in order to do *His great work* in the deliverance of His people. Knowing this, however, we should be very careful not to add more to the scripture than is given.

According to the text of Exodus, at which point God—and not Pharaoh himself—did the "hardening," it is unclear. (According to Hebrews 3:7-8, we can harden *our own* hearts by *our own* failures to respond to God's words.) Simply, the truth stands: In His foreknowledge and frugal wisdom, God chose not only *to keep* Pharaoh (one who had deserved an earlier execution of judgment for his own hardness) and *to raise him up* into his position of kingship, but He also chose *to redeem*

Pharaoh unto Himself for a greater display of His glory.[6]

God's ways are consistent. Just as God did with Pharaoh, it is not strange that He should have delayed Israel's forewarned judgment in order that, through her judgment, also a greater work might be accomplished for His glory. Furthermore, just as God chose to do with Pharaoh, He can harden, consequential to sin, whomever He wants. We, therefore, should all fear—we should never presume upon God's mercy. In view of God's dealings with Pharaoh and His elect Israel, we all should be careful to heed at first call. Although God "takes no pleasure in the death of the wicked" (Ezekiel 33:11) and "mercy triumphs over judgment" (James 2:13), there may come a time when all sensitivity of conscience is taken away. Then, in so doing, God would still be just.

"VESSELS" IN THE HANDS OF *THE POTTER*

But indeed, O man, who are you to reply against God? Will the thing formed say to him who formed it, "Why have you made me like this?" (21) Does not the potter have power over the clay, from the same lump to make **one vessel for honor and another for dishonor**? (22) What if God, wanting to show His wrath and to make His power known [on Pharaoh and Israel alike], endured with much longsuffering the **vessels of wrath** prepared for destruction, (23) and that He might make known the riches of His glory on the **vessels of mercy**, which He had prepared beforehand for glory, (24) even us whom He called, not of the Jews only, but also of the Gentiles? (Romans 9:20-24 NKJV)

Paul's descriptions of various "vessels," in the hands of a potter, similarly have fueled, within the minds of some, the thought of a predestined and "unconditional election." Again, although the intention of Paul's deep expressions of thought can be difficult to determine for certain, the statements made do not support the conclusion of an "unconditional election." There is other likely intention for Paul's analogy.

---

[6] See the chapter entitled "God's Sovereignty Over the Hearts of Men."

Instead of an "unconditional election," Paul's references to "vessels of honor" and "vessels of dishonor," within verse 21, probably simply relate to the vessels that God chooses to keep, in contrast to the vessels that He chooses to readily discard. **"Vessels of honor" are not for just any ordinary use—they are *kept* for special use**—whereas "vessels of dishonor" are for ordinary use, and then just thrown away.

In light of Paul's preceding discourse from verses 17-18 (which speaks of Pharaoh's and Israel's like *keeping* and *hardening* for God's further use and glory) and Paul's next statement in verse 22 (which speaks concerning God's endurance of vessels *deserving of earlier destruction*), the contrast between "vessels of honor" and "vessels of dishonor" does gain its likely meaning. **Both Pharaoh and Israel, alike, had judgments awaiting them; yet, they were *kept* (and not discarded) for God's greater purposes**. In any case, Paul argues, God—the Potter—will do whatever He pleases with that which He makes.

Additionally, although some might also propose that "vessels of honor" are synonymous with "vessels of mercy," and, likewise, "vessels of dishonor" with "vessels of wrath," in such a case, an *unconditional* selection is still not implied. Simply, just as verses 22 and 23 specify, **the "vessels of wrath" and the "vessels of mercy"** (the nation Israel and the ones "grafted in" through Christ) **both had been "prepared"— even by *their own* doings—ahead of time**. Then God, in turn, had also rendered accordingly.[7]

ISRAEL'S FAILURE AND THE GENTILES' GAIN

What shall we say then? That Gentiles, who did not pursue righteousness, have attained to righteousness, even the righteousness of faith; but Israel, pursuing the law of righteousness, has not attained to the law of righteousness. Why? **Because they did not seek it by faith, but**

---

[7] See Isaiah 65:6-7; Jeremiah 17:10; 1 Corinthians 2:9-10; the chapter "Our Real Effect upon Our Salvation"; and the discussion of Romans 1, found within the chapter "Inconsistencies—Part 2."

as it were, by the works of the law. For they stumbled at that stumbling stone. (Romans 9:30-32 NKJV)

In truth, Israel had sought after God; nonetheless, although that nation had displayed an outward "zeal for God" (Romans 10:2), they had not submitted to *God's chosen way*—which is "the just shall live by faith" (Romans 10:1-4; Habakkuk 2:4). Instead, in great haughtiness, the children of Israel had repeatedly refused Him and chosen to go their own ways—even in the midst of His continued displays of kindness (Isaiah 65:2-7).

Indeed, God had been longsuffering—reaching out to Israel even "all day long" (Romans 10:21). Yet, in the end, only His way would stand. Provoking Israel to jealousy (10:19; 11:11), and in fulfillment to that which He had spoken, He would be found (Romans 10:22) by a people who had no "form of godliness" (2 Timothy 3:5). He would be found by a people who had not been "called by [His] name" (Isaiah 65:1). Breaking off *the natural*, God would graft in *the spiritual* in her stead, and Paul would remind the Romans of the thing that God had foretold:

> "I will call them My people, who were not My people, and her beloved, who was not beloved. And it shall come to pass in the place where it was said to them, 'You are not My people,' there they shall be called sons of the living God." (Romans 9:25-26 NKJV)

In Christ, not only would a faithful Jewish remnant (Romans 11:1-5, 7, 17, and 23-24) remain, but Gentiles would become candidates as God's *elect* as well (Romans 9:24; 10:11-15). Moreover, in response to Israel's failure, and until such time as the elect *nation* be restored and grafted in again,[8] alongside the church (11:23-29), the church alone—Abraham's *spiritual* "seed of promise"—would shine forth as His "light" and as His glory upon the earth (Romans 9:7-8; Matthew 5:14; Ephesians 5:8; Philippians 2:15).

---

[8] **Important**: See the discussions concerning God's frugal workings with vessels "prepared ["readied"] for destruction" and God's purpose to "bring back" the elect nation found within the chapter "God's Sovereignty Over the Hearts of Men."

IN CONCLUSION

Had God been just? Had God's word failed concerning Israel? Had man been given no real choice concerning his salvation? Certainly, Paul was purposeful in the things that he spoke.

Even as Paul expounded, not only had God been just in choosing other vessels on which to display His glory—a people who would accept a salvation *through His arm and not their own works* (Romans 11:5-6; Romans 10:11-13; Isaiah 51:4-6)—but He also had been just in sustaining and in hardening Israel for His greater work of salvation. As Paul declared, the nation had long been overdue consequences for its continued resistance to His ways. Long before, the nation had been *readied* for destruction (Romans 9:22).

Furthermore, not only had God's ways been just concerning Israel and His word not failed, but the word of the Lord was actually being fulfilled. Israel had not been clueless concerning that which God intended to do. Many times, His plans had been spoken through the prophets (Romans 10:19-21). God's works had been foretold—and Paul would carefully remind the Romans of the words that God had spoken.

Finally, although Paul's discourse to the Romans has been mistakenly applied by many, it is, nonetheless, very significant in what it speaks to us today. To be certain, although God's "election of grace"[9] is not an *unconditional* election, God does determine the ones He receives—the ones who will receive His favor. Likewise, just as the elect nation was "cut off" temporarily because of unbelief, *as individuals*, we, too, can still be cut off if, in haughtiness, we wane in fearing God (Romans 11:20-22). Then, today—"lest [we] should be wise in [our] own opinion" *with regard to Israel* (Romans 11:25)—perhaps the apostle Paul would still remind us of God's great and irrevocable promise. Even as the church stands *elect* in accordance with "the election of grace" (Romans 11:5), Israel, too, shall remain *elect*—"beloved for the sake of the fathers" (Romans 11:28-29).

---

[9] Note: For a specific discussion of "the election of grace," see the chapter entitled "Who Are the *Elect*?".

Chapter 16

Another Look at Various Scriptures

Specifically, there are several passages of Scripture, involving the terms "predestination," "foreknowledge," "elect," or "chosen," which are often used to support the Calvinist interpretation of election—that God *unconditionally* chooses those individuals who will be *irresistibly* drawn toward Him and, thus, saved. There is meaning to these scriptures—the writers were not just speaking to the wind. May I suggest, however, that, contrary to the meanings often attributed, there are other credible interpretations that flow well with the context of the scriptures? The following section is a look at some of those passages.

ROMANS 8:28-30

> And we know that all things work together for good to those who love God, to those who are the called ["being called" IGNT] according to His purpose. (29) For whom He foreknew, He also predestined to be conformed to the image of His Son, that He might be the firstborn among many brethren. (30) Moreover, whom He predestined, these He also called, whom He called, these He also justified; and whom He justified, these He also glorified. (NKJV)

This passage of Scripture is so deep. So much truth can be gleaned from this passage that I feel very careful regarding anything I say. For sure, there will be special meaning conveyed upon one's own personal study. Nevertheless, because all three verses of this passage contain complex wordings which some have considered supportive of the Calvinist Reformed doctrine of *unconditional election*, I will share other perspective.

Context

Surrounding the words of Romans 8:28-30, there is important context. In marked similarity to the words of Paul found in Ephesians 1 (see "Another Look at Ephesians 1"), throughout all of Romans 8, Paul is emphasizing *the great inheritance* given to all who fully identify with Christ—who live according to the Spirit and not according to the flesh. There is justification and payment for sins. There is victory over the sinful nature and power to fulfill the righteous requirements of the law. What is more, for those led by the Spirit—for those who are even willing to suffer with Christ—there awaits the promise of a future glory!

Paul seemed to be after total confidence in the hearts of all who would hear his words. He understood the difficulties of their sufferings, and he knew of the battles to be waged against the flesh of their sinful natures. Yet, he also knew of the victory that awaits *all who truly love God and will continue to hope in Him.* Paul saw the need for God's people to hold onto their hope of glory—to persevere until the end, waiting patiently for God's reward (vv. 24-25). It was in response to Paul's heart for total confidence on the part of the saints that he would write the strong words of consolation and hope found in verses 28-30, as well as in the rest of the chapter.

Verse 28

Most importantly, with verse 28, Paul is encouraging those who love God—those who would even suffer with Christ—that, in the greatness of His care, God is even causing *all things* to work together for their good. What a wonderful truth! It is then as well—in consideration of Paul's latter words—that there also has been confusion.

From verse 28, some have viewed the words "the *called* according to His purpose" (emphasis mine) as meaning something in support of the interpretation of "election" being countered. Moreover, the words "according to His purpose" also have been construed by some as being indicative of God's planning *everything* ahead of time. Consequently, the interpretation that *specific individuals* are called, because of a predetermined plan to *unconditionally* choose them, also has been made.

332

Yet, may I suggest, instead, that, as Paul defines the ones for whom God "works all things together for good," he simply may be limiting further the ones who truly love God and receive His perfecting to those who "according to *His* purpose"—that of "the Spirit" and not of "the flesh"—are being called/invited to continue with Him? For sure, there is only one way for individuals to be invited in—and that is the way of Jesus.

(Significantly, chapter eight of Romans begins with emphasis on *the way of the Spirit* bringing God's life and promise. Then, shortly thereafter, in chapters nine through eleven, Paul continues to stress that having only a zeal for righteousness, by the works of the law, never will hit the mark before God. One must know God's righteousness and enter in *His* way—in order to be one of God's choice [Romans 9:11] and in accordance to His plan!)

Moreover, although Paul may have been referring to God's intent/plan, which is "according to the Spirit," there is also other likely meaning. Because of the strong ties between verses 28 and 29, perhaps Paul's interjection—"to those who are the called ["being called" IGNT] according to His purpose"—also begins making the strong point of God's *settled intent* to work all things to perfect His people. Not only would God cause all things to work together for good *to those who love Him* (and will submit to His ways), but He also would continue His invitation *toward glory* until the very end. (Note: According to the Greek Interlinear, "His" does not appear in the original Greek rendering of verse 28. Only "according to purpose" is written.)

Verse 29

Next, Paul's words of verse 29 expound on the truth given in verse 28. By the Greek conjunction *hoti* (rendered as "for" in NKJV and giving "emphasis on the cause, and expressive of the reason or matter of a communication, etc."),[1] the words of verse 29 give emphasis to, and the

---

[1] E.W. Bullinger, *A Critical Lexicon and Concordance to the English and Greek New Testament* (Grand Rapids, MI: Kregel Publications, 1999; orig. pub. 1908), pp. 296, 298, 769, xiii.

cause of, the thing just said in verse 28. The words of verse 28 are made sure and immutable by the words of verse 29! God's purposed intent—that "all things work together for good to those who love God"—is settled forever because, as verse 29 states, God has even "predestined" that it be so!

Very significantly, however, although some might assert verse 29 to be supportive of the doctrine of *unconditional election*, because of its references to God's "foreknowledge" and "predestination," such a conclusion should not be made. Although Paul does speak of "predestination," Paul is very specific in his reference to *what* is predestined. **It is not an unconditional election of specific individuals, but conformity of His people "to the likeness of His Son" that is being predestined.** Additionally, although Paul does describe the ones loving God as being ones He even "foreknew," such a reference should also only be taken according to its most literal meaning—not according to its often presumed relationship with the idea of *unconditional election.*[2]

In truth, God has foreknown a people—a people who will be corporately "in Christ"—since the beginning of creation (Ephesians 1:4-6; Ephesians 3:9-11). For all times, He has foreknown a people who will love Him—a people who will hope only in Him. These are the ones He has predestined to be to the praise of His glory and to be "conformed into the image of His Son." The ones He has foreknown—those who would continue in Him according to the work of Christ—*will* be conformed into the image of His Son throughout all life's circumstances. (Today even, as a people, he would encourage our prayerful agreement with His promise!)

Notwithstanding, although the Lord has surely predestined *a glorious Bride*, because the intent of Paul's writing appears to have been that of encouraging *individuals*, there also may be further meaning. Perhaps, in regards to the foreknowledge of God, Paul is making note that God has even known, ahead of time, those *individuals* who would love Him with all their hearts and look to Him for all their needs. Because of His foreknowledge, God has not been hindered, nor shall He be hindered,

---

[2] See the discussion of the words "foreknow" and "foreknowledge" within the chapter "The Foreknowledge of God."

in working "all things"—the pleasant things and the hard things (even the details before birth)—for the good of those who love Him (Romans 8:29, 33).

Verse 30

Lastly, in verse 30, Paul writes the words: "Moreover whom He predestined, these He also called; whom He called, these He also justified; and whom He justified, these He also glorified." With this statement, Paul makes strong inference, from the statement of verse 29, concerning God's settled intent toward those foreknown by Him. He continues his words—concerning the greatness of God's involvement in the lives of those who love Him—with even more to bring strong confidence. Not only is there unfailing *purpose* with God to cause all things to work together for the good of those *foreknown*—who love Him—but there is unfailing purpose to bring them into glory as well.

In right context, "predestination" brings the strong confidence that, because of His foreknowledge of those who are His, God has been and will remain in control of all that may happen *to those who love Him.* No weapon formed against His people shall prosper; and He will see to it that nothing shall happen that He cannot work for good.

God's care is great and continuous! Even as the words of Romans 8:31 conclude: "If God is for us, who can be against us?" Every step of the way—before birth, throughout life's circumstances, and even to the end—God watches over and is at work in the lives of the ones who love Him—justifying and making His own "more than conquerors" (v. 37). The end result for "those who love Him" is definitely sure and glorious.

1 PETER 1:1-2

Peter, an apostle of Jesus Christ, to the strangers scattered throughout Pontus, Galatia, Cappadocia, Asia, and Bithynia, **elect according to the foreknowledge of God the Father**, through sanctification of the Spirit, unto

obedience and sprinkling of the blood of Jesus Christ:
Grace unto you, and peace, be multiplied. (KJV)

For aid in proper examination, the text, according to the Interlinear Greek-English New Testament, is as follows:

Peter an apostle of Jesus Christ to [the] chosen sojourn-
ers of [the] dispersion of Pontus, of Galatia, of Cappadocia, of Asia and of Bithynia, according to [the] foreknowledge of God Father, in sanctification of spirit, to
obedience and sprinkling of [the] blood of Jesus Christ.
(IGNT)

The point of discussion appears in the opening to Peter's first letter to the churches "scattered." Some might interpret Peter's words—"elect according to . . . foreknowledge"—as being a support to the idea of an *unconditional* predestination of specific souls unto salvation. Yet, with respect to the words of Peter, one need not draw such a conclusion. There is other likely intent.

Peter begins his letter with a greeting and a blessing to God's *chosen* or *elect.* To be sure, the people of God, to whom he is writing ("the strangers scattered throughout the world"), are God's e*lect*, His *chosen* people—selected by His grace alone, and not by any of their works.[3] In so bringing his greeting, Peter emphasizes the truth of God's choice to, *Himself,* purchase and set apart a people for His own. (Later in the let-ter, in 1 Peter 2:9-10, Peter would even elaborate, again, on this great privilege we have been given as His chosen people.)

Then, by mentioning "foreknowledge," Peter also is likely reiterating the truth of God's greatness—that, concerning the work and sufferings of Christ, *nothing had taken Him by surprise.* For sure, many other times in Scripture, as is addressed in my preface to the chapter "Anoth-er Look at Ephesians 1," the early apostles would make the point of *God's foreknowledge and appointed purpose in Christ.*

---

[3] See Romans 11:5-6 and the chapter "Who Are the *Elect?*".

In particular, Peter had a history of noting God's eternal plan—His choice to bring salvation, through Christ, *from the beginning of time.* Peter's messages, as recorded in Acts 2:22-36, Acts 3:17-26, and Acts 4:27-28, demonstrate the significance this truth held in Peter's heart. Perhaps, as well, Peter's messages in Acts give us a glimpse into what he might have been reiterating as he wrote his letter to the church at large:

> God has always been on the throne. God knew in ad-
> vance. God's plan of *who His people would be* was
> foreknown. The *choice* God had made from the begin-
> ning of creation—to redeem a people and to have them
> for His own—had been determined, had been God's
> heart, and, since earlier times, even had been shared
> with His faithful prophets. (Significantly, it was only a
> few verses later, in 1 Peter 1:10-12, that Peter would
> again emphasize this great salvation previously revealed
> to the prophets.)

Finally, there is also other possible motive for Peter's descriptive greeting. (Definitely, from Peter's greeting, one can glean some very high standards.) By his mention of God's foreknowledge, perhaps Peter also wanted to give an important reminder (see 2 Peter 1:10-12) of what God foresees and desires all His "elect"—*the ones remaining with Him until the end*—to look like:

> *God's people* shall be continually submitted to the work
> of the Holy Spirit, they shall be obedient followers of
> Jesus Christ (being continually cleansed by His blood),
> and they shall stand—set apart as *strangers* in this
> world.

Truly, God has foreseen His people as a glorious people—as a people to the praise of His name—for all time! Yet significantly, although, as individuals, we all have the high calling toward sanctification and the obedience of Christ, the fullness of that sanctification—a sanctification even to be seen within His people, *corporately*—shall only become realized at the end of the age. (See 1 Peter 1:11-12 and Hebrews 11:39-40.)

1 PETER 2:8

> Now to you who believe, this stone [Jesus] is precious. But to those who do not believe, "The stone the builders [Israel] rejected has become the capstone," and "a stone that causes men to stumble and a rock that makes them fall." They stumble because they disobey the message— **which is also what they were destined for**. (1 Peter 2:7-8 NIV1984)

First of all, the NIV1984 word rendered "destined" is actually the Greek word *tithemi*, more accurately meaning "to put, set, place . . . appoint."[4] In contrast to "predestining," *tithemi* simply means something is made to happen (something is *determined*). **The word does *not* infer a decision being eternally predestined**, with no regard to anyone's response.[5]

Secondly, the context of 1 Peter 2:8 is that of the unbelief of most of Israel, in rejecting and not trusting in Jesus. Even as had been foretold numerous times in the past by her prophets (Romans 9: 27-29; Isaiah 10:22-23; Isaiah 65:1-7; Romans 11:7-8), and also as was spoken by Jesus (Matthew 13:10-15; John 9:39-41), beforehand, God had already determined a judgment upon Israel for her constant stubbornness and unwillingness to listen. Because of Israel's past failures to respond to His initiatives (Luke 13:34), God's judgment for many was an inability to perceive and to understand the identity of His Son. Their hearts were hardened so they could not receive. *Because of their previous responses*, God had "appointed" them such as this:

> " 'Hearing you will hear and shall not understand, and seeing you will see and not perceive; For the hearts of this people have grown dull. Their ears are hard of hearing, and their eyes they have closed, lest they should see with their eyes and hear with their ears, lest they should

---

[4] Bullinger, *A Critical Lexicon and Concordance to the Greek and English New Testament*, pp. 60, xiii.
[5] See the chapter "The *Will* of God."

understand with their hearts and turn, so that I should heal them.' " (Matthew 13:14-15 NKJV)

Although 1 Peter 2:8 has been given by some, to be a support for the doctrine of predestined salvation and predestined wrath, hopefully, there is now more clarity. God *does* make determinations and decree judgments that no man can thwart. He *did* decree a judgment on those in Israel—those given much who had claimed to see, having no need for a savior (Luke 8:18; John 9:39-41). We *do* need to fear God, being careful how we use what we have been given. God may execute judgments, and He may harden—not granting repentance. Notwithstanding, although He does appoint wrath and judgments do come, they do not come undeserved or *unconditionally* predestined.[6]

1 THESSALONIANS 1:2-10

Speaking to the church in Thessalonica, Paul mentioned God's election. He spoke to them as follows:

We give thanks to God always for you all, making mention of you in our prayers, remembering without ceasing your work of faith, labor of love, and patience of hope in our Lord Jesus Christ in the sight of our God and Father, **knowing, beloved brethren, your election by God**. For our gospel did not come to you in word only, but also in power, and in the Holy Spirit and in much assurance . . . And you became followers of us and of the Lord, having received the word in much affliction, with joy of the Holy Spirit, so that you became examples to all in Macedonia and Achaia who believe. . . . Your faith toward God has gone out, so that we do not need to say anything. For they themselves declare concerning us what manner of entry we had to you, and how you turned to God from idols to serve the living and true God, and to wait for His Son from heaven, whom He raised from the dead,

---

[6] See the chapters "The *Will* of God," "Our Real Effect upon Our Salvation," and "God's Sovereignty Over the Hearts of Men."

even Jesus who delivers us from wrath to come. (1 Thessalonians 1:2-10 NKJV)

If the reality of God's election is rightly understood,[7] this passage of Scripture should cause no difficulty. In particular, Paul *knew* the hearts of those within the church in Thessalonica. He knew their relationships with Christ were genuine. He took great delight in them, and he knew their heavenly Father did as well. Even as Paul would describe within 1 Thessalonians, as well as within 2 Thessalonians, the fruit of the Thessalonians was very evident.

2 THESSALONIANS 2:13-14

This passage, according to most translations, reads something like the following:

> But we are bound to give thanks to God always for you, brethren beloved by the Lord, because God **from the beginning chose you** for salvation through sanctification by the Spirit and belief in the truth, to which He called you by our gospel, for the obtaining of the glory of our Lord Jesus Christ. (NKJV)

Understandably, at first glance, the words "from the beginning chose you" might appear to some to be supportive of the Calvinist teaching of *unconditional election*. Given right context, however, this is not the case.

"Firstfruits"

Notably, although the previous translation of "from the beginning" is very likely and in many translations, another possible rendering of "firstfruits" also exists. Not only can "firstfruits" be found in certain other translations (i.e., English Standard Version and Douay-Rheims

---

[7] See the chapters "Significant Scriptures—Part 2," "Another Look at Romans 9 –11," and "Who Are the *Elect*?".

Bible), but this fact is also acknowledged in a New American Standard Bible footnote to 2 Thessalonians 2:13, which states that one early manuscript reads "first fruits."[8] According to the Interlinear Greek-English New Testament, 2 Thessalonians 2:13-14 even reads:

> But we ought to thank – God always concerning you, brothers having been loved by [the] Lord, because **chose you – God firstfruit** to salvation by sanctification of spirit and faith of (in)[the] truth, to which also He called you through the gospel of us, to obtainment of [the] glory of the Lord of us Jesus Christ. (IGNT, parentheticals as found)

How can there be such differences in translation? Notably, concerning the translations of "from the beginning," E.W. Bullinger (author of *A Critical Lexicon and Concordance to the English and Greek New Testament*) gives hint to the confusion. While noting the corresponding Greek words, as are found in both Lachmann's and Tregelles's texts of the ancient Greek, Bullinger describes the word as "**[aparche], an offering of first-fruits, instead of [ap arche], from the beginning.**"[9] It becomes understandable, therefore, how a mistake from the original Greek (perhaps a penmanship error made while copying)—and consequently, the differences in translations—*may* have transpired. For certain, the two Greek renderings do look very much alike! Accordingly, depending upon which manuscript is chosen, the translations do become either "from the beginning" or "firstfruits."

Specifically, when "firstfruits" should be rendered, one Greek word, *aparche* (meaning "an offering of first-fruits"),[10] is given. Noticeably, it is the same Greek word as is translated "firstfruit(s)" in all the following passages: Romans 8:23, Romans 11:16, 1 Corinthians 15:20 and 23, James 1:18, and Revelation 14:4.[11] In contrast, however, when "from the beginning" is to be rendered, two Greek words, *ap* and *arche*,

---

[8] *New American Standard Bible—Updated Edition* (La Habra, CA: The Lockman Foundation, 1995).

[9] Bullinger, *A Critical Lexicon and Concordance to the Greek and English New Testament*, pp. 92, 309, xiii.

[10] Ibid., p. 289.

[11] Ibid.

are given (*apo* meaning "from, away from"[12] and *arche* meaning "beginning, origin"[13]). These words, *ap* and *arche* (and their *correct* rendering, together, as "from the beginning"), likewise can be observed, using the Greek Interlinear, within many other scriptures as well (e.g., Matthew 19:4, 8; Matthew 24:21; and Mark 10:6).[14] Even one such scripture is given as follows:

> For then there will be great distress, unequaled from [*ap*] the beginning [*arche*] of the world until now . . .
> (Matthew 24:21 NIV1984)

So then, contextually, would such a rendering of "firstfruits" make sense? Perhaps. Significantly, as Paul makes the statement in 2 Thessalonians 2:13, he *is* praising God for the life of Christ that he sees in the church of Thessalonica. In 2 Thessalonians 1:3-4, concerning the Thessalonian church, Paul had even just declared:

> We are bound to thank God always for you, brethren, as it is fitting, because your faith grows exceedingly, and the love of every one of you all abounds toward each other, *so that we ourselves boast of you among the churches of God* . . . (NKJV, emphasis mine)

Additionally, it was not uncommon for Paul even to speak of other faithful believers as "firstfruits" offerings. For example, Paul similarly had made the following references:

> Greet my beloved Epaenetus, **who is the firstfruits** [*aparche*][15] **of Achaia** [Asia] **to Christ**. (Romans 16:5 NKJV)

> . . . ([Ye] know **the house of Stephanas, that it is the firstfruits** [*aparche*][16] **of Achaia**, and that they have ad-

---

[12] Ibid., pp. 308, xiii.
[13] Ibid., pp. 92, xiii.
[14] Ibid., p. 92.
[15] Ibid., pp. 289, xiii.
[16] Ibid.

dicted themselves to the ministry of the saints,) . . . (1
Corinthians 16:15 KJV)

Hence, in contrast to the translation "from the beginning," it is possible
that, while rejoicing over the Thessalonians (who were some of the first
to believe in Europe[17]), Paul, again, may simply have been rejoicing in
the honorable and distinguished position that they had—as "firstfruit"
offerings to the work of Jesus Christ.

"From the Beginning"

Notwithstanding, although the original intent of the words may well
have been "firstfruits," **given the surrounding context, a rendering of
"from the beginning" also is very likely** (and favored by me as well).
Furthermore, such a translation need not be deemed supportive of the
teaching of *unconditional election.*

Significantly, just preceding the words of verses 13-14, Paul had been
speaking very sobering words concerning *impending judgments* for
those who would not embrace a love for the truth or follow after righteousness (see 2 Thessalonians 2:9-12). Those unrighteous even would
be given over to "strong delusion" to believe the lies of Satan. Thus,
contextually, it *is* very likely that, being persuaded (because of their
fruit) of better things accompanying salvation, as well as noting the
tribulations that the church endured, Paul felt it more expedient *to encourage* the Thessalonians concerning God's *keeping* power and their
solid hope in Christ.

Indeed, although Paul still would encourage the Thessalonians concerning their part both *to heed* and *to continue* standing firm in Christ (see 1
Thessalonians 2:3 and 15; and 3:4-7, and 14), Paul's second letter
mainly was one of consolation and encouragement *to the faithful* (2
Thessalonians 2:16-17). Very much like Paul's words of encouragement found in Romans 8:28-30 and Ephesians 1, the context of Paul's
words to the Thessalonians seemed to be: Stand strong. You shall make

---

[17] Jack Hayford, *Hayford's Bible Handbook* (Nashville, TN: Thomas Nelson, Inc.,
1995), p. 401.

it. There *is* a future hope. For certain, Paul had seen *sure* evidence that their lives were committed to Christ. (See 1 Thessalonians 1:2-10; 2 Thessalonians 1:3-7; and 2 Thessalonians 3:3-4.)

Thus, understanding God's predestined purpose both *to keep* and *to perfect*, in Christ, *those whose hearts are His*, Paul would give thanks to God, not only for the Thessalonians, but also for His promise and His power to bring, even out of tribulation, all that would be to His glory. Paul did not fret because of the painful ordeals being suffered, nor did he fret because of the ones who would distort. He knew God's greatness—that, even from the beginning, God has watched over the lives of all who would love Him—to establish His truth and His glory. (See Romans 8:29-39, 2 Timothy 2:19, Jude 24, Psalm 37:5-6, and Psalm 138:8.)

ACTS 13:48

When the Gentiles heard this, they were glad and honored the word of the Lord; and all who were **appointed** for eternal life believed. (NIV1984)

Contextually (see vv. 13-48), this statement of Acts 13:48 is made concerning those who had believed after *both* Jews and Gentiles had had the gospel preached to them. Although, at first, even many Jews had appeared soft and open to hearing the words of Paul and Barnabus concerning Jesus, in the end, jealousies had arisen, and they had stopped listening (v. 45). Furthermore, when the concluding statement of verse 48 was penned by the writer, the words of Paul, found within verse 46, also just had been recorded. Notably, these words of verse 46 would express the *personal* responsibility of the Jews who had ended up not listening. Just as the apostle was quoted: ". . . *Ye [the Jews who stopped listening] put it from you, and judge yourselves unworthy of everlasting life, lo we turn to the Gentiles"* (Acts 13:46 KJV, emphasis mine). **Hence, *the Jews* had put themselves in a place "unworthy" to receive eternal life.**

Then, significantly, in Acts 13:48, the Greek word rendered as "appointed" is *tasso*.[18] According to Bullinger's Lexicon, the Greek word *tasso* simply means "to arrange, put in order, *especially in military sense*, to draw up *soldiers*, array; *then, mid.*, to appoint or order *anything* to be done, to appoint."[19] From an examination of scriptures where this Greek word is used, one point also becomes clear: *Tasso* either can be done by a person *to himself* or can be done by one to another. Consider, for example, the words of 1 Corinthians 16:15:

> I beseech you, brethren, (ye know the house of Stephanas, that it is the firstfruits of Achaia, and that **they have addicted** [*tasso* / "appointed" IGNT] **themselves** to the ministry of the saints, (KJV)

So, as can be seen by the *tasso* usage in 1 Corinthians 16:15, one can order or appoint *his own* life unto one thing or another.

Moreover, Ralph Earle, author of *Word Meanings of the New Testament*, also agrees with the middle use of *tasso* and makes the following comment concerning its use in Acts 13:48:

> This is the perfect passive participle of the verb *tasso*, which was used primarily in a military sense: "draw up in order, arrange in place, assign, appoint order" (A-S, p. 440). The participle may be taken in the middle sense: "as many as had set themselves unto eternal life."[20]

Consequently, because of the uncertainty of *who ordered whom*, it is not perfectly clear the intent of what is being said in Acts 13:48. The writer of Acts may be speaking in the context of *those unbelievers' personal responsibility* for "ordering" their lives into positions ready *to hear* the words of eternal life in Jesus (remember that verse 46 alluded to the unbeliever's own responsibility). On the other hand, the writer may just be referring to the Father's place *to give* unto Jesus—to open

---

[18] Bullinger, *A Critical Lexicon and Concordance to the Greek and English New Testament*, pp. 559, xiii.
[19] Ibid.
[20] Ralph Earle, *Word Meanings in the New Testament* (Peabody, MA: Hendrickson Publishers, Inc., 1997), p. 109.

eyes to see. For sure, we do know that many Jews were not given eyes to see who Jesus was—a rendered judgment upon much of Israel for not having responded earlier to what *was* given.

At any rate, although presumed by many to support a predestination of individuals unto eternal life, Acts 13:48 should not be taken so far. One's being "appointed" and one's being "predestined" are not one in the same. This scripture should only be used to support the truth that one's heart needs to be *readied*—to be *put in order* to see and to believe on Jesus—or he will not be enabled to see.

GENESIS 18:19

Please note the following translations:

"For I **know** [*yada* / Hebrew; *eido* / Greek] him, **that** [*hoti* / Greek] he will command his children and his household after him, and they shall keep the way of the LORD, to do justice and judgment; that the LORD may bring upon Abraham that which he hath spoken of him." (KJV)

"For I **have chosen** him, **so that** he will direct his children and his household after him to keep the way of the LORD by doing what is right and just, so that the LORD will bring about for Abraham what he has promised him." (NIV 1984)

"For I **have known** him, **in order that** he may command his children and his household after him, that they keep the way of the LORD, to do righteousness and justice, that the LORD may bring to Abraham what He has spoken to him." (NKJV)

"For I **have chosen** him, **so that** he may command his children and his household after him to keep the way of the LORD by doing righteousness and justice, so that the

LORD may bring upon Abraham what He has spoken about him." (NASB)

As is with Psalm 139:16, there is great and serious variance in the way Genesis 18:19 has been translated by different translations. Genesis 18:19 is a very significant scripture to get right. Wrong translation can lead to some seriously wrong conclusions.

Contextually, God is expressing *how* and *why* He can say that Abraham will "become a great and mighty nation, and all the nations of the earth shall be blessed in him" (v. 18 KJV) when the discrepancies in translation occur. Specially, from the flow of the KJV, we simply are given God's perception/understanding of Abraham—that he will command his household—as being the reason the promise will be fulfilled. Yet, from the other three translations referenced, God is seen "making" Abraham command his household. Then as well, from the NIV1984 and NASB translations, God's *choice* of Abraham is given as *the reason* Abraham will be *made* to command his household and to receive the fulfillment of His words. In like manner, the NIV1984 and NASB both state: "For I have chosen him."

Upon examination, however, *the King James Version seems to stand truest* to the original words of God, as are recorded in Genesis 18:19. Such a determination can be made because the original words—words whose varied renderings are cited above—do give specific meaning. From an examination of the original Hebrew, as well as from an examination of the Greek Septuagint, the meanings of these words are made clear.

In particular, *yada*, the Hebrew word rendered both as "know" *and* as "chosen" in the differing translations,[21] should receive special scrutiny. Clearly, *yada* does *not* mean "choose" (which *is* often rendered by the specific Hebrew word *bachar*[22])! Instead, according to *Wilson's Old Testament Word Studies*, and in alignment with "know" (as it *is* translated in the KJV), *yada* brings the meaning: "to perceive, to be sensible

---

[21] Edward W. Goodrick and John R. Kohlenberger, *The NIV Exhaustive Concordance* (Grand Rapids, MI: Zondervan Publishing House, 1990), p. 1466.
[22] Ibid., p. 1395.

of, by sight, . . . to understand, observe . . . to come to the knowledge of, by seeing, by hearing, and by experience . . . to know, to be acquainted with . . . ."[23] *Notably, and with agreement*, this definition for *yada* even aligns with the definition of the Septuagint rendering's corresponding Greek word, *eido*,[24]an obsolete root like *oida*, which means ". . . to have knowledge of, to know." According to Bullinger's Lexicon, and in alignment with the meaning of *yada*, the use of either *eido* or *oida* likewise "implies that the subject has simply come within the knower's sphere of perception or circle of vision."[25]

Most importantly, however, the differing translations bear witness to the basic meaning of *yada*, as is given by Wilson. Of the 949 times *yada* is used in the Old Testament,[26] most all of the time it is translated along the line of "know." (Note: *The NIV Exhaustive Concordance* for the ways *yada* is translated in the NIV1984, just alone.) Moreover, within a footnote of the passage, the New American Standard Bible, itself—although rendering *yada* as "chosen" —substantiates the word "known" as being the literal meaning of the word *yada*.[27]

Then additionally, not only is it important to understand the most literal translation of *yada*, but the rendering of the second cited word also is quite significant for proper interpretation of the passage. Indeed, using the Greek Septuagint and noting the Greek word that corresponds to the English word rendered as "that" (in the KJV), one *can* discern what probably *is* the most accurate translation of this part of the passage.

Specifically, the Greek word *hoti* is the Septuagint word corresponding to "that."[28] According to Bullinger's Lexicon, *hoti* pointedly means the following: " 'that,''because,' with emphasis on the cause, and expres-

---

[23] William Wilson, *Wilson's Old Testament Word Studies* (Peabody, MA: Hendrickson Publishers, 1993), pp. 239-240.
[24] R. Tan and D. A. deSilva, *The Lexham Greek-English Interlinear Septuagint* (Bellingham, WA: Logos Bible Software, 2009), Ge 18:19.
[25] Bullinger, *A Critical Lexicon and Concordance to the Greek and English New Testament*, pp. 434, xiii.
[26] Goodrick and Kohlenberger, *The NIV Exhaustive Concordance*, p. 1466.
[27] *New American Standard Bible—Updated Edition* (La Habra, CA: The Lockman Foundation, 1995).
[28] R. Tan and D. A. deSilva, *The Lexham Greek-English Interlinear Septuagint*, Ge. 18:19.

sive of the reason or matter of a communication, etc. [*hoti*] is objective, having reference not to the design, but to the cause." For clarity, Bullinger even gives further illustration of the use of *hoti* as contrasted with another Greek word, *ina* (which *does* mean "that, in order that, to the end that, with emphasis on the purpose, design, and result . . .").[29] He explains:

> "Hope" is followed by [*hoti*], which presents the object of the hope [e.g., "I hope *that* (*hoti*) I can go"], while "prayer" is followed by [*ina*], showing the purpose and design of the prayer [e.g., "laboring fervently for you in prayers, that (*ina*) you may stand perfect and complete" (Colossians 4:12 NKJV)].[30]

Furthermore, as a help, the distinct intent of *hoti* also can be seen in all the following scriptures: Matthew 2:22; Matthew 4:12; Matthew 5:17, 20, and 21; and 2 Corinthians 1:13-14.[31] Two of the examples are given as follows:

> But when he heard **that** [*hoti*] Archelaus was reigning in Judea in place of his father Herod, he was afraid to go there. (Matthew 2:22 NIV1984)

> When Jesus heard **that** [*hoti*] John had been put in prison, he returned to Galilee. (Matthew 4:12 NIV1984)

Clearly, a rendering of "in order that" or "so that" would not have made sense in the above *hoti* examples, as *does* the word "that." Perhaps as well, in consideration of Genesis 18:19, the word "that" should be substituted for all the other renderings that were given where *hoti* corresponds.

To be sure, Scripture must be translated as literally as possible. God's words are pure and holy, and they are enough. In light of the specific

---

[29] Bullinger, *A Critical Lexicon and Concordance to the Greek and English New Testament*, pp. 769, xiii.

[30] Ibid., pp. 769-773, xiii.

[31] Ibid.; *The Zondervan Parallel New Testament in Greek and English*, 8th ed. (New York: Zondervan Publishing House, 1982), pp. 522-523.

meanings of the original words, hopefully, Genesis 18:19 now will be considered in new light—and not as a scripture which supports the thought that, on account of *God's* choices, individuals are *made* to do what they do.

IN CONCLUSION

Because of the complexity of many passages of scripture, at first glance, there can be confusion regarding man's responsibility and God's impartiality towards men. Without careful inspection of the original words used, without the context in which the statements of scripture are found, and without the confirmation that other scriptures provide (Matthew 18:16), there can be serious misapplication. Within this chapter, therefore, I have sought the Lord for *His* counsel that can be established through many witnesses.

Furthermore, within *several* chapters, I have discussed scriptures that some may feel support the idea of *unconditional election*. If, therefore, a scripture of interest has not appeared here, it possibly may appear within another chapter that is closely related by subject.

CONCLUSION

Chapter 17

In Conclusion

God is God. Even as the heavens are high above the earth, His ways are high above our ways. We may never put God in *our* box. There are things about God to which we will never attain access. In His jealousy, He *would* have us know—*there is none like Him.*

Nonetheless, this I know. *God loves all mankind and has made provision so that none need perish.* This truth is established solidly in His Word. This is the gospel message, and to this I must testify.

God is sovereign. He rules. And He will do what He wants to do. (We *must* acknowledge His greatness and His reigning power to do *whatever He decides to do.*) Nonetheless, as King, our God must never be held responsible for that which He has even said He is not responsible. His name is *holy*—and must never be so maligned.

God has given all men the real ability to choose Him and to attain life incorruptible (Romans 1:18-20). He has set before all men life and death (Deuteronomy 30:19). At the same time, by foreknowledge, He has been greater than all men's doings—knowing and keeping the ones who truly are His in heart (even for all time).

How can this be? Although some may feel there is paradox between these two truths, there need not be confusion. There need not be confusion if we will remember who He is. *God is God, and He is not like us; therefore, we should never reason Him to our level.* Likewise, His time realm is not like ours. It is different from our own.

The two—God's foreknowledge and man's responsibility—exist simultaneously. Understanding this, the apostle Paul even wrote to Timothy concerning these coexisting truths of God's solid foundation:

> Nevertheless the solid foundation of God stands, having this seal: **"The Lord knows those who are His,"** and, **"Let everyone who names the name of Christ depart**

from iniquity." (2 Timothy 2:19 NKJV)

Other places speak of these coexisting truths as well.

Truly, we may have a solid confidence that the Lord will take care of His own. Even within the context of the serious consequences of men's own choices, Paul gave equal acknowledgement of God's greatness over all (even bringing reminder of God's intimate and unceasing knowledge). Paul understood that, no matter what a man might do, nothing shall be greater than the Lord's ability to do—*and* His covenantal promise to do—for those whose hearts are His (the ones even seen through foreknowledge). Foremost, Paul understood that God—who sees into the hearts of all men—is always greater.[1] (See also Philippians 3:3 and Hebrews 13:6.)

HIS GREATNESS *AND* HIS HEART FOR ALL MEN

The Lord reigns over all. He *allows*—and nothing can get by Him. Just as the writer of Lamentations understood:

> Who is he who speaks and it comes to pass, when the LORD has not commanded it? Is it not from the mouth of the Most High that woe and well-being proceed? (Lamentations 3:37-38 NKJV)

For sure, nothing may bypass God. Yet, although the Lord should be rightly acknowledged for His greatness, His character and His heart must be rightly acknowledged as well. Without such knowledge of *His goodness* and *His faithful workings*, one's hope is lost. Particularly, the writer of Lamentations understood the significance of this balance and also wrote:

> Though He causes grief, yet He will show compassion according to the multitude of His mercies. **For He does**

---

[1] Significantly, a right knowledge of God's greatness and His *keeping* power is the safeguard we all need against "falling from grace" and getting wrongly into *our own* works. Throughout all, it remains *His* work.

not afflict willingly, nor grieve the children of men.
To crush under one's feet all the prisoners of the earth,
to turn aside the justice due a man before the face of the
Most High, or subvert a man in his cause—the LORD
does not approve. (Lamentations 3:32-36 NKJV)

Even as the writer of Lamentations declared, the Lord does not do anything He does just to cause harm to a man. He loves. It is for redemptive purposes that He may afflict.

Truly, without a proper perspective of God's greatness over every matter *and* His heart of goodness toward every man, one cannot have hope.
Even as the writer of Lamentations encouraged himself to have hope,
while reflecting on these two truths, these truths also will give hope to
others who may find themselves under similar affliction. Knowing
God's goodness and faithful workings—while knowing His greatness
over *all* that may happen—together, these things are the basis for a *solid* hope in God.

A RIGHT BALANCE

Concerning *election*, in truth, God's people are *chosen—elected* by
Him. Nonetheless, contrary to the Calvinist Reformed teaching of *unconditional election*, they are not *unconditionally* elected. His people
choose to fear Him, hope in Him, and wholeheartedly love Him. They
count the cost and willingly give up all else for Him. Likewise, His
people continue in the faith, enduring with Him until the end.

Today, there is important truth in both camps of Arminians and Reformed Calvinists—and the Lord would restore truth. Yet, as truth is
being restored, we should note our enemy. Strategically, the enemy
would distort that which is real (Acts 20:30; 2 Peter 3:16), and the enemy would take *off balance*. Notwithstanding, and in agreement with
God's greatness, it is my prayer and expectation that those who truly
love Him will be set free from "every high thing" that has exalted itself
above the knowledge of God (2 Corinthians 10:5). He is great to do! It
is also my prayer and expectation that He will be seen clearly for who

He truly is, and that, knowing Him, His people will rise up and bear His name well.

APPENDICES

Appendix A

The Meaning of the Acronym TULIP

The following definitions corresponding to TULIP are taken from a book by David N. Steele and Curtis Thomas, entitled *Romans: An Interpretative Outline*.[1] The acronym TULIP comes from the five points of Calvinism. (**Please note: I am not espousing these doctrines; I am only referencing them for the reader's information**.)

THE FIVE POINTS OF CALVINISM

Total Inability or Total Depravity

Because of the fall, man is unable of himself to savingly believe the gospel. The sinner is dead, blind, and deaf to the things of God; his heart is deceitful and desperately corrupt. His will is not free, it is in bondage to his evil nature, therefore, he will not—indeed he cannot—choose good over evil in the spiritual realm. Consequently, it takes much more than the Spirit's assistance to bring a sinner to Christ—it takes regeneration by which the Spirit makes the sinner alive and gives him a new nature. Faith is not something man contributes to salvation but is itself a part of God's gift of salvation—it is God's gift to the sinner, not the sinner's gift to God.

Unconditional Election

God's choice of certain individuals unto salvation before the foundation of the world rested solely in His own sovereign will. His choice of particular sinners was not based on any foreseen response of obedience on their part, such as faith, repentance, etc. On the contrary, God gives faith and repentance to each individual whom He selected. These acts are the result, not the cause of

---

[1] David N. Steele and Curtis Thomas, *Romans: An Interpretive Outline* (P & R Publishing, 1963), pp. 144-146.

God's choice. Election therefore was not determined by or conditioned upon any virtuous quality or act foreseen in man. Those whom God sovereignly elected He brings through the power of the Spirit to a willing acceptance of Christ. Thus God's choice of the sinner, not the sinner's choice of Christ, is the ultimate cause of salvation.

Limited Atonement or Particular Redemption
Christ's redeeming work was intended to save the elect only and actually secured salvation for them. His death was substitutionary endurance of the penalty of sin in the place of certain specified sinners. In addition to putting away the sins of His people, Christ's redemption secured everything necessary for their salvation, including faith which unites them to Him. The gift of faith is infallibly applied by the Spirit to all for whom Christ died, therefore guaranteeing their salvation.

Irresistible or Efficacious Grace
In addition to the outward general call to salvation which is made to everyone who hears the gospel, the Holy Spirit extends to the elect a special inward call that inevitably brings them to salvation. The internal call (which is made only to the elect) cannot be rejected; it always results in conversion. By means of this special call the Spirit irresistibly draws sinners to Christ. He is not limited in His work of applying salvation by man's will, nor is He dependent upon man's cooperation for success. The Spirit graciously causes the elect sinner to cooperate, to believe, to repent, to come freely and willingly to Christ. God's grace, therefore, is invincible; it never fails to result in the salvation of those to whom it is extended.

Perseverance of the Saints
All who are chosen by God, redeemed by Christ, and given faith by the Spirit are eternally saved. They are kept in faith by the power of Almighty God and thus persevere to the end.

Appendix B

"Foreknow" and "Foreknowledge"
Their Most Literal Meanings

A proper interpretation of the words "foreknow" and "foreknowledge" is needed because some have taken great license in their interpretation of the meanings of the words. Curiously, however, because the Greek words rendered as "foreknow" and "foreknowledge" in Scripture are very precise and clear in the definitions they bring, ambiguity over the words' definitions should *not* be a problem. Consider again, therefore, the meanings of "foreknow" and "foreknowledge" as relayed by the original Greek.

According to E. W. Bullinger's *A Critical Lexicon and Concordance to the English and Greek New Testament*, the verb "foreknow" comes from the Greek verb *proginosko*.[1] It is a word formed from a combination of the root word *ginosko* (meaning "to perceive, observe, obtain a knowledge of or insight into")[2] and the preposition/prefix *pro* (meaning "before, forward").[3] Similarly, "foreknowledge" comes from the Greek noun *prognosis*.[4] It is a word formed from a combination of the noun *gnosis* (meaning: "knowing, or recognition, the knowledge or understanding of a thing")[5] and the preposition/prefix *pro* ("before, forward").

Straightforwardly, then, *proginosko,* which is rendered as "foreknow," means "to know, perceive, learn or understand beforehand, to take note of before."[6] Similarly, according to Bullinger, the noun *prognosis,* which is rendered as "foreknowledge," simply means "a perceiving beforehand."[7] As a help, Bullinger even suggests a correlation of the

---

[1] E. W. Bullinger, *A Critical Lexicon and Concordance to the English and Greek New Testament* (Grand Rapids, MI: Kregel Publications, 1999; orig. pub. 1908), pp. 302, xiii.

[2] Ibid., pp. 434, xiii.

[3] Ibid., pp. 434, 435, xiii, xx.

[4] Ibid., pp. 302, xiii.

[5] Ibid., pp. 436, xiii.

[6] Ibid., pp. 302, xiii.

[7] Ibid.

meaning of the medical term "prognosis" with right interpretation of the noun "foreknowledge" (*prognosis*).

Hopefully, it is now clearer to the reader that the verb "foreknow" and the noun "foreknowledge," in simplest terms, have to do with *knowing ahead of time*. That would be their most literal meanings. Also, as is so with the rendering of any words of Scripture, hopefully one will agree that "foreknow" and "foreknowledge" *only* should be rendered in their simplest forms—and not according to man's speculation, which can lead to serious error.

SOURCES

Sources

The Holy Spirit: "When He, the Spirit of truth, has come, He will guide you into all truth" (John 16:13 NKJV).

Arndt, William F., and Gingrich, F. Wilbur. *A Greek-English Lexicon of the New Testament and Other Early Christian Literature.* Chicago, IL: The University of Chicago Press, 1957.

Brown, Colin. *The New International Dictionary of New Testament Theology, Vol. 2.* Grand Rapids, MI: The Zondervan Corporation, 1976.

Brown, Driver, Briggs, and Gesenius. *Theological Word Book of the Old Testament.* Available: http://www.biblestudytools.net/Lexicons.

Bullinger, E.W.. *A Critical Lexicon and Concordance to the English and Greek New Testament.* Grand Rapids, MI: Kregel Publications, 1999.

Earle, Ralph. *Word Meanings in the New Testament.* Peabody, MA: Hendrickson Publishers, 1997.

Goodrick, Edward W., and Kohlenberger, John R.. *The NIV Exhaustive Concordance.* Grand Rapids, MI: Zondervan Publishing House, 1990.

Great People of the Bible and How They Lived. Pleasantville, NY: The Reader's Digest Association, Inc., 1974.

Green, Jay P., Sr.. *The Interlinear Hebrew-Aramaic Old Testament.* Peabody, MA: Hendrickson Publishers, 1985.

Hayford, Jack. *Hayford's Bible Handbook.* Nashville, TN: Thomas Nelson, Inc., 1995.

The Holy Bible, King James Version. Nashville, TN: Thomas Nelson, Inc., 1976.

The Holy Bible, New International Version. Grand Rapids, MI: Zondervan Publishing House, 1984.

The Holy Bible, New King James Version. Nashville, TN: Thomas Nelson Publishers, 1994.

The Interlinear Greek-English New Testament: Samuel Bagster and Sons LTD, 1958.

New American Standard Bible—Updated Edition. La Habra, CA: The Lockman Foundation, 1995.

Online Parallel Bible. Available: http://www.biblestudytools.com/parallel-bible/

Packer, J. I.. *Concise Theology: A Guide to Historic Christian Beliefs.* Carol Stream, IL: Tyndale House Publishers, Inc., 2001.

Roget's International Thesaurus. New York, NY: Thomas Y. Crowell Company, 1962.

Steele, David N., and Thomas, Curtis. *Romans: An Interpretive Outline.* Phillipsburg, NJ: P & R Publishing, 1963.

Strong, James, LL.D., S.T.D.. *Strong's Complete Word Study Concordance.* Chattanooga, TN: AMG Publishers, 2004.

Tan, R., and deSilva, D. A.. *The Lexham Greek-English Interlinear Septuagint.* Bellingham, WA: Logos Bible Software, 2009.

Thayer and Smith. *The New Testament Greek Lexicon.* Available: http://www.biblestudytools.net/Lexicons.

Trenchard, Warren C.. *Complete Vocabulary Guide to the New Testament.* Grand Rapids, MI: Zondervan Publishing House, 1998.

Webster's New World Dictionary of the American Language, College Edition. Cleveland and New York: The World Publishing Company, 1968.

Wilson, William. *Wilson's Old Testament Word Studies*. Peabody, MA: Hendrickson Publishers, 1993.

Young, Robert. *Young's Literal Translation of the Holy Bible*. Grand Rapids, MI: Baker Book House, 1898.

The Zondervan Parallel New Testament in Greek and English, 8th ed. New York, NY: Zondervan Publishing House. 1982.

SCRIPTURE INDEX

Scripture Index

375

Made in the USA
Las Vegas, NV
17 October 2024

97007871R00213